COLLECTOR'S ENCYCLOPEDIA OF

DEPRESSION GLASS

FIFTEENTH EDITION

GENE FLORENCE

COLLECTOR BOOKS

A Division of Schroeder Publishing Co., Inc.

PRICING

All prices in this book are retail prices for mint condition glassware. This book is intended to be only a guide to prices as there are a few regional price differences that cannot reasonably be dealt with herein. You may expect dealers to pay from 30% to 50% less than the prices quoted. Glass that is in less than mint condition, i.e., chipped, cracked, scratched, repaired, or poorly moulded, will bring only a small percentage of the price of glass that is in mint condition — if wanted at all.

Prices have become reasonably well established due to national advertising by dealers, the Depression glass shows held from coast to coast, and the Internet. I have my own web page operated for books and glass (www.geneflorence.com). However, there are still some regional differences in prices due partly to glass being more available in some areas than in others. Companies distributed certain pieces in some areas that they did not in others. Generally speaking, prices are about the same among dealers from coast to coast.

Prices tend to increase swiftly on rare items and they have increased as a whole due to more collectors entering the field and people becoming aware of the worth of Depression glass.

One of the important aspects of this book is the attempt to illustrate as well as realistically price those items that are in demand. All items listed are priced. The desire is to give you the best factual guide to collectible patterns of Depression glass available.

MEASUREMENTS

To illustrate why there are discrepancies in measurements, I offer the following sample from just two years of Hocking's catalog references:

Year	Item	Ounces	Item	Ounces	Item	Ounces
1935	Pitcher	37, 58, 80	Flat Tumbler	5, 9, 13½	Footed Tumbler	10, 13
1935	Pitcher	37, 60, 80	Flat Tumbler	5, 9, 10, 15	Footed Tumbler	10, 13
1936	Pitcher	37, 65, 90	Flat Tumbler	5, 9, 13½	Footed Tumbler	10, 15
1936	Pitcher	37, 60, 90	Flat Tumbler	5, 9, 13½	Footed Tumbler	10, 15

All measurements in this book are exact as to some manufacturer's listing or to actual measurement. You may expect variance of up to ½" or 1 – 5 ounces. This may be due to mould variations or reworking worn moulds or changes by the manufacturer as well as rounding off measurements for catalog listings.

The current values in this book should be used only as a guide. They are not intended to set prices, which vary from one section of the country to another. Auction prices as well as dealer prices vary greatly and are affected by condition as well as demand. Neither the author nor the publisher assumes responsibility for any losses that might be incurred as a result of consulting this guide.

On the Cover:
Colonial plate white, $3.00; Colonial cream soup, $60.00; Manhattan relish set, $85.00; American Sweetheart plate with decal, $20.00; Moondrops powder jar, $160.00.

Cover design by Beth Summers
Book design by Beth Ray

Searching For A Publisher?

We are always looking for people knowledgeable within their fields. If you feel that there is a real need for a book on your collectible subject and have a large comprehensive collection, contact us.

Collector Books
P.O. Box 3009
Paducah, KY 42002-3009
www.collectorbooks.com

Gene Florence

P.O. Box 22186
Lexington, KY 40522   or   P.O. Box 64
Astatula, FL 34705

CONTENTS

ACKNOWLEDGMENTS

I cherish all the information dealers, collectors, and readers have shared with me through writing, e-mailing, calling, and talking to me directly in various regions of the country. Thanks for transporting those newly encountered pieces to shows for inspection and sending pictures. Thanks for the 30s coupon advertisements that you've shown me promoting products from seeds to farm equipment with Depression glass "lures." Thank you for your special knowledge regarding the glass you collect, what you find and can't find in the region in which you live. All this has been valuable to me and to collectors as a whole. All has combined to add to the body of knowledge regarding Depression glass.

I have treasured the shows that Depression glass clubs and show promoters have invited me to and have found them to be an inestimable source of information about the glass. Hopefully, I helped to promote the glass and show to all our benefits. I know I certainly tried. However, 30 years of doing this are beginning to take a toll on both, my wife, Cathy, and me; I hope you will forgive us for slowing down our scampering about the country and cutting back on many of the shows we've been privileged to be a part of in the past. Cathy's help is immeasurable; quite frankly, these books would not exist without her, beginning with her typing my first chicken scratched longhand manuscript. She has worked many long hours at my side as my chief editor, critic, proofreader and, lately, research assistant — all while wearing her other hats of wife and mother. She was always the labor end of unpacking, packing, sorting, and labeling the glass. Unfortunately, as her job descriptions expanded, so did her stress levels, which were not being resolved by our helter-skelter schedule. Regretfully, we decided our shows and travel should be dramatically reduced and have taken steps to do so.

Specific thanks regarding this particular book need to go to Dick and Pat Spencer, Dan and Geri Tucker, Joe and Florence Solito, Sam and Becky Collings, Barbara Grgurich, Glen and Carolyn Robertson, Barbara Wolfe and Marianne Jackson at Anchor Hocking, and various readers throughout the United States and Canada for glass photos and information provided. There have also been snippets forthcoming from readers out of the United States, in Australia, New Zealand, England, Canada, and Puerto Rico.

Photographs herein were artistically captured by Richard Walker of New York and Charles R. Lynch of Kentucky. They both labored long over hundreds of setups during one 13-day session and several smaller sessions scheduled throughout the two-year period since the last book. Glass arranging, unpacking, sorting, carting, and repacking was completed by Jane White, Zibby Walker, Dick and Pat Spencer, and Cathy Florence. Billy Schroeder and some other members of the Collector Books' shipping crew simplified loading and unloading vans. In addition, Jane White and many of the crew previously mentioned helped on several other photography sessions.

Thanks for the expertise of the editorial department at Collector Books, especially Beth Ray, who know how to take my mailings and make them into a book.

If you write me please enclose a SASE (self-addressed, stamped envelope) that is large enough to return your photos if you wish them back. Writing books from January through May (four this year) leaves precious little time for answering the stacks of letters that arrive each week. I want to thank the thoughtful people who send postcards with the possible answers to their questions for me to check off the correct response. Those are a delight. I want to inform people who forget to include the SASE that they're wasting their time writing; they'll not be answered. I want to encourage you to send pictures of items you hope to have identified, or even pencil rubbings of the pattern, rather than descriptions. I want to explain that my expertise, such as it is, lies in knowledge of the patterns presented in my books. I know quite a bit about the collectible patterns I have researched and will gladly help you any way I can with those when time permits. I don't know the names, manufacturers, line numbers, and worth of every single piece of Depression glassware made nor do I have the time to research them for you. I now have two *Glassware Pattern Identification* books that contain over 900 patterns identified for you by names, dates, colors, companies, and how many pieces were made when known. They should save you searching in over 300 books on your own. No, I don't provide lists or prices for those patterns. The books are for identifying your patterns only. We're trying to document those "wonder who made this" type pieces you see at markets but never in books. Please know these are not so much sour grapes as self-preservation. I'm suffering from a tidal wave of questions I have no knowledge of and it's a waste and frustration for both of us. I would hate coming to the place where I'd discourage your writing me at all; but these questions on everything other than the glassware in my books is giving me pause to consider that.

I need to thank my children who come to my rescue from time to time. Marc, my youngest, who is trying to oversee my web page while handling a full-time work schedule teaching computer technology all over the country. No, I do not have much time to surf the net myself. These books take more of my time than I care to admit or than you could ever imagine. Chad, my eldest, is drilling/pulling underground fiber optics all over the country, but taking time out to fit in help at a show or search the house for research information needed and left behind. Thanks, too, to Cathy's mom and dad, Sibyl and Charles, who have helped us wash, sort, pack, repack, shelve, measure, and otherwise do whatever was needed to be done both for photography sessions and shows. Any way you slice it, there's an enormous amount of work that must be accomplished by many hands before these books come to you with a wealth of current information systematically prepared between glossy covers.

This book was written in Florida, sitting before my computer which faces the lake, where I usually can watch my fishing poles set up on the dock, watch the alligators cruise by, and see the fellow anglers motoring along and occasionally hauling up a fish. The water levels are down and the fishing is so bad that I don't have to worry about missing the fish. Oh, well; I wouldn't be fishing in Kentucky either.

As we go to press with this fifteenth edition, thank you once again, my readers, for making this America's #1 bestselling book on glass. Do enlighten your friends on Depression glass. Point them to, or give them, a book. In the grand scheme of things, it appears that only a few of us realize this glass's inherent, as well as monetary, value. I receive letters nearly every day from people who have just learned about Depression glass — or who just discovered they essentially gave away some family heirlooms at a sale. If you get a chance, educate and delight yourself. Take in a Depression glass show. They're awesome and wonderful fun and well worth the price of admission.

PREFACE

As I sit down to write this fifteenth book, I have to remind myself that, every day, new people are discovering this beautiful, old Depression era glassware; and I have to try to somehow acquaint them with all the information I've gathered over 30 years and to do it in a way that the readers who have heard it all before, are not totally bored. It's a trickey responsibility, but here goes, once again. For those who don't know, for 30 years these books have been on a two-year rotation; every two years they are completely rewritten to include all the latest facts, finds, and prices noticed by me.

First, I need to address the slow-down economy pricing that is going to appear in some pattern pieces. Remember, I don't *set* these prices; I merely report what is happening in the market. As I write this, people are talking about Mr. Greenspan's recession and some analysts are predicting two or three quarters more of the doldrums; and our beloved glass community is reflecting some of this market unrest. The wild, surplus monies that people had to throw around on glass a couple of years ago, are being parceled out more frugally; and some pattern pieces aren't presently supporting a price rise or have even slipped a fraction from those prices reported two years ago. This has happened before, so don't panic. Now is the time to pick up some bargains. I remember my publisher being very concerned when I reflected lower prices once before. Then, as now, I stated my job was to report market prices as accurately as I knew how. This is how it is now as I write and price this book. Do I expect it to continue in this mode? I doubt it. It didn't before; but I wasn't born with a crystal ball and there are no guarantees with much of anything in this life. Glass collecting isn't all about money, anyway. The majority collect because of some emotional pull of the glass itself. I very much doubt that appeal is going to suddenly die.

Depression glass as defined in this book is the colored glassware made fundamentally during the Depression years in the colors of amber, blue, black, crystal, green, pink, red, yellow, and white. There are other colors and some glass made before, as well as after, this time; but primarily, the glass within this book was manufactured from the late 1920s through 1940. Further, this publication is mostly concerned with the inexpensively made dinnerware turned out by machine in bulk and sold through smaller stores or given away as publicity or premium items for other products of that time. Depression glass was often packaged in cereal boxes and flour sacks or given as incentive gifts for buying tickets or products at the local movie theaters, gasoline stations, and grocery stores. Merchandise was offered with magazine subscriptions, for buying (or selling) certain amounts of seeds or in return for amounts of coupons garnered with butter or soap purchases. One collector showed me an ad with a picture of a butter dish that could be had by buying a cream separator, something dairy operators might know.

Collectors have also been seeking later made patterns encompassing the time from 1940 to the 1960s which has led to a companion book, entitled *Collectible Glassware from the 40s, 50s, 60s...*, now in its sixth edition. However, to correctly date glassware from this latter period, it was necessary to move some patterns previously exclusive to this Depression glass book into the time frame encompassed by the 50s book. If your pattern is no longer found within this Depression book, you should seek it in the 40s, 50s, 60s.... Too, there were more elegant, etched tablewares being manufactured during this 20s through 60s time frame which are highly collectible, today; and those have been covered in my *Elegant Glassware of the Depression Era* book.

There have been significant changes in collecting Depression glass since my first book was published on the subject in 1972. Prices have soared; seemingly plentiful patterns have been gathered into countless collections throughout the world and removed from the marketplace. Collectors, rather than accumulating complete sets of dishes, have branched into collecting items only from many different patterns, i.e., cups and saucers, pitchers, shakers, tumblers, shot glasses, cruets, sugar and creamer sets, luncheon plates. Smaller Depression patterns and previously ignored crystal and satinized wares have attracted clientele; collecting a rainbow (many colors) of one, or more, patterns is now in vogue, rather than the one color collecting of old. Truthfully, anything that is Depression glass, a recognized pattern or not, suddenly has added importance and collectibility. Glass is sold on the Internet, which has had great impact on the collectibles market in just the two years since last book. Very learned glass collectors are more the norm than the exception, and they are crossing fields and branching into other areas of glass appreciation. This ever-broadening interest has prompted me to research twelve more books in the field of Depression glass, the Elegant and 50s previously mentioned, one on kitchenware items of the Depression, six others on the very rare glassware of those times, not to mention the latest ones on stemware identification and two on pattern identification. Regarding these last three, I have had several dealers write or seek me out to express their gratitude in saving them endless hours of searching through their libraries of books to identify some new piece they've acquired. I've even had letters from readers thanking me for having written all these books and contributed to their pleasure in the glass. These words of encouragement are certainly appreciated, but truthfully, it certainly is not only my work anymore. Be sure and read the acknowledgments for the countless people who contribute to this body of work.

Over 30 previously unknown pieces have been added to the listings since the last edition, as well as some previously unseen colors. Those of you who feel nothing new is ever found should look closely at your favorite pattern. Similarly, there has been an expunging of a dozen pieces that have never been found. These are due to original catalog misinformation or misinterpretation, entry mistakes, or errors of measurements in the past. My publisher has noticed that many of these mistakes were copied, along with the rest of my 30 years' work, into another publication being sold as another author's work and selling for more money.

Information for this book comes from over 30 years of research and selling experience, via communication with fellow dealers and collectors throughout the country, and over 1,425,000 miles of traveling the country, hunting and locating glassware. I must say that some of the most interesting (and surprising) enlightenment has come directly from readers, sharing catalogs, magazines, photographs of glass, and the glass, itself. They may have a family member who worked at a plant, or talked with an engraver, or heard something at a market, or found something at a garage sale they thought significant. More importantly, they bothered to share it. It's invaluable and adds to the body of knowledge for us all.

ADAM JEANNETTE GLASS COMPANY, 1932 – 1934

Colors: Pink, green, crystal, some yellow, and Delphite blue. (See Reproduction Section.)

Jeannette's Adam pattern is a favorite with collectors. It has some of the Deco era shapes, triangles, squares, and linear lines, combined with a kind of Art Nouveau scrolled center motif of fern-like leaves surrounded by a garland of dainty flowers. Then, there's the ancient biblical garden story of Adam encompassed in the name itself. Add to that the many pieces made in the line and the fact that the glass experienced a three-year production period, and you have a winning combination. Having said that, thirty years ago, nearly every booth at markets displayed something in the Adam pattern. Today, you're lucky to encounter a few pieces. Therefore, new collector, you must appreciate the fact that it will probably take you quite some time to gather an entire set piece by piece. However, the fun thing about collecting these days is that table settings don't have to match. Any woman's magazine you pick up shows myriad combinations of wares delightfully presented. So, with imagination, you can successfully use whatever you find.

Facts to know include pitchers coming with both square and round bases. The square has the motif on the base while the round has only concentric rings. Candy and sugar lids are interchangeable. *Any round* plates or saucers you stumble upon are *rare*. There are at least five pieces found in crystal, i.e. pitcher, ashtray, coaster, divided relish, and grill plate, and almost nobody cares even though they could be classified as rarely seen dishes.

You should always look for inner rim damage on bowls, which have been used and stacked in cabinets for about 70 years. Ads say "irr" for inner rim roughness. You may be in less than mint condition too, after that many years, but you don't want to pay *mint prices* for damaged wares. There are skilled people who can smooth these chips out, now, if they aren't too bad. Don't automatically assume everybody grinding glass is skilled, however; they are not. Some will do more harm to your piece than if you'd left it alone. The good ones fix pieces so you can't tell there was damage. If you can see where they fixed it, they're less skilled than you need.

There is an extremely rare pink butter dish *top* that sports *both* the Adam (outside) motif and the Sierra (inside) mold design. It's *one top* having *two* designs and if you find one, it will bring you big bucks in today's market place. It sold for $250 in 1974. The ripoff artists reproduced a regular pink butter and lid years ago and it is no big deal, now, because I've told you how to tell old from new in the Reproduction Section at the back of the book. (Do not apply that telltale old from new concept to any piece other than the butter.) Prices on butters dipped temporarily then, but are back to normal. There is, also, a rare lamp to be found. It's made from a notched sherbet, frosted to hide the cord and covered with a metal cover, which holds a tall bulb. One just sold on the Internet for over $2,000.00. However, in talking with a retired machinist, he said, given the parts, he could make one up in no time at all. Therefore, the cord, bulb, switch, and metal part of any you see should show 70 years of age somewhere. A similar one is pictured with Floral pattern. Iced tea tumblers, though not exactly rare, and cereal bowls will be hard to come by as they have faded from the markets into collections.

	Pink	Green			Pink	Green
Ashtray, 4½"	30.00	28.00	**Cup	30.00	25.00
Bowl, 4¾", dessert	25.00	25.00	Lamp	495.00	495.00
Bowl, 5¾", cereal	55.00	55.00	Pitcher, 8", 32 ounce	45.00	45.00
Bowl, 7¾"	30.00	30.00	Pitcher, 32 ounce, round base	75.00	
Bowl, 9", no cover	45.00	45.00	Plate, 6", sherbet	11.00	11.00
Bowl cover, 9"	25.00	45.00	***Plate, 7¾", square salad	18.00	17.00
Bowl, 9", covered	75.00	95.00	Plate, 9", square dinner	35.00	32.00
Bowl, 10", oval	35.00	40.00	Plate, 9", grill	28.00	23.00
Butter dish bottom	30.00	65.00	Platter, 11¾"	33.00	35.00
Butter dish top	80.00	360.00	Relish dish, 8", divided	20.00	25.00
Butter dish & cover	110.00	425.00	Salt & pepper, 4", footed	100.00	125.00
Butter dish combination			****Saucer, 6", square	6.00	6.00
with Sierra pattern	1,650.00		Sherbet, 3"	33.00	38.00
Cake plate, 10", footed	30.00	32.50	Sugar	25.00	35.00
*Candlesticks, 4", pair	95.00	115.00	Sugar/candy cover	25.00	45.00
Candy jar & cover, 2½"	115.00	115.00	Tumbler, 4½"	35.00	30.00
Coaster, 3¼"	22.00	20.00	Tumbler, 5½", iced tea	65.00	65.00
Creamer	28.00	28.00	Vase, 7½"	435.00	95.00

* Delphite $225.00   ** Yellow $100.00   *** Round pink $60.00; yellow $100.00   **** Round pink $75.00; yellow $85.00

"ADAMS RIB" LINE #900 DIAMOND GLASSWARE, CO., c. 1925

Colors: Amber, blue, green, pink; some marigold; milk and crystal w/marigold iridescence, vaseline; and colors decorated w/gold, silver, white enamel, florals; and flashed colors of blue and orange w/black trim.

Several books ago, a collector asked me why I didn't put this pattern in my book. So, finally, this is one of the new patterns included. It has taken a while to gather enough examples for a picture. The annoying thing about that is, we have other pieces we've purchased to show, but they weren't in the box that came out at photography. Sorry!

I doubt that the listing below is complete. You may find other pieces and I would very much appreciate a notice of such. Some of the pieces listed below were shown in a 1928 Sears catalog which touted six orange and black "ribbed" pieces for $1.32. That further dates the orange/black dish craze that was afoot then.

You should know that there is a pedestal candy made by Fenton which closely resembles the "Adams Rib" one. The knob of the Diamond Company's candy has a tiny protrusion, whereas the one made by Fenton is smooth.

Many of the flat based bowls were originally presented on black, three-toed pedestal bases, also a glass fashion of the time. Black, in fact, may be a color possibility, though I couldn't document or find any. The iridized pieces are prized by carnival glass people; so, you will have competition vying for those. There are iridized blue and green pitchers that most collectors have not found mugs to accompany. So, keep your eye out for those.

Though the company had long been in business, this is one of those unfortunate factories that burned in the early thirties. The #900 line was one of their last big successes.

	Non Iridescent	Iridescent
Base, black, pedestal, 3 toe (for flat bowls)	15.00	
Bowl, vegetable, flared (belled) rim	60.00	
Bowl, flat, rolled edge	40.00	
Bowl, console, pedestal foot	55.00	175.00
Bowl, 8", 3-footed, salad	45.00	
Candy, 3-footed bonbon w/lid	45.00	
Candy, oval, flat	65.00	
Candy, footed jar and cover	55.00	
Candle, blown	30.00	50.00
Candle, tall	35.00	60.00
Cigarette holder, footed	25.00	
Compote, cheese, non-ribbed	25.00	
Comport, small	35.00	
Comport, 6½" tall	40.00	80.00
Comport, large fruit	60.00	100.00

	Non Iridescent	Iridescent
Cup	18.00	
Creamer	25.00	45.00
Mayonnaise, 6", w/ladle	45.00	
Mug (or lemonade)	35.00	85.00
Pitcher, lemonade, applied handle	200.00	350.00
Plate, dessert	10.00	
Plate, lunch	18.00	
Plate, cracker, w/center rim	30.00	
Saucer	6.00	
Sandwich, center flat top handle		50.00
Sandwich, center ½ hex handle	30.00	55.00
Sherbet, flat rim	20.00	
Sugar, open	25.00	45.00
Tray, oval sugar/creamer (8½x6¼")	20.00	35.00
Vase, fan	35.00	65.00
Vase, 8½", footed, flair rim	75.00	110.00
Vase, 9¾"	95.00	150.00

"ADDIE," "TWELVE POINT" LINE #34 NEW MARTINSVILLE GLASS MFG. CO., c. 1930

Colors: Black, crystal, cobalt, green, jade green satin, pink, red; and w/Lotus Glass Co. silver decoration.

This is another of the new additions to this book. The name I've mostly heard this called in the marketplace is "Twelve Point," simply because it has that many points. However, when I started doing the research, I found that twenty years ago author Heacock had named the pattern in honor of Addie Miller, a pioneer author for New Martinsville Glass Company wares. The company designated it Line #34.

Notice the lions/heraldry design on the black saucer. Since this decoration turns up on various colors of Line #34 and at least one other New Martinsville blank (see pg. 122, of my *Elegant Glassware*, 9th edition), is it a Lotus or a New Martinsville decoration?

I had both blue and red pieces at a show last year; and more people seemed drawn to the cobalt blue color. I suspect once people come across the jade green satin, that's going to capture major attention. The jade green was marketed with the black, a striking combination — and definitely in keeping with the bi and tri-colored glass presentations of that era.

Again, it's possible you're going to find other colors or pieces and I'd appreciate notification of what you turn up. Also, any measurements you could supply would be helpful.

	Black/Cobalt/ Jade/Red	All other colors
Bowl, large flare rim, vegetable	45.00	35.00
Candlestick, 3½"	30.00	20.00
Creamer, footed	22.00	10.00
Cup, footed	12.50	8.00
Mayonnaise, 5"	25.00	15.00
Plate, lunch	12.50	8.00
Sandwich tray, 2-handle	35.00	25.00
Saucer	5.00	2.50
Sherbet, footed	15.00	10.00
Sugar, open, footed	22.00	10.00
Tumbler, footed, 6 oz., juice	15.00	10.00
Tumbler, footed, 9 oz., water	22.50	15.00

AMELIA, "STAR MEDALLION," "BOXED STAR" LINE #671, IMPERIAL GLASS COMPANY, c. 1920s

Colors: Amber, blue, Clambroth, crystal, green, pink, Rubigold Iridescent, Smoke; Azalea, Turquoise, and Verde, 1960s; Pink carnival, 1980s.

This pattern has been around for a long time, but not all pieces are to be found in all colors. The items I see most often at markets are the milk or hotel pitcher and sugar in either crystal or Rubigold, Imperial's name for their marigold carnival color. However, I'm noticing I have failed to pick up a set for the photo. I assume I thought I already had it.

In the 1980s, just before their demise, Imperial put out a pink carnival, crimped rim compote which turns up frequently in malls. It's pretty.

The custard cups were just that. They have no known carnival punch bowl to accompany them; and finding the carnival colored nut bowl is "a hard nut to crack" so to speak.

We've been looking for this pattern a while now, and as you can see from the photo, colored Amelia is hard to locate these 80 years later. We haven't even found the 1960s colors, which attests to people liking the pattern and hanging on to what they have.

If your piece comes with an "IG" mark, it's been made since 1951 when Imperial began so marking their wares.

	Clambroth	Rubigold	Smoke	All other colors
Butter w/cover, round				45.00
Bowl, 5", lily				15.00
Bowl, 5½", square	25.00	30.00	45.00	15.00
Bowl, 5½", deep nut, ftd.		35.00		20.00
Bowl, 6", round nappy	20.00	25.00	40.00	15.00
Bowl, 6¼", oval preserve				20.00
Bowl, 7", oval				20.00
Bowl, 7½", berry, flare (belled) rim			25.00	
Bowl, 8", round berry				35.00
Cup, custard		25.00		12.50
Compote, straight rim				20.00
Compote, crimped rim (late)	35.00	35.00		15.00

	Clambroth	Rubigold	Smoke	All other colors
Creamer				20.00
Celery, 2-handle				30.00
Celery vase, footed	80.00	90.00	150.00	40.00
Goblet, wine		50.00	75.00	20.00
Pitcher, milk or hotel	30.00	37.50	80.00	25.00
Plate, 6½", dessert		35.00		12.00
Plate, 9½", lunch	40.00	50.00	70.00	25.00
Spoon holder (open sugar)				20.00
Sugar w/cover				30.00
Tumbler, 4"		30.00	50.00	20.00
Tumbler, 4½", lemonade, flare rim	30.00	50.00	20.00	

AMERICAN PIONEER LIBERTY WORKS, 1931 – 1934

Colors: Pink, green, amber, and crystal.

The company that made this pattern started life in 1903 as a Cut Glass Works, which was then a part of its name. I've been told many times by devotees of American Pioneer that this looks like "better glass" than your run of the mill Depression era wares. It probably is. Once it started manufacturing Depression type tableware lines, Liberty management was aiming to be ahead of its time, innovative with its wares. Unfortunately, the plant suffered fire damage in 1931 and couldn't recover financially from this blow.

The candy jar lids are interchangeable even though the two candies are shaped differently. One looks like a normal footed candy, the other is taller and has the shape of a footed vase. There are two versions of cups, one being a bit more flared than the other. One has a 4" diameter and is 2½" tall; the other has a 3⅜" diameter and is 2⅜" tall. These variances are very minute and may well be mold differences; but collectors have noticed them enough to say the flared rim cup is the more commonly found. Lids for covered vegetable bowls are hard to find; and one collector insisted there are three sizes, not the two I have listed; but I never received any confirmation of this. Be on the lookout for the third possibility. Amber cocktails have been discovered in two sizes; but none have surfaced in any other color. One holds three ounces and is 3¹³⁄₁₆" high; the other holds 3½ ounces and is 3¹⁵⁄₁₆" tall. Liner plates for the elusive urns, or pitchers in today's jargon, are the regular six and eight inch plates. The six inch plate in pink is rare. Both sizes of urns have turned up in amber. So, we can no longer say amber was marketed only as a luncheon set. Dresser sets are coveted pieces in American Pioneer and one has recently surfaced in crystal. Oh yes! Thirty years and hundreds of thousands of people collecting Depression glass later, heretofore *unknown* items and colors are still being found. This is what makes collecting exciting. There's the possibility that any collector can find something rare in the next shop.

You do need to study the design. It must have those plain banded, horizontal rib areas in order to be American Pioneer. Numerous companies made hobbed patterns that are similar in shape.

	Crystal, Pink	Green		Crystal, Pink	Green
* Bowl, 5", handled	25.00	25.00	Lamp, 5½", round, ball shape, amber $150.00	175.00	
Bowl, 8¾", covered	125.00	150.00	Lamp, 8½", tall	125.00	150.00
Bowl, 9", handled	30.00	38.00	Mayonnaise, 4¼"	60.00	90.00
Bowl, 9¼", covered	125.00	150.00	Pilsner, 5¾", 11 ounce	150.00	150.00
Bowl, 10¾", console	60.00	70.00	** Pitcher, 5", covered urn	175.00	225.00
Candlesticks, 6½", pair	110.00	135.00	*** Pitcher, 7", covered urn	195.00	250.00
Candy jar and cover, 1 pound	95.00	110.00	Plate, 6"	12.50	15.00
Candy jar and cover, 1½ pound	100.00	135.00	* Plate, 6", handled	12.50	15.00
Cheese and cracker set (indented platter and comport)	60.00	70.00	* Plate, 8"	11.00	12.00
Coaster, 3½"	35.00	35.00	* Plate, 11½", handled	30.00	40.00
Creamer, 2¾"	25.00	20.00	* Saucer	4.00	5.00
* Creamer, 3½"	20.00	22.00	Sherbet, 3½"	16.00	20.00
* Cup	12.00	12.00	Sherbet, 4¾"	40.00	45.00
Dresser set (2 colognes, powder jar, indented 7½" tray)	450.00	450.00	Sugar, 2¾"	20.00	22.00
Goblet, 3¹³⁄₁₆", 3 oz., cocktail (amber)	40.00		* Sugar, 3½"	20.00	22.00
Goblet, 3¹⁵⁄₁₆", 3½ oz., cocktail (amber)	40.00		Tumbler, 5 ounce, juice	40.00	45.00
Goblet, 4", 3 oz., wine	40.00	55.00	Tumbler, 4", 8 ounce	40.00	55.00
Goblet, 6", 8 oz., water	45.00	57.50	Tumbler, 5", 12 ounce	50.00	65.00
Ice bucket, 6"	65.00	75.00	Vase, 7", 4 styles	110.00	135.00
Lamp, 1¾", w/metal pole 9½"		80.00	Vase, 9", round		250.00
			Whiskey, 2¼", 2 ounce	50.00	100.00

* Amber — Double the price of pink unless noted   **Amber $300.00   ***Amber $350.00

AMERICAN SWEETHEART MacBETH-EVANS GLASS COMPANY, 1930 – 1936

Colors: Pink, Monax, ruby, and cobalt; some Cremax and color trimmed Monax.

This line was produced for seven years and it was well received judging from the remaining pieces found by the collecting public in these last thirty years. Although the ware is rather delicate looking, it was surprisingly durable. You might be interested to know that a Louisville Tin & Stove Company catalog dated 1937, offered a 32-piece set of Monax American Sweetheart for $2.75 or a 42-piece set (including a two-piece sugar) for $4.15.

The pitchers and water tumblers came only in pink and there are similar shaped pitchers having no design that were sold with plain, Dogwood shaped tumblers. These are not considered to be American Sweetheart, though some people do buy them to go with their sets. If it doesn't have the pattern, don't pay American Sweetheart prices for it.

Both pink and Monax (white, with translucent edges) shakers are rarely found and infinitely desirable to collectors, many of whom do not have them for their sets. You will find plates in Monax that come in two styles, with and without the center motif. You will also find luncheon pieces in Monax, that were trimmed in gold. These were made near the end of American Sweetheart's production run, but are not looked upon very favorably by today's collector. In fact, many people purposely remove the gold with a pencil eraser. Monax pieces are found with colored edgings of yellow, green, pink, and smokey/black, any piece of which is highly collectible. Rarely found items, such as the sugar lid (with two different styles of knobs), large (18", triple wide, flat rim) and small console bowls appear in Monax, and the larger ones were also manufactured in red and blue.

Dessert sets consisting of four cups, saucers, four 8" luncheon plates, creamer, sugar, and 12" cake server were made in the mid-30s in ruby and cobalt and these colors are prized by collectors. In England, they would call this a tea service. Also appearing in the opaque colors were tidbit servers (stacked plates with a center rod), 15" sandwich plates, and the aforementioned large console bowl. Tidbit servers have been made up by enterprising individuals over the years; so, you need to check for older hardware; but I know of no way to tell original from newly made other than that.

You will find sherbet dishes in ruby and cobalt that are shaped like American Sweetheart but which do not carry the moulded design. These are not considered to be American Sweetheart though many of this pattern's collectors will purchase them as novelty items. Sherbets were made in two sizes, with the smaller 3¾" one being harder to find. Sherbets also appear in crystal with metal holders. Another author reported these to have been made in Amethyst; but I have never seen any.

Cremax items appeared from the company in the mid-30s, ostensibly to compete with the china trade. Cremax is a beige color that doesn't appeal to today's crowd. Back then, getting people to set their dining tables with *glass* dishes was a marketing chore; so, they tried to make their glass look more like china.

For those who believe all the good glass has already been found and no bargains appear any more, I offer this. Two weeks ago on my way to a southern show, to take a break from driving, we stopped by a shop near a busy highway and plucked two of those scarce American Sweetheart tumblers from a shelf for a third of their worth. How many of you have waited ten years to buy the latest book because you already had an older edition?

It is still possible to collect this much appreciated pattern in basic pieces to use and enjoy; and harder pieces do still turn up. Though we in the trade all feel that *everybody* knows about Depression glass by now, I know for a fact they do not. New people to the glass write, call, e-mail, or drop by shows all the time, fascinated by this glass and wanting to know more about it. The sadder ones are those who *just* gave away, sold for pennies at a garage sale, or trashed their aunt's or grandmother's dishes because they had no clue they were worth this much. Help spread the word.

AMERICAN SWEETHEART

	Red	Blue	Cremax	Smoke & Other Trims
Bowl, 6", cereal			16.00	50.00
Bowl, 9", round, berry			50.00	250.00
Bowl, 9½", soup				165.00
Bowl, 18", console	1,100.00	1,250.00		
Creamer, footed	165.00	195.00		110.00
Cup	120.00	150.00		110.00
Lamp shade			495.00	
Lamp (floor with brass base)			795.00	
Plate, 6", bread and butter				22.00
Plate, 8", salad	120.00	130.00		30.00
Plate, 9", luncheon				45.00
Plate, 9¾", dinner				100.00
Plate, 12", salver	195.00	265.00		125.00
Plate, 15½", server	325.00	425.00		
Platter, 13", oval				225.00
Saucer	20.00	25.00		17.50
Sherbet, 4¼", footed (design inside or outside)				110.00
Sugar, open footed	165.00	195.00		110.00
Tidbit, 2 tier, 8" & 12"	250.00	335.00		
Tidbit, 3 tier, 8", 12" & 15½"	625.00	750.00		

	Pink	Monax
Bowl, 3¾", flat, berry	85.00	
Bowl, 4½", cream, soup	90.00	120.00
Bowl, 6", cereal	17.00	20.00
Bowl, 9", round, berry	55.00	75.00
Bowl, 9½", flat, soup	75.00	90.00
Bowl, 11", oval, vegetable	70.00	80.00
Bowl, 18", console		495.00
Creamer, footed	15.00	10.00
Cup	20.00	9.00
Lamp shade		495.00
Plate, 6" or 6½", bread & butter	6.00	6.50
Plate, 8", salad	14.00	10.00
Plate, 9", luncheon		12.00
Plate, 9¾", dinner	45.00	30.00
Plate, 10¼", dinner		27.00
Plate, 11", chop plate		25.00
Plate, 12", salver	24.00	24.00
Plate, 15½", server		250.00

	Pink	Monax
Platter, 13", oval	55.00	80.00
Pitcher, 7½", 60 ounce	995.00	
Pitcher, 8", 80 ounce	795.00	
Salt and pepper, footed	595.00	475.00
Saucer	4.00	2.00
Sherbet, 3¾", footed	25.00	
Sherbet, 4¼", footed (design inside or outside)	22.00	22.00
Sherbet in metal holder (crystal only)	3.50	
Sugar, open, footed	15.00	8.00
* Sugar lid		500.00
Tidbit, 2 tier, 8" & 12"	60.00	60.00
Tidbit, 3 tier, 8", 12" & 15½"		325.00
Tumbler, 3½", 5 ounce	105.00	
Tumbler, 4¼", 9 ounce	95.00	
Tumbler, 4¾", 10 ounce	125.00	

*Three styles of knobs.

AUNT POLLY U.S. GLASS COMPANY, Late 1920s

Colors: Blue, green, and iridescent.

Just recently, I was treated to viewing a new piece of Aunt Polly. It was a ruffled edge vase created from the regular vase mold. The next best part was the fact it was in the collector's favorite blue color. They let me take a digital picture which is shown in the insert. I realize its not the best picture in the world, but these were "field" conditions with a new camera I'd just barely learned to turn on and I wanted you to see it.

So far, the covered candy shown in green has never appeared in blue; and there are distinctly different shades of green and blue to be found. Witness the colors shown. The footed, double handle candy shown in blue is a very desirable item. It is on most Aunt Polly collectors' wish lists, along with the oval vegetable, sugar lid, shakers, and butter dish. The Aunt Polly butter bottom is interchangeable with other U.S. Glass patterns of the time, namely Strawberry, Cherryberry, and U.S. Swirl; but none of those patterns was made in blue. Thus, blue Aunt Polly butter bottoms have always been scarce. The canary (vaseline) colored tumbler and the very blue one toward the back are moulded differently from the normally found one on the right in blue. The panels are wider and there is no design in the bottom. These are obviously from different molds and were, possibly, prototypes for the subsequent design. I learned that the "vaseline" term people use today to describe the yellow, glow-in-the-dark color factories back then called canary was coined from a reporter's trying to write a description of said color. He compared it to the new petroleum jelly product that had recently hit the market and had become so popular at that time. Hence the term, "vaseline" glass. Some creamers come with a more pronounced lip than others, accounted for by the fact these were made by hand with a paddle while the glass was still hot.

Aunt Polly, like most U.S. Glass patterns, suffers from mold roughness at the seams. This is off putting to some collectors. However, most accept that as part and parcel of the pattern, along with its charming, earlier, 1900s glass appearance.

AUNT POLLY

	Green, Iridescent	Blue
Bowl, 4¾", berry	8.00	18.00
Bowl, 4¾", 2" high	18.00	
Bowl, 5½", one handle	15.00	25.00
Bowl, 7¼", oval, handled, pickle	15.00	45.00
Bowl, 7⅞", large berry	20.00	50.00
Bowl, 8⅜", oval	75.00	145.00
Butter dish and cover	275.00	250.00
Butter dish bottom	100.00	100.00
Butter dish top	175.00	150.00
Candy, cover, 2-handled	75.00	
Candy, footed, 2-handled	30.00	60.00

	Green, Iridescent	Blue
Creamer	35.00	60.00
Pitcher, 8", 48 ounce		225.00
Plate, 6", sherbet	6.00	15.00
Plate, 8", luncheon		20.00
Salt and pepper		250.00
Sherbet	10.00	15.00
Sugar	25.00	35.00
Sugar cover	60.00	165.00
Tumbler, 3⅝", 8 ounce		38.00
Vase, 6½", footed	38.00	60.00

AURORA HAZEL ATLAS GLASS COMPANY, Late 1930s

Colors: Cobalt blue, pink, green, and crystal.

Aurora has a devoted following, mainly because of its cobalt blue pieces. I used to recommend this to new collectors as a pattern that was economical to collect, easy to find, and one which had fewer pieces to look for than in most patterns, a sort of "getting your feet wet," first experience pattern. That was before collectors found out the deep cereal bowl was rarely seen. Now, with the price that bowl is commanding, when it can be found, I hesitate to be so free with my recommendations, not knowing the state of everyone's pocketbook. Still, when compared to the cost of other patterns, if this is where your interest lies, then don't suppress your desires. If I've learned one thing in this business, it's that people have an emotional response to colored glass. If cobalt items uplift you when you see them, then by all means buy some and set them where you can enjoy them. Goodness knows, in this fast paced society we live in, small things affording daily pleasures are necessary treats for the psyche.

At least two readers have suggested that patterns with a tall creamer and no sugar, such as this one, should have the creamer listed as a milk pitcher. The reason I didn't list it as such was because milk pitchers usually held at least 16 ounces; this one was a little small for that. However, lending credence to that idea, a collector reported that creamers were given away as premiums for buying a breakfast cereal in her home town. She remembers boxed displays on the counter from which the proprietor handed you one with your purchase. Unfortunately, she could not remember the name of the cereal, but thought it might have been Corn Flakes. Her grandmother had several of the creamer/milk pitchers in her attic.

A few pieces have been found in pink, and these command a price similar to the blue due to their scarcity. The small bowl, creamer, and tumbler have, so far, never been seen in that color. A Canadian reader says pink and green are more readily found there than in the States.

Both green and crystal cereal bowls, cups, and saucers have been found. So far, only collectors of cups and saucers have been very excited over this news. One expressed dismay that there were additional sets to find. That person is probably not going to be happy with me adding all these new patterns to the book since their list was almost complete of having found a cup and saucer for every pattern in my book.

	Cobalt, Pink		Cobalt, Pink
Bowl, 4½" deep	65.00	Plate, 6½"	12.50
* Bowl, 5⅜" cereal	18.50	*** Saucer	4.50
Creamer, 4½"	25.00	Tumbler, 4¾", 10 ounce	27.50
** Cup	17.50		

*Green $7.00 or crystal $5.00   **Green $7.50   ***Green $2.50

19

"AVOCADO," "SWEET PEAR" NO. 601 INDIANA GLASS COMPANY, 1923 – 1933

Colors: Pink, green, crystal; white, 1950s; yellow mist, burnt honey, and water sets in myriad frosted and transparent colors for Tiara Home Products, 1974 – 1998. (See Reproduction Section.)

This #601 line was originally called "Sweet Pear" by authors of pattern glass books.

I doubt it was anything but the line number to Indiana. I have one of their early catalogs and no names are presented anywhere. However, the "Avocado" nickname is more widely known in Depression glass circles. Tiara catalogs showing yellow and amber items made in the 1980s refer to those wares as Sweet Pear. So, Indiana did use that name later.

"Avocado" is a popular pattern among collectors; there just isn't enough of the older green and pink surfacing these days for new collectors to get interested. I recently bought a collection of both colors. I had people calling me about the pitcher and tumblers almost before I got them unwrapped, which should indicate how much collectors want those. The rest was sold in two shows, though, admittedly, dealers took a great liking to it.

I've had several inquiries, recently, regarding crystal "Avocado," heretofore, mostly ignored. So, if you see those items, perhaps you shouldn't dismiss them out of hand. To date, there are no known cups, saucers, or sherbets in crystal, but a pitcher has surfaced.

Milk glass items were produced in the mid-1950s and collectors for milk glass will vie for those. Do read the Reproduction Section telling about the various "Avocado" items and colors produced by Indiana for their Tiara Home Products line during their 1970 – 1998 life span. You don't want to be caught paying collectible prices for recent wares.

	Crystal	Pink	Green
Bowl, 5¼", 2-handled	10.00	30.00	35.00
Bowl, 6", footed relish	9.00	30.00	35.00
Bowl, 7", 1-handle preserve	8.00	30.00	35.00
Bowl, 7½", salad	12.00	50.00	70.00
Bowl, 8", 2-handled, oval	11.00	30.00	35.00
Bowl, 9½", 3¼", deep	22.00	150.00	200.00
*** Creamer, footed	12.00	35.00	40.00
Cup, footed, 2 styles		35.00	38.00

	Crystal	Pink	Green
* Pitcher, 64 ounce	350.00	1,000.00	1,500.00
*** Plate, 6⅜", sherbet	5.00	16.00	18.00
** Plate, 8¼", luncheon	7.00	17.00	22.00
Plate, 10¼", 2-handled, cake	14.00	55.00	65.00
Saucer, 6⅜",		22.00	24.00
*** Sherbet		60.00	70.00
*** Sugar, footed	12.00	35.00	40.00
* Tumbler	35.00	195.00	310.00

* Caution on pink. The orange-pink is new.
* White: Pitcher $425.00; Tumbler $35.00.

** Apple design $10.00. Amber has been newly made.
*** Remade in dark shade of green.

20

BEADED BLOCK, #710 IMPERIAL GLASS COMPANY, 1927 – 1930s; Late 1970s – Early 1980s

Colors: Pink, green, crystal, ice blue, Canary, iridescent, amber, red, opalescent, and milk white.

Beaded Block, #710, manufactured by Imperial over the years in a bountiful array of colors, is still a sought commodity. Just this past week I was stopped by some collectors who recognized me at a market and asked if I had any opalescent trimmed pieces. They said they had accumulated over 25 in the years they'd been collecting. I was tempted to ask if I could borrow theirs for a photograph. In the last few years, more and more people are asking me for Beaded Block, particularly the opalescent trimmed items made in the late 1930s. The dilemma for collectors, now, is whether to pay the escalating prices being asked or to do without. Collectors appear to buy all colors, though I have noted some slow down in the Rubigold, marigold carnival colored wares. Whether the piece comes with the stippled, frosted square or the plain square block matters little at this point.

Square Beaded Block plates are commonly found while round plates are scarce. Most round plates were transformed into bowls. There are size variances in this pattern. The sizes listed here were all obtained from actual measurements of the pieces and not those listed in catalogs. The two-handled jelly which most companies called a cream soup measures from 4¾" to 5". Be sure to read the section on measurements on page 2. I have found company catalog size listings were more nearly approximations.

Imperial reissued pink and iridized pink (pink carnival) in the late 1970s and early 1980s. These pieces are easily spotted since they are marked IG in the bottom. When I visited the factory in 1981, I was told that the white was made in the early 1950s and the IG mark (for Imperial Glass) was first used about that time. Only a few marked pieces of Beaded Block are found, but they include the white covered pear pictured below. This two-part candy in the shape of a large pear is found infrequently and dates from the mid 50s. Pears have been found in yellow, green, pink, and amber. Amber seems to be the more easily found color and usually they are seen on the West Coast. These generally are priced in the $250 to $350 range; but I have seen them offered for $695. The key word is offered.

Pink and white Beaded Block pitchers are scarce when compared to green and crystal. Yet, this collecting surge for Beaded Block has even boosted the price for the green pitcher.

A red Lily bowl (4½") is the only Beaded Block item found in that color. It is on every collector's wish list. Several of these were found in central Ohio years ago, but I have seen only one lately.

New collectors should note that the 6" vases in cobalt and pink are really not Beaded Block. They have no beading and no scalloped edge as do all the other pieces except candy bottoms. Imperial called these tall pieces "footed jellies." These were attained at groceries with a product inside. One found with the original label read "Good Taste Mustard Seed, 3½ oz., Frank Tea & Spice Co., Cin., O." I recently noticed that that information was attributed to another author's publication written five years later than mentioned in my book. Remember, these are "go-with" pieces and not truly Beaded Block.

Uninformed dealers like to label Beaded Block as pricey, older Sandwich glass, which is either a compliment to Beaded Block or an insult to Sandwich glass. Come on, people. It was sold at Woolworth's. I've also seen at least one expert attributing the Sea Foam decoration to about four decades before it was made.

BEADED BLOCK

	*Crystal, Pink, Green, Amber	Other Colors
Bowl, 4⅞"-5", 2-handled, jelly	20.00	35.00
** Bowl, 4½", round, lily	20.00	40.00
Bowl, 5½", square	20.00	35.00
Bowl, 5½", 1-handle	20.00	35.00
Bowl, 6", deep, round	25.00	38.00
Bowl, 6¼", round	25.00	38.00
Bowl, 6½", round	25.00	38.00
Bowl, 6½", 2-handled, pickle	30.00	42.00
Bowl, 6¾", round, unflared	25.00	40.00
Bowl, 7¼", round, flared	30.00	45.00
Bowl, 7½", round, fluted edges	30.00	45.00
Bowl, 7½", round, plain edge	30.00	45.00
Bowl, 8¼", celery	38.00	60.00
Candy, pear shaped	325.00	395.00
Creamer	25.00	45.00
*** Pitcher, 5¼", pint jug	110.00	
Plate, 7¾", square	22.00	30.00
Plate, 8¾", round	30.00	45.00
Stemmed jelly, 4½"	25.00	38.00
Stemmed jelly, 4½", flared top	25.00	40.00
Sugar	25.00	45.00
Vase, 6", bouquet	25.00	45.00

* All pieces 25% to 40% lower.   ** Red $495.00   *** White $195.00, pink $175.00, crystal $85.00

"BERLIN," "REEDED WAFFLE," LINE #124 WESTMORELAND SPECIALTY COMPANY, c. 1924

Colors: Blue, crystal, green, pink; ruby, c. 1980s.

The names "Berlin" and "Reeded Waffle" for Westmoreland's Line #124 are holdovers from a pattern glass design first produced in the 1870s. The older ware could be found with colored stains of ruby or amber. Westmoreland made at least 15 pieces of this pattern in the prevailing Depression era colors. Thus, its inclusion here. We have set 3 items of Plaid in the photo, a milk pitcher and goblet at either end of row 1 and a compote in the center of the bottom row.

You should know that there's been some confusion between this pattern and one known as "Plaid" or "Open Plaid," which is similar at first glance. Plaid has an actual basketweave design and was only produced in crystal.

Consulting an assortment of pattern glass books, I found that the older "Berlin" design sported tumblers, wines, cracker jars, cruets, cups, butter dishes, etc. So, an abundance of items occur in this design, but were attributed to other companies.

I'm told Westmoreland made a ruby colored pitcher sometime in the 1980s, just before going out of business.

	*Crystal		*Crystal
Basket	27.50	Creamer	20.00
Bowl, bonbon, 1 handle	15.00	Mayonnaise	30.00
Bowl, 6½", round	15.00	Pitcher	65.00
Bowl, square	20.00	Plate, 9", lunch	15.00
Bowl, 2- handle cream soup	20.00	Sugar	20.00
Bowl, 7", round	20.00	Tray, 2- handle, celery	27.50
Bowl, 7½", round	25.00	Vase, footed	35.00
Bowl, oval, pickle	22.50	* Double price of crystal for colors.	

23

BLOCK OPTIC, "BLOCK" HOCKING GLASS COMPANY, 1929 – 1933

Colors: Green, pink, yellow, crystal, and some amber, blue, and clambroth green.

There are about 10 major Depression glass patterns, and Block Optic is one of that elite group. It's there due to availability through length of production, its charm of form and design, its variety of colors and, somewhat, to its history of being less expensive to collect, the economic factor. There are a few pricey items, but, by and large, most collectors can afford to pursue this pattern.

Lately, I've run into quite a few collectors looking for crystal Block, something mostly ignored in the past. One of those told me she picked that because she thought it had a wonderful Deco quality about it. Also, at shows, a few have been asking for the black footed stems, something else glanced over in the past. Around the 1928 – 1932 period, glass companies got in a big way of making bi-colored wares, either by decorating that way, or by actually fusing two (or three) colors and the Deco black was a big part of that. Hence, firing the foot of Block stems with black.

Due to a marked paper stopper found in one of the Block tumble-up (night) sets, we now know those were acquired with Baree Fragrance Bath Salts. The bottom of that is much more easily found than the little barrel shaped tumbler and is priced accordingly. Several people have gleefully told me about lucking onto those little tumblers for next to nothing in junk shops. So, keep a sharp eye out. You might do the same.

Thanks to some reader input, we also know that the lack of butter bottoms is due, in part, to the those ice box marvels of the time which came with a Block Optic top on a *metal* bottom, rather than a glass one. Thus, there are many more tops than bottoms available.

Some oddities are to be found in this pattern. Pieces come satinized or frosted, also a big push of that era. It was relatively easy to do by using camphoric acid and it gave the items a totally different look. In fact, I understand that today's crafters are etching things much the same way. In the early days of collecting, no one wanted anything to do with the satinized wares. However, that, too, is changing. Quite a few collectors are beginning to embrace them. One told me once she knew it was "a genre of that time" that was all the impetus she needed to really look at it and develop a liking for it. You can find a few items with painted decorations which probably means they were used in some special promotional product line.

Newcomers to collecting should know that Block Optic has five variations of sugars and creamers, due to their variety of handles, their being footed or flat, or their having rayed or nonrayed bottoms. In yellow Block, only the fancy handled sugar and creamer are found. The thicker, 4¼" diameter bowl with a height of 1½" is hard to find, as is the mayo, the blown Cameo style vase, grill plates, the 3½" short wine, and the 7" salad bowl.

A majority of collectors look for green Block. Pink Block has nearly all been swallowed up into collections, even the pieces which were a lighter pink which were disregarded at first. Stems are difficult to find, now. Many people liked their shape and capacity whether they collected much glass or not. Yellow Block, though very striking, comes in far fewer items than the green and is seen much less often. Both yellow and green fluoresce in black light, a display technique being used more and more often. Do *not* fall for the tale that this guarantees glass to be old, however; it simply means there's uranium oxide among the mix, something being produced by some factories today.

Grill plates, those plates with the "T" shaped dividers most often associated with diner and grill eateries are infrequently found in pink and crystal; in yellow and green, they're impossible. I've held two yellow ones in my hands, one of which a worker in my home managed to annihilate in the 1980s. The other is pictured in my *Florence's Glassware Pattern Identification I* book.

BLOCK OPTIC

	Green	Yellow	Pink
Bowl, 4¼" diam., 1⅜" tall	11.00		12.00
Bowl, 4½" diam., 1½" tall	27.50		40.00
Bowl, 5¼", cereal	12.00		40.00
Bowl, 7¼", salad	175.00		175.00
Bowl, 8½", large berry	35.00		35.00
* Bowl, 11¾", rolled-edge console	75.00		75.00
** Butter dish and cover, 3" x 5"	50.00		
Butter dish bottom	30.00		
Butter dish top	20.00		
*** Candlesticks, 1¾" pr.	120.00		80.00
Candy jar & cover, 2¼" tall	65.00	75.00	60.00
Candy jar & cover, 6¼" tall	60.00		150.00
Comport, 5⅜" wide, mayonnaise	90.00		90.00
Creamer, 3 styles: cone shaped, round, rayed-foot & flat (5 kinds)	13.00	13.00	15.00
Cup, four styles	7.00	8.00	6.00
Goblet, 3½", short wine	500.00		500.00
Goblet, 4", cocktail	40.00		40.00
Goblet, 4½", wine	40.00		40.00
Goblet, 5¾", 9 ounce	28.00		33.00
Goblet, 7¼", 9 ounce thin		38.00	
Ice bucket	45.00		80.00
Ice tub or butter tub, open	65.00		110.00
Mug	40.00		
Pitcher, 7⅝", 54 ounce, bulbous	95.00		295.00
Pitcher, 8½", 54 ounce	65.00		50.00
Pitcher, 8", 80 ounce	100.00		150.00
Plate, 6", sherbet	3.00	3.00	3.00
Plate, 8", luncheon	7.00	8.00	8.00
Plate, 9", dinner	27.50	45.00	38.00
Plate, 9", grill	95.00	65.00	

	Green	Yellow	Pink
Plate, 10¼", sandwich	25.00		25.00
Plate, 12¾"	30.00	30.00	
Salt and pepper, footed	45.00	95.00	90.00
Salt and pepper, squatty	125.00		
Sandwich server, center handle	75.00		75.00
Saucer, 5¾", with cup ring	10.00		8.00
Saucer, 6⅛", with cup ring	10.00		8.00
Sherbet, non-stemmed (cone)	3.75		
Sherbet, 3¼", 5½ ounce	6.00	10.00	7.50
Sherbet, 4¾", 6 ounce	18.00	21.00	18.00
Sugar, 3 styles: as creamer	12.50	12.50	12.50
Tumbler, 3 ounce, 2⅝"	25.00		28.00
Tumbler, 5 ounce, 3½", flat	25.00		28.00
Tumbler, 9½ ounce, 3¹³⁄₁₆", flat	15.00		15.00
Tumbler, 10 or 11 oz., 5", flat	20.00		18.00
Tumbler, 12 ounce, 4⅞", flat	30.00		30.00
Tumbler, 15 ounce, 5¼", flat	50.00		45.00
Tumbler, 3 ounce, 3¼", footed	30.00		30.00
Tumbler, 9 ounce, footed	18.00	27.50	17.00
Tumbler, 6", 10 ounce, footed	35.00		38.00
Tumble-up night set	75.00		
Tumbler, 3" only	60.00		
Bottle only	15.00		
Vase, 5¾", blown	350.00		
Whiskey, 1⅝", 1 ounce	42.50		45.00
Whiskey, 2¼", 2 ounce	32.00		32.00

 * Amber $45.00

 ** Green clambroth $250.00, blue $550.00, crystal $135.00

*** Amber $50.00

26

"BOWKNOT" ATTRIBUTED TO BELMONT TUMBLER COMPANY, Probably late 1920s

Color: Green.

Newcomers to Depression glass should know that most dealers do not display some of these smaller patterns such as "Bowknot" at glass shows because they take up the same valuable space as more costly items. Space is at a premium in a show booth and expenses include gas, food, motel, and booth rent before the first customer even arrives. Therefore, if you've chosen a smaller pattern, you'll probably have to inquire if the dealers have any pieces in inventory. I have found that "Bowknot" pieces sell well, when you can find them. Since this ware was heavily used, it is very necessary to check them for inner rim roughness (irr), particularly on the bowls and sherbets. Cereal bowls and tumblers are on many collectors' wish lists; and there are two styles of tumblers, a footed and a flat version (pictured in my *Florence's Glassware Pattern Identification I* book).

To date, no saucer has turned up for the cup. However, it was the custom back then to produce custard cups alone. This is perhaps one of those. People don't drink custard much these days, but judging from the pages of these found in older company catalogs, it seems to have been a very popular beverage back then, equivalent to our ice cream consumption, today. I suppose they could make custard without ice, a troublesome, costly product to obtain. Cathy's grandfather regaled us once, years ago, with a tale of cutting the ice off ponds in winter, hauling it on sleds to the backyard ice house/storm cellar (underground storage area) and packing it in layers between straw to help cool the foods stored there and provide ice to freeze ice cream, which that family loved. He said it would last until "well up in summer" that way.

Bowl, 4½", berry	25.00	Sherbet, low footed	25.00
Bowl, 5½", cereal	35.00	Tumbler, 5", 10 ounce	25.00
Cup	12.00	Tumbler, 5", 10 ounce, footed	25.00
Plate, 7", salad	15.00		

CAMEO, "BALLERINA," or "DANCING GIRL" HOCKING GLASS COMPANY, 1930 – 1934

Colors: Green, yellow, pink, and crystal w/platinum rim. (See Reproduction Section.)

Cameo could arguably be called *the* most beloved pattern in Depression glass. It was manufactured by Hocking Glass Company in the early 1930s, evidently incorporating a pattern design named "Springtime" from Monongah Glass Company (bought by Hocking). Several of their patterns were altered or continued by Hocking. Monongah's glass was *plate* etched, made in crystal, and usually gold trimmed. Collectors now are seeking "Springtime" which is relatively scarce in comparison to Cameo.

I need to stress that *all* miniature pieces with the Cameo design are newly made in the last 15 years. These were never made originally. See the Reproduction Section regarding these "Jennifer" sets. I've now seen the miniature comport touted as rare or as a salt dip on the Internet auctions and commanding outlandish sums from the uninformed. While we are discussing what isn't Cameo, I should remind you of the imported, weakly patterned shakers that appeared a few years ago in pink, and a darker green and cobalt blue color that were never made originally. Don't pay more than $12 for these fakes.

The Cameo centered-handled sandwich server and short, 3½" wines are choice Cameo collectibles. A couple of these shorter pink wines have surfaced in the last three years, but no green ones, lately. I bought a center-handled server that had been purchased 10 years ago for $125 at an auction in Lancaster, Ohio, the home of Anchor Hocking. You might want to check out the price that piece commands, today, when they can be found. It beats the stock market.

I receive more letters and calls about Cameo saucers than any other piece of Cameo. The rare Cameo saucer has a recessed, 1¾" diameter cup ring. Hocking made very few of these recessed ring saucers. They ordinarily made a smooth center, dual purpose saucer/sherbet plate for their patterns which will accommodate the foot of a sherbet. No recessed ring, yellow Cameo saucers have ever been confirmed.

The yellow Cameo butter dish and milk pitcher are remarkably evasive; but yellow Cameo cups, saucer/sherbet plates, footed tumblers, grill, and dinner plates were heavily promoted by Hocking. These five pieces are abundant, although prices on these commonly found yellow items have begun to climb. If you like it, now would be the time to gather it.

You can still assemble a large set of green Cameo, the most collected color, without investing an enormous amount of money as long as you stay away from buying the rarer pieces and purchase only one or two sizes of stems or tumblers when they can be found. Should you find a size you don't want at a bargain price, however, don't pass it up as you can reap a reward for it from another collector who does.

Cameo has two styles of grill ("T" shape divider bars) plates. One has tab handles and one does not. Both styles are common in yellow. However, the green grill with the tab or closed handles is harder to find and priced accordingly. The 10½" rare, rimmed dinner or flat cake plate is like the heavy edged (no tabs) grill plate without the dividers. The regular dinner plate has a large center as opposed to the small centered sandwich plate. The less expensive sandwich plate is often priced as the more expensive dinner plate. Avoid that trap!

Darker green bottles with the Cameo design (shown below) are marked on the bottom "Whitehouse Vinegar" These were sold with vinegar and a cork. Glass stoppers, however, should be found atop water bottles. These stoppers do not have a Cameo pattern on them, but are plain, paneled stoppers with hollow centers and are often absent on the bottles.

CAMEO

	Green	Yellow	Pink	Crystal, Plat
Bowl, 4¼", sauce				6.00
Bowl, 4¾", cream soup	195.00			
Bowl, 5½", cereal	40.00	35.00	150.00	6.50
Bowl, 7¼", salad	65.00			
Bowl, 8¼", large berry	45.00		175.00	
Bowl, 9", rimmed soup	75.00		225.00	
Bowl, 10", oval vegetable	35.00	42.00		
Bowl, 11", 3-legged console	90.00	125.00	75.00	
Butter dish and cover	250.00	1,500.00		
Butter dish bottom	140.00	500.00		
Butter dish top	95.00	1,000.00		
Cake plate, 10", 3 legs	30.00			
Cake plate, 10½", flat	110.00		175.00	
Candlesticks, 4", pair	125.00			
Candy jar, 4", low, and cover	95.00	110.00	595.00	
Candy jar, 6½", tall, and cover	195.00			
Cocktail shaker (metal lid) appears in crystal only			950.00	
Comport, 5⅜" wide, mayonnaise	45.00		225.00	
Cookie jar and cover	65.00			
Creamer, 3¼"	25.00	22.00		
Creamer, 4¼"	30.00		125.00	
Cup, 2 styles	18.00	9.00	85.00	5.50
Decanter, 10", with stopper	195.00			250.00
Decanter, 10", with stopper, frosted (stopper represents ⅓ value of decanter)	40.00			
Domino tray, 7", with 3" indentation	195.00			
Domino tray, 7", with no indentation			275.00	150.00
Goblet, 3½", wine	1,000.00		750.00	
Goblet, 4", wine	80.00		245.00	
Goblet, 6", water	65.00		195.00	
Ice bowl or open butter, 3" tall x 5½" wide	195.00		750.00	295.00

	Green	Yellow	Pink	Crystal, Plat
Jam jar, 2", and cover	225.00			175.00
Pitcher, 5¾", 20 ounce syrup or milk	295.00	2,000.00		
Pitcher, 6", 36 oz., juice	68.00			
Pitcher, 8½", 56 oz., water	70.00		1,500.00	500.00
Plate, 6", sherbet	5.00	3.00	90.00	2.00
Plate, 7", salad				3.50
Plate, 8", luncheon	15.00	11.00	35.00	4.00
Plate, 8½", square	55.00	250.00		
Plate, 9½", dinner	25.00	12.00	85.00	
Plate, 10", sandwich	20.00		55.00	
** Plate, 10½", rimmed, dinner	110.00		175.00	
Plate, 10½", grill	15.00	10.00	50.00	
Plate, 10½", grill with closed handles	75.00	6.00		
Plate, 10½", with closed handles	18.00	14.00		
Platter, 12", closed handles	30.00	40.00		
Relish, 7½", footed, 3 part	35.00			175.00
* Salt and pepper, ftd. pr.	75.00		900.00	
Sandwich server, center handle	7,000.00			
Saucer with cup ring	225.00			
Saucer, 6" (sherbet plate)	5.00	3.00	90.00	
Sherbet, 3⅛", molded	16.00	40.00	75.00	
Sherbet, 3⅛", blown	18.00		75.00	
Sherbet, 4⅞"	38.00	85.00	125.00	
Sugar, 3¼"	23.00	20.00		
Sugar, 4¼"	30.00		125.00	
Tumbler, 3¾", 5 oz., juice	33.00		90.00	
Tumbler, 4", 9 oz., water	30.00		80.00	9.00
Tumbler, 4¾", 10 oz., flat	30.00		95.00	
Tumbler, 5", 11 oz., flat	40.00	60.00	95.00	
Tumbler, 5¼", 15 oz.	80.00		135.00	
Tumbler, 3 oz., footed, juice	70.00		135.00	
Tumbler, 5", 9 oz., footed	33.00	17.50	115.00	
Tumbler, 5¾", 11 oz., ftd.	70.00		135.00	
Tumbler, 6⅜", 15 oz., ftd.	500.00			
Vase, 5¾"	250.00			
Vase, 8"	55.00			
Water bottle (dark green) Whitehouse vinegar	30.00			

* Beware reproductions
** Same as flat cake plate

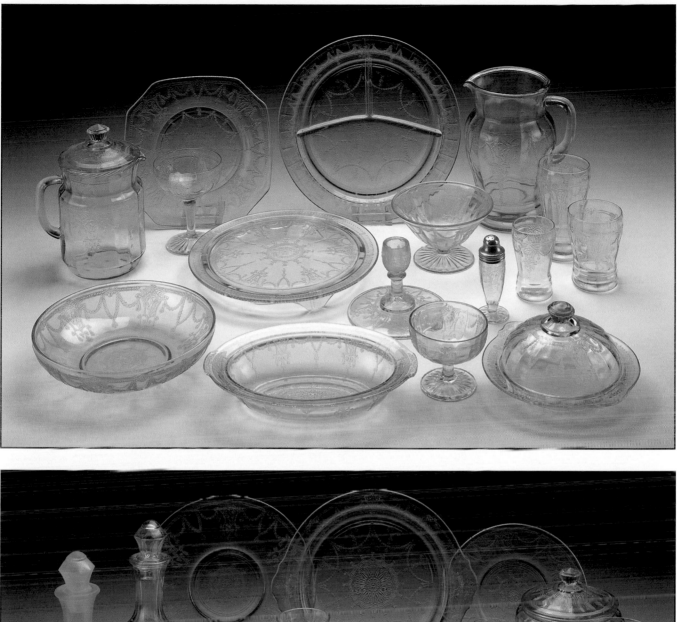

CHERRYBERRY U.S. GLASS COMPANY, Early 1930s

Colors: Pink, green, crystal; some iridized.

There is now a small cadre of collectors for the Cherryberry pattern, first noticed by Strawberry collectors who thought this pattern was theirs until closer inspection revealed cherries rather than strawberries in the design. Though this U.S. Glass pattern has relatively few pieces, there are other collectors vying for some of those items, namely, carnival glass supporters looking for the iridized pitchers, tumblers, and butter dishes, the most valuable pieces. Then, there are "item" collectors of butters and pitchers who snare those, too. So, there's quite a bit of competition for the few pieces surfacing.

Crystal is the rarest color though only a few seek it. As with other U.S. Glass Company patterns, many pieces have rough mould seams. Color inconsistencies of green cause an additional problem. Green can be found from a very yellow hue to a blue one. There is not as much color variance with the pink, but there are some pieces that are distinctly lighter than others. If you are a collector who is concerned about matching color hues, this may not be the pattern for you. If you can accept that this old glassware was made under less controlled circumstances than is presently used, and that the resulting burned out and imperfect color matches were part of that glass package, then there's no problem.

This is another U.S. Glass pattern that has no cup or saucer and has a plain butter base. If all these U.S. Glass patterns are "sister" patterns, then Strawberry and Cherryberry are twins. You can only differentiate them by an inspection of the fruits.

	Crystal, Iridescent	Pink, Green		Crystal, Iridescent	Pink, Green
Bowl, 4", berry	6.50	15.00	Olive dish, 5", one-handled	9.00	22.00
Bowl, 6¼", 2" deep	50.00	150.00	Pickle dish, 8¼", oval	9.00	22.00
Bowl, 6½", deep, salad	20.00	25.00	Pitcher, 7¾"	185.00	195.00
Bowl, 7½", deep, berry	20.00	32.00	Plate, 6", sherbet	6.00	12.00
Butter dish and cover	150.00	210.00	Plate, 7½", salad	8.00	20.00
Butter dish bottom	80.00	100.00	Sherbet	6.50	10.00
Butter dish top	70.00	110.00	Sugar, small ,open	12.00	24.00
Comport, 5¾"	18.00	28.00	Sugar, large	15.00	30.00
Creamer, small	12.00	24.00	Sugar cover	30.00	50.00
Creamer, 4⅝", large	18.00	42.50	Tumbler, 3⅝", 9 ounce	23.00	40.00

CHERRY BLOSSOM JEANNETTE GLASS COMPANY, 1930 – 1939

Colors: Pink, green, Delphite (opaque blue), crystal, Jadite (opaque green), and red. (See Reproduction Section.)

Almost all pieces in pink Cherry Blossom (and most in green) have increased in price, indicating a stream of new buyers; but prices on basic dinnerware pieces have really pulled this pattern past those beginning 1973 reproduction doldrums. Reproductions do not seem to bother anyone today as enlightened collectors treat them as just a nuisance part of all collecting. If you are a beginner, turn to the Reproduction Section in the back of the book and educate yourself on Cherry Blossom reproductions. (See page 244 – 245). I will be picking up around $3,000.00 worth of pink Cherry in a couple of days. It is a good seller which I was pleased to be offered, or I wouldn't be looking at it for any price.

Remember only two pairs of original pink Cherry Blossom shakers were ever documented and as far as I know, these have never resurfaced for sale. Therefore that price has remained constant. (Original ones are pictured on page 34.) However, the country has been absolutely flooded with reproduction Cherry shakers with their squared, jut wing collars. I continue to get many calls, letters, and e-mails on pink Cherry Blossom shakers. Someone sent pictures over the Internet for my "expert" opinion. When I said these shakers were not old, he replied that I only said that in order to buy them for a small price. I did not offer to buy them nor would I have touched them with a barge pole since they were not old. Please don't ask my opinion if you might not like the answer. The odds are not on your side for finding genuine pink Cherry shakers today, but I've learned never to say never.

That 9" platter is the most difficult piece to find (after genuine shakers). I have only seen one green 9" platter. (Measure this platter outside edge to outside edge.) I have calls for verification if I really mean outside edge. I do. The 11" platter measures 9" from the inside to inside rim and that common piece is not the rare 9" platter. The mug is the next piece rarely found. I have only seen a couple since I closed my shop in 1993.

Cherry Blossom has a propensity for inner rim chips, nicks, or those famous "chigger bites" as auctioneers like to call chips. Inner rim roughness (irr) was caused as much from stacking glass together as from using it. Of 13 berry bowls in a set I was offered, only one was mint. You can safely store dishes (bowls or plates) with proper sized paper plates or bowls between them. This is particularly true at glass shows where stacks of items are often handled over and over. Why do customers handle every plate only to announce that they already have those — and leave the booth? I guess that's called "appreciative touching."

Additional Cherry Blossom items that are hard to acquire include the aforementioned 9" platter, mugs, flat iced teas, soup and cereal bowls, and the 10" green grill plate. That grill plate has never even been found in pink, although there are two sizes found in green. The 9" one can be found without much difficulty. Mint condition grill plates are a prize. You may notice that the price for these has risen considerably over the last two years — mint being the key word here.

Crystal Cherry Blossom is sometimes spotted. Generally, it is the two-handled bowl that sells in the $20.00 to $25.00 range. Crystal is scarce, but there is not enough found to be collectible as a set. A few red (both opaque and transparent) and yellow pieces have surfaced, but the reproduction red wiped out most collectors' desire to own red. The original red was glossy and quite beautiful.

Letters AOP in listings and advertisements stand for "allover pattern" on the footed tumblers and rounded pitcher. The large, footed tumblers and the AOP pitcher come in two styles. One style has a scalloped or indented foot while the other is merely round with no indentations. Sherbets are also found like that. The letters PAT stand for "pattern at the top," illustrated by the flat-bottomed tumblers and pitchers.

There are some known experimental pieces of Cherry such as a pink cookie jar, pink five-part relish dishes, orange with green trim slag bowls, and amber children's pieces. You can see most of these pieces pictured in past *Very Rare Glassware of the Depression Era* books. Pricing on experimental items is extremely difficult to determine; but do not pass them up if the price is right — for you. There is always market demand for rare items of Depression glassware and particularly for those found in major patterns such as Cherry Blossom. The latest rarity being circulated in Cherry Blossom is a green casserole dish. I saw a damaged one about five years ago in Florida. Keep your eyes peeled for another one. Just be sure the piece is old and not a modern day plaything from Taiwan or dupe artists.

CHERRY BLOSSOM

	Pink	Green	Delphite
Bowl, 4¾", berry	20.00	22.00	16.00
Bowl, 5¾", cereal	52.00	47.50	
Bowl, 7¾", flat soup	100.00	90.00	
* Bowl, 8½", round, berry	52.00	50.00	50.00
Bowl, 9", oval vegetable	52.00	50.00	50.00
Bowl, 9", 2-handled	50.00	75.00	28.00
** Bowl, 10½", 3-leg, fruit	110.00	120.00	
Butter dish and cover	90.00	125.00	
Butter dish bottom	20.00	25.00	
Butter dish top	70.00	100.00	
Cake plate (3 legs), 10¼"	35.00	40.00	
Coaster	12.00	12.00	
Creamer	25.00	25.00	22.00
Cup	24.00	23.00	20.00
Mug, 7 oz.	395.00	360.00	
*** Pitcher, 6¾", AOP, 36 ounce			
scalloped or round bottom	75.00	75.00	80.00
Pitcher, 8", PAT, 42 ounce, flat	75.00	75.00	
Pitcher, 8", PAT, 36 ounce			
footed	75.00	75.00	
Plate, 6", sherbet	8.00	10.00	10.00
Plate, 7", salad	27.00	25.00	
**** Plate, 9", dinner	28.00	28.00	20.00
***** Plate, 9", grill	38.00	34.00	

	Pink	Green	Delphite
Plate, 10", grill		125.00	
Platter, 9", oval	950.00	1,100.00	
Platter, 11", oval	60.00	60.00	45.00
Platter, 13" and 13" divided	75.00	75.00	
Salt and pepper			
(scalloped bottom)	1,300.00	1,100.00	
Saucer	4.00	5.00	5.00
Sherbet	20.00	20.00	16.00
Sugar	14.50	17.50	20.00
Sugar cover	20.00	20.00	
Tray, 10½", sandwich	30.00	33.00	22.00
Tumbler, 3¾", 4 ounce,			
footed, AOP	18.00	20.00	25.00
Tumbler, 4½", 9 ounce,			
round, footed, AOP	40.00	40.00	25.00
Tumbler, 4½", 8 ounce,			
scalloped footed, AOP	40.00	40.00	25.00
Tumbler, 3½", 4 ounce,			
flat, PAT	22.00	33.00	
Tumbler, 4¼", 9 ounce,			
flat, PAT	17.00	25.00	
Tumbler, 5", 12 ounce,			
flat, PAT	75.00	85.00	

* Yellow $395.00
** Jadite $325.00
*** Jadite $325.00
**** Translucent green $225.00
***** Jadite $85.00

CHERRY BLOSSOM — CHILD'S JUNIOR DINNER SET

	Pink	Delphite
Creamer	52.00	50.00
Sugar	52.00	50.00
Plate, 6"	12.50	14.00 (design on bottom)
Cup	40.00	50.00
Saucer	7.50	7.25
14 piece set	350.00	380.00

Original box sells for $35.00 extra with pink sets.

CHINEX CLASSIC MacBETH-EVANS DIVISION OF CORNING GLASS WORKS, Late 1930s – Early 1940s

Colors: Ivory, ivory w/decal decoration.

Collectors of Chinex Classic strive to match items from among different florals found on ivory tint and affiliated Cremax ware. It is troublesome enough to ferret out the scroll decorated Chinex Classic pattern; but locating a piece you lack, only to have it embellished with a decal other than the one you want, is vexing. Windsor castle decal items are the most fascinating decoration to collectors; darker blue trims appear to be more popular than the lighter blue or brown. Notice that the brown Windsor castle comes with or without a brown trim. I see more brown, but that is less than twenty pieces a year.

I favor the dark blue trimmed Windsor castle decal decoration but have never located enough lighter blue to have a setting for a picture. I found a butter bottom as you can see in the Windsor castle photo. Can you confirm whether the top has a Windsor castle decal or just a blue trim? I have had readers say they found butters without a castle scene on the top. One was kind enough to sell me a Chinex floral top, but I have been unable to find the bottom for that one. The floral decal on that top is like those pieces on the right of the lower photograph. Have you any butter parts to match those missing in the photos?

The Pittsburgh area is where I have been able to find Chinex. Of course, MacBeth-Evans was just down the road and I suspect that has a great deal to do with this. A major portion of recent finds, however, have been in Canada where Corning was a mainstay in glass production. Chinex was advertised as ware resistant to crazing and chipping which helps explain its relatively good condition, today. It was made to compete with the chinaware then which did craze and chip. So, that was an excellent selling point.

Few collect plain, undecorated ivory pieces; but note how they mixed with the floral decorations in our photo. Maybe you could fill in those missing floral decals with this less expensive Chinex.

I was told by a collector that the undecorated Chinex worked in the microwave and reported that. However, I had an irate letter from a reader who blew up a piece of decorated ware, and it was all my fault. So, you do this at risk.

Notice the butter bottom looks like the Cremax pattern on the edge rather than Chinex. The butter tops have the scroll-like design that distinguishes Chinex, but this scroll design is missing from the butter bottoms. The bottom has a plain "pie crust" edge (like Cremax). The floral or castle designs will be inside the base of the butter, and apparently surrounding the knob of the top if the top has a floral decoration.

	Browntone or Plain Ivory	Decal Decorated	Castle Decal
Bowl, 5¾", cereal	5.50	9.00	15.00
Bowl, 6¾", salad	12.00	20.00	40.00
Bowl, 7", vegetable	14.00	25.00	40.00
Bowl, 7¾", soup	12.50	25.00	40.00
Bowl, 9", vegetable	11.00	25.00	40.00
Bowl, 11"	17.00	35.00	45.00
Butter dish	55.00	75.00	150.00
Butter dish bottom	12.50	27.50	50.00
Butter dish top	42.50	47.50	100.00
Creamer	5.50	10.00	20.00
Cup	4.50	6.50	15.00
Plate, 6¼", sherbet	2.50	4.00	7.50
Plate, 9¾", dinner	4.50	9.00	18.00
Plate, 11½", sandwich or cake	7.50	15.00	28.00
Saucer	2.00	4.00	6.00
Sherbet, low footed	7.00	11.00	27.50
Sugar	6.00	10.00	20.00

CHINEX CLASSIC

37

CIRCLE HOCKING GLASS COMPANY, 1930s

Colors: Green, pink, and crystal.

Green Circle can be collected in sets with time and patience. It is reasonably priced, though not easily found. Pink seemingly occurs only in a luncheon set. As you can see by the dearth of pink in the picture, I am having no luck acquiring it. I haven't seen a pink luncheon plate in years even though I have been looking. The last ones I saw were a stack of a dozen or so priced as a lot, but I only wanted one for photography. Looking back now, I should have bought the stack. Lots of pieces thought to be common in the early days of collecting are not. If you have a piece of pink not in the listing, please, let me know.

Both the 9⅜" and 5¼" green bowls pictured, have ground bottoms. At Hocking, ground bottoms usually suggest early production pieces. The 5" flared bowl is shown in the right foreground of the photograph. It is clearly a darker shade of green when compared with the other pieces. Different shades of green occur in a few patterns made by Hocking; Cameo comes to mind.

Two different styles of cups add to the idiosyncrasies of Circle. The flat bottomed style fits a saucer/sherbet plate while the rounded cup takes an indented saucer. I finally found an indented saucer for my round, pink cup, but no saucer/sherbet plate for the flat one.

Green stems with crystal tops are more easily found than all green stems. In many Elegant patterns, two-toned stems are often more expensive. This is not the case for Circle. Few currently desire crystal topped items. Thus, you can buy these rather inexpensively.

Collectors of kitchenware (particularly reamer collectors) often buy Circle. They treasure that 80 ounce pitcher with the reamer top. Color contrasts on these pitchers make it difficult to obtain a reamer separately that correctly matches the green hue of the pitcher. That 80 ounce pitcher shown here is a darker green (similar to the flared bowl) than the other green items. Notice that the bowls have jumped in price due to many collectors searching for them. Demand is always the driving factor in prices; rarity only helps.

	Green	Pink
Bowl, 4½"	14.00	
Bowl, 5¼"	20.00	
Bowl, 5", flared, 1¾" deep	18.00	
Bowl, 8"	30.00	
Bowl, 9⅜"	35.00	
Creamer	9.00	20.00
Cup (2 styles)	6.00	10.00
Goblet, 4½", wine	15.00	
Goblet, 8 ounce, water	11.00	
Pitcher, 60 ounce	75.00	
Pitcher, 80 ounce	35.00	
Plate, 6", sherbet/saucer	2.00	5.00

	Green	Pink
Plate, 8¼", luncheon	6.00	10.00
Plate, 9½"	12.00	
Plate, 10", sandwich	14.00	
Saucer w/cup ring	2.50	3.00
Sherbet, 3⅛"	5.00	10.00
Sherbet, 4¾"	7.00	
Sugar	7.00	20.00
Tumbler, 3½", 4 ounce, juice	8.00	
Tumbler, 4", 8 ounce, water	9.00	
Tumbler, 5", 10 ounce, tea	18.00	
Tumbler, 15 ounce, flat	25.00	

CLOVERLEAF HAZEL ATLAS GLASS COMPANY, 1930 – 1936

Colors: Pink, green, yellow, crystal, and black.

Cloverleaf pattern has easy recognition going for it. The "good luck" associated with these little shamrocks may be what you'll need to find it. I have seen any number of wonderful club show displays using various colors of this pattern.

Pictured below is every piece of yellow Cloverleaf known. The grill plate (divided in three parts) must suffice as a dinner-sized plate. The candy dish, shakers, and bowls are all difficult to find in yellow. I have seen only one yellow bowl at all the glass shows I attended in the last year. You will be able to find the other pieces; but, know that all yellow items are getting scarce and pricey.

There appear to be equal numbers of collectors for black or yellow Cloverleaf. Few pursue pink or crystal. Besides luncheon pieces in pink, a berry bowl and a flared, 10 ounce tumbler exist. That pink tumbler was sparcely distributed and has not been found in crystal at all. How many pink berry bowls have you seen? Prices for these bowls are beginning to surge. I've seen more yellow berry bowls than pink.

Green Cloverleaf is the color most in demand. Every known piece of green is pictured. The 8" bowl and tumblers will sell briskly. All the bowls (in any color), as well as grill plates and tumblers are becoming more difficult to gather. Of the three styles of tumblers pictured, it is the flat, straight-sided one available only in green that is rarely found.

Black Cloverleaf prices have been rather steady over the last few years with only a little increase on a few pieces. Small ashtrays are being ignored while the larger ones sell infrequently. The black sherbet plate and saucer are the same size. The saucer has no Cloverleaf design in the center, but the sherbet plate does. Notice the price difference. These sherbet plates still turn up in stacks of saucers occasionally; so keep your eyes open.

Cloverleaf pattern can be found moulded on both sides of the pieces, inside or outside. In order for the black to show the pattern, moulds had to be designed with the pattern on the visible side of pieces, otherwise it looked plain black. On transparent pieces, the pattern could be on the bottom or the inside and it would still show. Over the years, transparent pieces were made using the moulds designed for the black; so, you now find these pieces with designs on both sides. This does not make a difference in value or collectibility.

CLOVERLEAF

	Pink	Green	Yellow	Black
Ashtray, 4", match holder in center				65.00
Ashtray, 5¾", match holder in center				90.00
Bowl, 4", dessert	40.00	40.00	40.00	
Bowl, 5", cereal		50.00	55.00	
Bowl, 7", deep salad		75.00	85.00	
Bowl, 8"		95.00		
Candy dish and cover		65.00	125.00	
Creamer, 3⅝", footed		10.00	22.00	18.00
Cup	9.00	9.00	11.00	18.00
Plate, 6", sherbet		10.00	10.00	40.00
Plate, 8", luncheon	11.00	8.00	14.00	15.00
Plate, 10¼", grill		25.00	28.00	
Salt and pepper, pair		40.00	135.00	100.00
Saucer	3.00	3.00	4.00	5.00
Sherbet, 3", footed	10.00	12.00	14.00	22.00
Sugar, 3⅝", footed		10.00	22.00	18.00
Tumbler, 4", 9 ounce, flat		65.00		
Tumbler, 3¾", 10 ounce, flat, flared	30.00	50.00		
Tumbler, 5¾", 10 ounce, footed		30.00	40.00	

COLONIAL, "KNIFE AND FORK" HOCKING GLASS COMPANY, 1934 – 1936

Colors: Pink, green, crystal, and Vitrock.

Green is still the preferred color of Hocking's Colonial pattern. Pink prices are equal to those of green, however, because of rarity. If pink were as sought as green, there is no telling how high the prices would soar. Did you notice the white cream soup on the cover? A white water pitcher was found a couple of years ago and we now have cream soups to add to those already discovered cups, saucers (two styles), luncheon plates, creamers, and sugar bowls. No top has been spotted for that sugar. White has been largely ignored due to the small number of pieces first found, but it's beginning to look like a set might be possible. There was speculation once that this white was Corning made, but it looks like Hocking's Vitrock to me. Crystal Colonial can still be found, but it is no longer inexpensive. In crystal, Colonial looks very like older pattern glass. Indeed, Cathy has found a crystal bowl that is slightly cone shaped that probably is pattern ware; and it has this Colonial design. Perhaps that's why the company gave it the Colonial name; it had its basis in an older glass design.

The true shortage of crystal stemware is now being discovered. Since no stems are found in pink, some collectors mix crystal stems with their pink sets. I have noticed that buyers for both crystal and pink items have picked up recently. The problem with collecting anything other than green is limited availability.

There are three sizes of footed tumblers and five sizes of stems in Colonial. Footed tumblers are not stems despite erroneous reports (and photographs) identifying them as such in a competing publication on Depression glass. Errors can occur in writing; but to not be able to identify simple pieces that any casual glass research would point out, has already created some problems for new collectors — as well as old authors. When they ask *me* why so and so said such and such and they've just found out that isn't at all correct, I *want* to say you've purchased bad information from someone who obviously doesn't know the basics of glassware. Yet, I can't really say that. It puts us all in a bad light when things like this happen. This isn't the only faux pas in this book by a long shot. It just happens to be the most recent one brought to my attention at a show. Only footed tumblers are found in pink; do not mistake these as Colonial stems.

The first green, beaded top Colonial pitcher to appear is shown on page 42. Notice that it is gold trimmed, a heavily used decorating technique in the first third of the twentieth century. A pink one was bought at an auction in the Cincinnati area in 1975. I bought the green one 30 miles north of there 20 years later. To date, only one of each color has been spotted — though I doubt only one of each was made.

Colonial soup bowls (both cream and flat), cereals, mint shakers, and dinner plates are still difficult to obtain in all colors. The vertical ridges on Colonial have a tendency to chip; when examining a piece, look at those ridges first. Always take the top off of any shaker to check for damage. I once bought a shaker with a top I couldn't loosen and when I soaked it free, I found it had been glued on to cover a large chip in the top edge.

Coveted Colonial mugs are seldom seen today. The 11 ounce Colonial tumbler measures 2¾" across the top while the 12 ounce measures exactly 3". These two tumblers are repeatedly confused. It is easier to measure across the top than to measure the contents if you are out shopping. The spooner stands 5½" tall, while the sugar without a lid is only 4½" high. That inch makes a huge difference in price.

The cheese dish consists of a wooden board with an indented groove upon which the glass lid rests. One is pictured below.

COLONIAL

	Pink	Green	Crystal
Bowl, 3¾", berry	60.00		
Bowl, 4½", berry	18.00	20.00	10.00
Bowl, 5½", cereal	65.00	100.00	35.00
Bowl, 4½", cream soup, white $60	75.00	80.00	65.00
Bowl, 7", low soup	65.00	65.00	30.00
Bowl, 9", large berry	30.00	30.00	25.00
Bowl, 10", oval vegetable	40.00	40.00	22.00
Butter dish and cover	700.00	55.00	42.00
Butter dish bottom	450.00	32.50	25.00
Butter dish top	250.00	22.50	17.00
Cheese dish		250.00	
Cream/milk pitcher, 5", 16 oz.	65.00	15.00	18.00
Cup, white 8.00	10.00	14.00	7.00
Mug, 4½", 12 ounce	500.00	800.00	
+ Pitcher, 7", 54 ounce	50.00	55.00	35.00
*+ Pitcher, 7¾", 68 ounce, white $3.00	70.00	80.00	45.00
Plate, 6", sherbet	7.00	8.00	3.00
Plate, 8½", luncheon	10.00	11.00	6.00
Plate, 10", dinner	55.00	65.00	30.00
Plate, 10", grill	25.00	25.00	15.00
Platter, 12", oval	35.00	25.00	20.00

	Pink	Green	Crystal
Salt and pepper, pair	150.00	160.00	65.00
Saucer/sherbet plate, white 3.00	7.00	8.00	3.00
Sherbet, 3"	25.00		
Sherbet, 3⅜"	12.00	14.00	8.00
Spoon holder or celery, 5½"	135.00	130.00	90.00
Stem, 3¾", 1 ounce, cordial		30.00	18.00
Stem, 4", 3 ounce, cocktail		25.00	14.00
Stem, 4½", 2½ ounce, wine		30.00	14.00
Stem, 5¼", 4 ounce, claret		25.00	20.00
Stem, 5¾", 8½ ounce, water		30.00	25.00
Sugar, 4½"	25.00	16.00	8.00
Sugar cover	65.00	27.00	16.00
Tumbler, 3", 5 ounce, juice	22.00	25.00	15.00
** Tumbler, 4", 9 ounce, water	22.00	22.00	15.00
Tumbler, 5⅛" high, 11 ounce	35.00	42.00	22.00
Tumbler, 12 ounce, iced tea	52.00	52.00	24.00
Tumbler, 15 ounce, lemonade	65.00	75.00	45.00
Tumbler, 3¼", 3 ounce, footed	17.00	25.00	10.00
Tumbler, 4", 5 ounce, footed	32.00	42.00	20.00
*** Tumbler, 5¼", 10 ounce, footed	50.00	50.00	27.50
Whiskey, 2½", 1½ ounce	16.00	16.00	12.00

*Beaded top $1,100.00   **Royal ruby $110.00   ***Royal ruby $160.00   +With or without ice lip

COLONIAL BLOCK HAZEL ATLAS GLASS COMPANY, Early 1930s

Colors: Green, crystal, black, pink, and rare in cobalt blue; white in 1950s.

Green Colonial Block is the most seen color and therefore, most collectors stick to buying it rather than pink. You will find an infrequent crystal piece and white creamer and sugar sets. A few black and frosted green Colonial Block powder jars are being found. A cobalt blue Colonial Block creamer is shown in my *Very Rare Glassware of the Depression Years, Second Series.* So far, no sugar bowl has been found to match it. That creamer can be found with Shirley Temple's image in white. Hazel Atlas also made a different creamer with the same Shirley image which has now been reproduced.

Many pieces of Colonial Block are *marked HA,* but not all. *The H is on top of the A,* which confuses some inexperienced people who assume that this is the symbol for Anchor Hocking. The anchor is a symbol used by Anchor Hocking and that was not used until after the 1930s.

Green 4" and 7" bowls, butter tub, sherbets, and the pitcher are the pieces most often lacking in Colonial Block collections. The 5 ounce footed juice is rare. You can check out one of these tumblers in *Very Rare Glassware of the Depression Years, Fifth Series.* How does a small pattern like this can have so many hard to find pieces? To begin with, it most likely was regionally distributed; and some of those hard-to-find pieces may have been premiums for a product that did not sell well.

The goblet to the right of the green pitcher is Colonial Block and not Block Optic as it is often called at markets. Some Block Optic collectors use these heavy goblets with their sets because they are more reasonably priced than those in Block Optic. Too, the heavier Colonial Block goblets are probably more durable than the thinner Block Optic. More green sherbets are now finding their way into collections. These were discovered about ten years ago and shortly thereafter, the floodgates opened and we were awash with sherbets.

U.S. Glass made a pitcher similar in style to Hazel Atlas's Colonial Block. There is little difference in them except most Hazel Atlas pitchers are marked and the one in the photo is not so marked. Collectors today are not as inflexible in their collecting principles as they once were. Many collectors will buy either pitcher to go with their set. That is why items that are similar to a pattern, but not actually a part of it, are referred to as "go-with" or "look-alike" pieces. In general, these items are more reasonably priced. Original ads called colonial block a modernistic design.

	Crystal	Pink, Green	White		Crystal	Pink, Green	White
Bowl, 4"	4.00	10.00		Goblet	6.00	14.00	
Bowl, 7"	10.00	22.00		Pitcher	22.00	45.00	
Butter dish	30.00	45.00		*Powder jar w/lid	12.00	17.50	
Butter dish bottom	5.00	12.50		Sherbet	4.00	8.00	
Butter dish top	25.00	32.50		Sugar	6.00	10.00	8.00
Butter tub	25.00	45.00		Sugar lid	6.00	15.00	7.50
Candy jar w/cover	22.00	40.00		Tumbler, 5¼", 5 oz., footed		65.00	
Creamer	6.00	12.00	8.00				

*Black $22.50

43

COLONIAL FLUTED, "ROPE" FEDERAL GLASS COMPANY, 1928 – 1933

Colors: Green and crystal.

Unlike other patterns, there has not been a new discovery in Colonial Fluted since I started writing 30 years ago. The "F" in a shield, usually found in the center of many Colonial Fluted pieces, is the symbol used by the Federal Glass Company. Not all pieces of Federal Glass are marked. No, that "F" does not stand for Fire-King as one person asked. Many Federal made kitchen items look similar to Fire-King ware. That recent Fire-King buying frenzy has people checking everything they see for Fire-King.

Colonial Fluted was a functional pattern that was relentlessly used; you will find most flat pieces with scratches. Knife use wears away the surface of most glassware and Colonial Fluted is testimony to that. I rarely find any plates that are not white with wear. When you find Colonial Fluted, it usually is priced moderately enough to use; so, if you like it, do so. Treat this older glass with respect, but enjoy using it.

Colonial Fluted used to be an inaugural set for beginning collectors; now, quantities are so limited that new collectors could become disheartened looking for it. A few collectors find it an ideal bridge set. Indeed, much of the original advertising for this pattern was centered around bridge parties, which are not as in vogue now as they were in the 1930s. Crystal decorated pieces with hearts, spades, diamonds, and clubs are very collectible. We hope to photograph a set in the future,

Colonial Fluted can be mixed with other sets, too, which is a present trend with collectors. There is no dinner plate in the Colonial Fluted pattern. There is a dinner-sized plate made by Federal that goes very well with this which has the roping around the outside of the plate, but not the fluting. There is, also, a grill plate that goes well with the pattern. It has no roping either. Both of these pieces can expand the number of items in your set and give you larger serving pieces to use. Federal made those items mentioned, so they match in color.

	Green			Green
Bowl, 4", berry	12.00		Plate, 6", sherbet	4.00
Bowl, 6", cereal	16.00		Plate, 8", luncheon	8.00
Bowl, 6½", deep (2½"), salad	35.00		Saucer	2.00
Bowl, 7½", large berry	22.00		Sherbet	7.00
Creamer	10.00		Sugar	10.00
Cup	8.00		Sugar cover	20.00

COLUMBIA FEDERAL GLASS COMPANY, 1938 – 1942

Colors: Crystal, some pink.

Columbia is not too plentiful, today. Columbia tumblers have always been scarce; but, presently, there are other difficulties. Two sizes of Columbia tumblers have now been validated, the 2⅞", 4 ounce juice and 9 ounce water. An "analogous" tumbler has surfaced which it is marked "France" on the bottom. Devotees of Columbia need to be aware of this before paying for foreign-made glassware. You might find Columbia water tumblers with advertisements for dairy products printed on them. These were used as containers for cottage cheese.

Pink Columbia sells extremely well for a pattern that has only four pieces. Prices have stabilized for the moment. Crystal Columbia bowls, plates, and even the cups have increased in value since the last book.

The formerly elusive (except in Colorado) snack tray has begun to turn up in quantities unknown before causing the price to stay in the $30.00 range. Many collectors have not known what to look for since it is an unusual piece and shaped differently from most Columbia. The pictures in recent editions have shown the tray so well that collectors are finding these to the point that supply is over running demand right now. These snack plates were found with Columbia cups in a boxed set almost 30 years ago in northern Ohio. Federal Glass Company labeled the box "Snack Sets." No mention was made of Columbia on the box. Snack trays are also being found with Federal cups other than the Columbia pattern, which is probably why so many are being located after all these years.

I have pictured a snack tray that has the "winged" tab handles. There are bowls and snack set that are designed like the Columbia snack tray. They do not have the center design but do have the "winged" tab handles. These are being found in original Federal boxes labeled "Homestead."

You will find Columbia butter dishes with diverse flashed colors and floral decal decorations. Some were even satinized (frosted); others were flashed with color after the satin finish was applied. Federal must have fervently promoted these since many are found today. The supply for this butter dish exceeds the demand.

Satinized, pastel-banded, and floral-decaled luncheon sets in Columbia have been seen. These sets are scarce. In the past, they were difficult to sell, unless you found a complete set. It was too difficult to find matching pieces. Today, with all the mixing and matching colors that is going on, there is not the onus for having everything the same at the table as was once de rigeur.

	Crystal	Pink		Crystal	Pink
Bowl, 5", cereal	18.00		Cup	9.00	25.00
Bowl, 8", low soup	25.00		Plate, 6", bread & butter	4.00	15.00
Bowl, 8½", salad	22.00		Plate, 9½", luncheon	11.00	35.00
Bowl, 10½", ruffled edge	22.00		Plate, 11", chop	17.00	
Butter dish and cover	20.00		Saucer	2.00	10.00
Ruby flashed 22.00			Snack plate	30.00	
Other flashed 21.00			Tumbler, 2⅞", 4 ounce, juice	25.00	
Butter dish bottom	7.50		Tumbler, 9 ounce, water	30.00	
Butter dish top	12.50				

45

CORONATION, "BANDED RIB," "SAXON" HOCKING GLASS COMPANY, 1936 – 1940

Colors: Pink, green, crystal, and Royal Ruby.

Coronation was first made in 1936 and was probably so named because of the coronation fanfare going on in England at that time. It was certainly headline news then. Many collectors first noticed Coronation because of its tumblers. Coronation's tumblers were invariably confused with the rarely found Old Colony ("Lace Edge") tumblers. Note the fine ribs above the middle of the Coronation tumbler. These ribs are missing on the Old Colony footed tumbler. (Perhaps you can make a cerebral link between an actual coronation (a crown above) and Coronation pattern with its ribs above the middle. Maybe you could visualize a crown above ribs. Whatever helps in identification. Look at the bottom of page 161 to see the differences. Some collectors intentionally buy Coronation tumblers to use with Old Colony since they can buy three Coronation tumblers for the cost of one Old Colony. Both are the same shape and color and made by the same manufacturer. Just don't accidentally confuse the two since there is quite a price disparity. Of course, if you see Old Colony tumblers priced as Coronation, that's a "smile" price.

Royal Ruby Coronation cups were sold with crystal saucers. Those crystal saucer/sherbet plates are the only common crystal pieces found in Coronation. A few other crystal pieces are turning up besides the crescent salad, but there is little demand for now. No Royal Ruby Coronation saucer/sherbet plates have ever been seen. Royal Ruby is the name of the red glass that was made by Hocking and only their red glassware can be called Royal Ruby.

Coronation pitchers are rarely seen in person, but I have provided you two views on page 47. That pitcher is the one piece missing from most collections of Coronation. Most of these were bought long ago by collectors of pitchers and tumblers because Coronation collectors thought they were way too expensive. Few pitchers are being marketed for today's collectors to buy.

The handles on Royal Ruby Coronation bowls are open; handles on the pink are closed. Two newly discovered bowls in pink have been without handles. They measure 4¼" and 8", like the previously discovered green ones. The smaller pink berry is like the green one in the foreground of the top photo. The items in green Coronation at the bottom of page 47 are shown compliments of Anchor Hocking. Additional green pieces now known include the luncheon plate and large or small berry bowls, shown in the upper photo. That green crescent salad plate is a rather interesting item for Depression glass. Crescent salads are more prevalent in Elegant patterns. A couple of these have also been detected in crystal.

The larger green tumbler in the lower photograph is 5⁷⁄₁₆" tall and holds 14¼ oz. Who knew Depression glass was going to be so significant? Even movie producers are increasingly concerned to show correct dishes in their period movies. Canadian dealers have reported selling large sets of Depression glass to be used in movies being made there. I know Cathy and I were viewing some flick recently and we both turned to each other with a "Did you see...?" when the camera panned a piece of Depression ware.

Beginning dealers often price those commonly found red handled Coronation berry bowls excessively. They have always been abundant and are somewhat difficult to sell. Some years ago a large accumulation was discovered in an old warehouse. They were still in the original boxes. Yet, I regularly see these priced for four to five times their worth. I once saw the large, two-handled berry priced for $75.00. It was marked "rare old pigeon blood." That "pigeon blood" term comes from older collectors who use it to describe dark, red glass (not made from the blood of dead birds). One dealer assured me that his Royal Ruby goblets were rare old pigeon blood pieces, and very valuable. He obviously thought so — since they were priced at $30.00 each two years ago. I checked; he still owns them. I offered an informative book, but he said he knows as much as he needs to know. I like to check his booth. My best bargain in his booth was a Jade-ite Fire-King pitcher for $75.00.

	Pink	Royal Ruby	Green
Bowl, 4¼", berry, handled	7.00	7.00	
Bowl, 4¼", no handles	80.00		55.00
Bowl, 6½", nappy, handled	6.00	18.00	
Bowl, 8", large berry, handled	15.00	20.00	
Bowl, 8", no handles	195.00		195.00
* Cup	5.50	6.50	
Pitcher, 7¾", 68 ounce	595.00		
Plate, 6", sherbet	3.00		
Plate, 8½", luncheon	4.50		60.00
** Saucer (same as 6" plate)	3.00		
Sherbet	10.00		85.00
Tumbler, 5", 10 ounce, footed	30.00		195.00

*Crystal $4.00   ** Crystal $.50

CRACKLE VARIOUS COMPANIES (L.E. SMITH, MCKEE GLASS, MACBETH EVANS, FEDERAL GLASS, U.S. GLASS, ET. AL.) c. 1924

Colors: Amber, green, crystal, canary, amethyst, pink, satin (frosted) colors, crystal with color trims.

I've had various collectors approach me from time to time wanting to know why I didn't include crackle in my books. Mostly, for so few collectors, I couldn't afford to spend the eons of research time trying to find out which of the multitudes of companies made what. So, I avoided the issue. A couple of years ago, a serious collector appeared at my book table at a show and told me in ardent terms of her love for this type glassware. I asked which company's wares she collected and she said, "Oh, it makes no difference. If it's crackled, that's all I need to know." Intrigued, I asked what type crackle she collected, the genuinely cold water cracked, reheated crackle, or the moulded type. "Oh, I'm only interested in the moulded type. I'm not really into broken looking glass. But," she added, "it would be nice to know what all is available and what kind of prices I should be paying." That got me to thinking. If I were to lump every moulded piece I could find into a listing, then that could serve some purpose; and getting it out there would eventually help ascertain what was available to collectors. So, here's what I've been able to learn. I'm sure there's more you can contribute and I look forward to hearing what you turn up. Again, we're only dealing with the moulded crackle wares that were advertised as making drink liquids "look like cracked ice" or putting you in "refreshing anticipation of a cool summer drink." Not everybody had ice available to them then. It cost money, it came in freezing, heavy square blocks, if you weren't affluent enough to have it delivered, had to be hauled home on towels, paper, or in boxes in the floor of your car; it had to be lifted and chipped apart with an ice pick, no delicate job; it melted; it required expensive ice boxes to keep; and the resultant water messes had to be dealt with. So, many companies hopped onto this "suggestion of ice" effect in their glassware lines, particularly in beverage sets; and judging by the available pieces found in markets, today, so did the buying public.

There were various finely stippled and crinkled effect wares, too. We're trying not to include them in this list, only the moulded items with the large veins making that cracked ice look. Let me hear what you know about wares with this design. For now, I'm pricing only crystal, using prices I've observed in the market. Colored crackle will fetch 20 – 25% more, except for canary, which will cost up to 50% more.

	*Crystal		*Crystal		*Crystal
Bottle, water	18.00	Jar, screw threads	22.00	Sherbet, round rim	8.00
Butter, small (powder jar style)	25.00	Pitcher, bulbous middle, water, no lid	25.00	Tray, 3-footed, flat	22.50
Bowl, console	20.00			Tumbler, 4¾" footed cone	8.00
Bowl, flare rim on black base	35.00	Pitcher, 64 ounce bulbous w/lid	40.00	Tumbler, 5 ounce, bowed middle, juice	10.00
Bowl, footed small vegetable	18.00	Pitcher, 9", cone, footed	45.00	Tumbler, 9 ounce, bowed middle, water	8.00
Bowl, ruffled vegetable	20.00	Pitcher, water, slant edge, flat bottom, optic, no lid	30.00	Tumbler, 12 ounce, bowed middle, tea	9.00
Bowl, hexagon cereal	12.00	Plate, dessert, round or octagon	8.00	Tumbler, juice, straight side	8.00
Caddy, center handle, 6 holder	10.00	Plate, salad, round or octagon	9.00	Tumbler, tea, straight side	6.00
Caddy, center handle, 4 holder	8.00	Plate, 8", round or octagon	10.00	Tumbler, water, straight side	8.00
Candle, cone	22.00	Plate, cloverleaf snack	13.00	Vase, squat, bulbous with flat rim	12.50
Candy box, hexagonal lid	25.00	Plate, cracker w/center rim	17.00		
Candy, footed, round, dome lid	25.00	Plate, server, 2-handle	20.00	*Colors add 20 – 25%, except canary, add 50%	
Compote, cheese (for cracker)	12.50	Sherbet, octagon rim	10.00		
Cup	10.00				

48

CREMAX MacBETH-EVANS DIVISION OF CORNING GLASS WORKS, Late 1930s – Early 1940s

Colors: Cremax, Cremax with fired-on colored trim or decals.

Cremax is a general designation for several tableware patterns that were manufactured in the ivory glass coloring (called Cremax). These patterns also identify the color as part of the pattern name. For illustration, there was Cremax Bordette line, with pink, yellow, blue, and green borders; Cremax Rainbow line with pastel pink and green borders; the Cremax Windsor line, with Windsor brown, blue, and green castle decals; and a plain ware simply called Cremax pattern. There was, also, a six-sided center floral ware called Princess pattern and one with a floral spray known as Flora. The blue or pink-bordered roses have more admirers than do the non-colored border items. The sandwich plate with red flowers on the back right (bottom of page 51) was called "Mountain Flowers." You might recognize it as a Petalware decoration, also.

The blue Cremax picture shown has created more collectors for this pattern. Although this blue is commonly seen in Canada and some states that border Canada, few other collectors realized that there were so many pieces of blue to gather. I have been informed that the lighter robin's egg blue was distributed by Corning almost exclusively in Canada. That darker blue shade is not as common in Canada. Many of the pieces I have bought have been in northern states, especially Michigan and New York.

The Delphite colored blue (shown below) has the same shapes as what we are familiar with, but the robin's egg blue (top of page 50) has a flat sugar and creamer and a slightly smaller cup. At this time, price both shades of blue about the same as the pieces with decals. Assembling a set of the light blue will take time.

Cremax Bordette demitasse sets were marketed in sets of eight. Some sets have been found on a wire rack. The usual make-up of these sets has been two sets each of four colors: pink, yellow, blue, and green. I have finally obtained three of these to show you but have not found a blue as yet. Notice that the interiors of these cups are plain.

The bottom to the butter dish in Chinex is often believed to be Cremax. The scalloped edges of the butter bottom are just like the edges on Cremax plates; however, the only butter tops ever found have the Chinex scroll-like pattern. Thus, if you find only the bottom of a butter, it is a Chinex bottom. See page 37 for an example.

The green Windsor castle decal is the most difficult colored decal to find on Cremax. The one piece pictured on page 50 is the only piece I have ever found. A Cremax set could be bought rather economically. It was advertised as resistant to chips and made to be in service for years. Most of what you find today is in good shape.

	Cremax	*Blue, Decal Decorated		Cremax	*Blue, Decal Decorated
Bowl, 5¾", cereal	3.50	10.00	Egg cup, 2¼"	12.00	
Bowl, 7¾", soup	7.00	25.00	Plate, 6¼", bread and butter	2.00	4.00
Bowl, 9", vegetable	8.00	18.00	Plate, 9¾", dinner	4.50	12.00
Creamer	4.50	10.00	Plate, 11½", sandwich	5.50	20.00
Cup	4.00	5.00	Saucer	2.00	3.50
Cup, demitasse	11.00	25.00	Saucer, demitasse	4.00	10.00
			Sugar, open	4.50	10.00

*Add 50% for castle decal

"CROW'S FOOT" LINE 412 & LINE 890 PADEN CITY GLASS COMPANY, 1930s

Colors: Ritz blue, Ruby red, amber, amethyst, black, pink, crystal, white, and yellow.

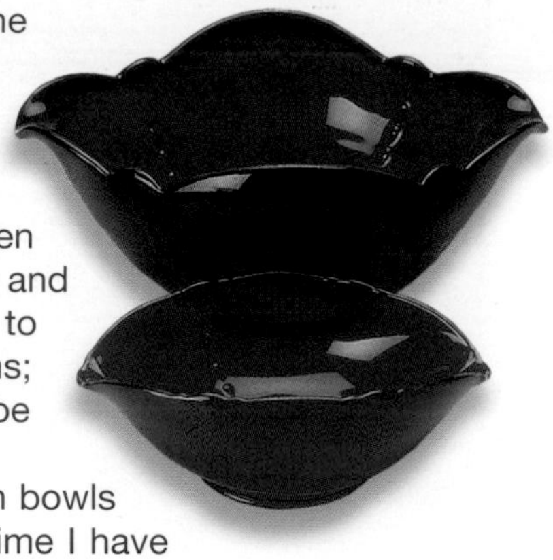

"Crow's Foot" is the most frequently used mould blank for Paden City etchings. The squared shape is Line #412, and the round is Line #890. When on display, plain "Crow's Foot" attracts new collectors. After all, not everyone can afford the popular "Cupid," "Orchid," or "Peacock & Wild Rose" etched patterns of Paden City. This new collecting attention has made red (Ruby) and cobalt (Ritz) blue "Crow's Foot" troublesome for dealers to keep in inventory. New collectors are being exposed to Paden City patterns through the Internet; and this exposure seems to be contagious as more and more people are asking for this smaller company's wares. Often, the first attraction is to the color and then the pattern. Some are concentrating on only round or square items; others are mixing them. Fewer are buying amber, crystal, or yellow; but small sets can be procured in these colors.

The red punch bowl has the telltale "Crow's Foot" pattern. There are similar punch bowls without the "Crow's Foot" on them. Similar is not enough. If I had a dollar for every time I have heard, "It's just like that, except..." over the years, I would not have to write any more books.

Silver decorated designs on cobalt are engaging, and even non-"Crow's Foot" collectors will buy them. Notice Paden City candles are square based. Black is not common, but white is really scarce. You may not like white glass, but this is one pattern you need to recognize if you see it in white.

Many Paden City red pieces are inclined to run toward amberina (especially tumblers). Some collectors will do without before they add a piece showing yellow color. Amberina is a collector's term for the yellowish tint of pieces that were supposed to be red. It was originally an improperly heated glass mistake and not a color that glass manufacturers tried to make. Despite this, there are now collectors who pursue amberina colored wares.

	Red	Black/Blue	Other Colors
Bowl, 4⅞", square	25.00	30.00	12.50
Bowl, 8¾", square	50.00	55.00	25.00
Bowl, 6"	40.00	35.00	15.00
Bowl, 6½", rd., 2½" high, 3½" base	45.00	50.00	22.50
Bowl, 8½", square, 2-handle	50.00	60.00	27.50
Bowl, 10", footed	75.00	75.00	32.50
Bowl, 10", square, 2-handle	75.00	75.00	32.50
Bowl, 11", oval	35.00	42.50	17.50
Bowl, 11", square	60.00	70.00	30.00
Bowl, 11", square, rolled edge	65.00	75.00	32.50
Bowl, 11½", 3 footed, round console	85.00	100.00	42.50
Bowl, 11½", console	75.00	85.00	37.50
Bowl, cream soup, footed/flat	22.00	22.50	10.00
Bowl, Nasturtium, 3 footed	185.00	210.00	90.00
Bowl, whipped cream, 3 footed	55.00	65.00	27.50
Cake plate, square, low pedestal foot	85.00	95.00	42.50
Candle, round base, tall	75.00	85.00	37.50
Candle, square, mushroom	37.50	42.50	20.00
Candlestick, 5¾"	25.00	30.00	12.50
Candy w/cover, 6½", 3 part (2 styles)	85.00	95.00	40.00
Candy, 3 footed, rd., 6⅛" wide, 3¼" high	150.00	185.00	75.00
Cheese stand, 5"	35.00	30.00	12.50
Comport, 3¼" tall, 6¼" wide	27.50	32.50	15.00
Comport 4¾" tall, 7⅜" wide	50.00	60.00	35.00
Comport, 6⅝" tall, 7" wide	60.00	75.00	30.00
Creamer, flat	12.50	15.00	6.50
Creamer, footed	12.50	15.00	6.50
Cup, footed or flat	10.00	12.50	5.00
Gravy boat, flat, 2 spout	95.00	100.00	50.00
Gravy boat, pedestal	135.00	150.00	65.00
Mayonnaise, 3 footed	55.00	65.00	30.00
Plate, 5¾"	2.25	3.50	1.25
Plate, 8", round	11.00	13.00	4.50
Plate, 8½", square	12.00	14.00	3.50
Plate, 9¼", round, small dinner	35.00	40.00	15.00
Plate, 9½", round, 2-handle	65.00	75.00	32.50
Plate, 10⅜", round, 2-handle	50.00	60.00	25.00
Plate, 10⅜", square, 2-handle	40.00	50.00	20.00
Plate, 10½", dinner	90.00	100.00	40.00
Plate, 11", cracker	45.00	50.00	22.50
Platter, 12"	55.00	60.00	15.00
Relish, 11", 3 part	95.00	100.00	45.00
Sandwich server, round, center-handle	65.00	75.00	32.50
Sandwich server, square, center-handle	45.00	50.00	17.50
Saucer, 6", round	2.50	3.00	1.00
Saucer, 6", square	3.00	3.50	1.50
Sugar, flat	11.00	13.50	5.50
Sugar, footed	11.00	13.50	5.50
Tumbler, 4¼"	75.00	85.00	37.50
Vase, 4⅝" tall, 4⅛" wide	75.00	80.00	40.00
Vase, 10¼", cupped	110.00	129.00	45.00
Vase, 10¼", flared	100.00	115.00	32.50
Vase, 11¾", flared	165.00	195.00	65.00

CUBE, "CUBIST" JEANNETTE GLASS COMPANY, 1929 – 1933

Colors: Pink, green, crystal, amber, white, Ultra Marine, canary yellow, and blue.

Cube is a geometric Depression glass design that non-collectors seem to appreciate. Cube is frequently confused with Fostoria's American by novice collectors, especially the crystal Cube 2⅝" creamer and 2⁹⁄₁₆" sugar on the 7½" round tray. Very little Cube was made in crystal and very little Fostoria American was made in green. The very scarce original pink Fostoria American was a lavender/pink color. Cube is less vibrant or brilliant in appearance when compared to the brighter, clearer quality of Fostoria's American pattern.

Alert: Any colored Cube-looking pitchers shaped differently than the ones pictured on page 55, are probably Indiana's Whitehall pattern that was recently produced. I get a lot of mail about these pitchers thought to be Cube or rare Fostoria. These have been advertised on the Internet as "rare" Cube. They are neither Cube nor rare. Other pieces of pink Whitehall, as well as a darker shade of green than Cube's original green, are also being made. Cube tumblers are flat and only come in one size, as pictured. If you see colored, footed tumblers, they are Whitehall.

The individual photo below shows a tab handled bowl in Cube. Normally, Jeannette called these lug soups in other patterns, but there is no listing in Cube for this bowl. In any case it sold for $95.00 to a very happy collector who had never seen it before.

Green Cube is more troublesome to find than the pink, but more collectors search for pink. The quandary in collecting pink (after finding it) is acquiring it in the right hue. Pink Cube varies from a light pink to an orange pink. You can see some different tints in the bottom photo on the next page although there is not an example of the orange pink. Pitchers generally look darker due to thickness, but you can see other color discrepancies. This is an example of how difficult it was for glass factories in the Depression to generate consistent quality glassware. As glass tanks got hotter, the pink color got lighter. However, as supplies of this historic glassware diminish, off shades are becoming more amenable than they once were. There are at least two shades of green. At present, the darker shade of green is not as desirable as the ordinarily found green. Both pink and green Cube cause matching difficulties when ordering through the mail or via the Internet. That it why it is preferable to attend Depression glass shows and observe what you are buying. You might actually be willing to pay a little more for that convenience. It also saves correspondence and shipping costs if there is a problem dealing the other way.

The green item on the left in the top photo is a topless candy. Had I been present when this shot was set up, I would have chosen to have a less conspicuous topless sugar since those lids are interchangeable. I am, usually, working ahead getting other photo groupings ready at these marathon sessions and little things like this get by. Last fall's session lasted almost two weeks although the crew took Sunday off so Cathy and I could organize several days of pictures to come.

Prices for Cube tumblers continue to rise. Almost all collectors are looking for four, six, or eight tumblers; as a result, it takes longer to find all these tumblers than the pitcher. Inspect the pointed sides of the tumblers and pitchers since they sometimes chipped before the heavy rims did.

The Cube powder jar is three footed. A few exceptional colors have turned up such as canary yellow and two shades of blue. Occasionally, these jars are found with celluloid or plastic lids. Powder jars were not made with those lids at the factory. These may have been replacements when tops were broken. Another possibility is that lone powder bottoms were sold to someone who made celluloid lids to match brush, mirror, or comb handles for sets they sold. In any case, prices below are for intact, original glass lids. The powder jars with other types of lids sell for half or less. A celluloid lid is better than no lid at all — and there are a few collectors for celluloid items.

	Pink	Green
Bowl, 4½", dessert , painted edge	9.50	9.00
* Bowl, 4½", deep	8.00	
** Bowl, 6½", salad	14.00	15.00
Bowl, 7¼", pointed edge	20.00	22.00
Butter dish and cover	70.00	65.00
Butter dish bottom	20.00	20.00
Butter dish top	45.00	45.00
Candy jar and cover, 6½"	30.00	30.00
Coaster, 3¼"	10.00	10.00
*** Creamer, 2⅝"	3.00	
Creamer, 3⁹⁄₁₆"	12.00	14.00
Cup	7.50	9.00
Pitcher, 8¾", 45 ounce	210.00	235.00
Plate, 6", sherbet	3.00	3.00
Plate, 8", luncheon	9.00	10.00
Powder jar and cover, 3 legs	33.00	35.00
Salt and pepper, pair	35.00	35.00
Saucer	2.50	2.50
Sherbet, footed	8.00	9.00
*** Sugar, 2⅜"	3.00	
Sugar, 3"	7.00	8.00
Sugar/candy cover	15.00	15.00
Tray for 3⁹⁄₁₆" creamer and sugar, 7½" (crystal only)	4.00	
Tumbler, 4", 9 ounce	75.00	80.00

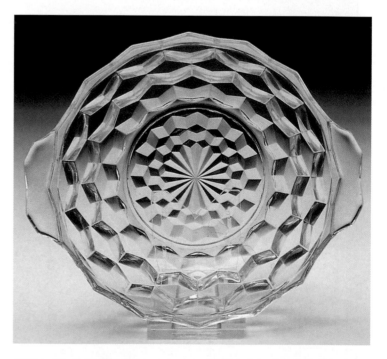

*Ultra Marine $50.00 **Ultra Marine $90.00
***Amber or white $3.00; crystal $1.00

"CUPID" PADEN CITY GLASS COMPANY, 1930s

Colors: Pink, green, light blue, peacock blue, black, canary yellow, amber, and crystal.

"Cupid" prices continue their upward trend, with the major impetus transpiring on Internet auctions. "Cupid" has, thus, been exposed to a whole new group of buyers who have found it as exciting as we did when Cathy first spotted it about 25 years ago.

Collectors are not finding much etched Paden City glassware in any design. Most Paden City etchings have increased at least 20% to 30% in the last few years. All that searching for "Cupid" must be working. I counted 31 items for sale at a recent show in Chicago. I suspect that more is being made available to the market right now due to price increases. Some wild prices are being paid to obtain pieces. Who knows? These *wild* prices might seem very tame in the future.

I reported the discovery of cup and saucers in the last book, but I didn't know at the time of the writing that a "Cupid" cup would be on the cover. No, I don't design covers. Collector Books has a very talented staff who does that.

The bottom to a tumble up has been found, but there have been no reports of a tumbler surfacing. A pink 10" vase with the bulbous bottom, commonly found in "Peacock & Wild Rose," has been seen with the "Cupid" etch; and several pink and green casseroles have been found. I previously pictured a casserole in black with a silver overlaid pattern.

The light blue "Cupid" remains quite rare. So far, only a 10½" plate, rolled edge candle, mayonnaise, and a 6¼" comport have made appearances. All have been previously pictured. I'd love to find a liner and spoon for that mayonnaise.

Samovars are rarely found, but are attracting major attention when they are. Big prices were being asked for the last three I saw. One has been making the show circuit for nearly two years, which has allowed many to see it that might not otherwise have. I might point out that to be a "Cupid" samovar, the "Cupid" pattern has to be etched on it. Mould shape alone does not make the pattern. I once had a plain samovar shipped to me as "Cupid"; so I speak of this from experience.

Prices are the most difficult part of writing this book. Even with all the help from other dealers around the country, prices never please everyone. If you own a piece, you want it to be highly priced; if you want to buy the same piece, you want the price to be low. Keep in mind that one sale at a high price does not mean that everyone would be willing to pay that. That is especially true of rare glass and any outrageous sum obtained on Internet auctions. If two people want something and have the money (or if one person simply doesn't want the other to get the item cheaply), then there may be any wild price paid. That does not mean that that identical item will sell for that price the next time — or ever again. Only you can determine whether a piece of glass is worth (to you) the price being asked.

Other information has been added regarding the "Cupid" design found on silver overlay vases marked "Made in Germany." These vases have been found in cobalt and lavender in Arizona, California, and Florida. The newest report concerns a silver overlay vase marked "Made in Czechoslovakia," which may help date these, at least. Stay tuned.

	Green/Pink		Green/Pink
Bowl, 8½", oval footed	275.00	Ice bucket, 6"	325.00
Bowl, 9¼", footed fruit	295.00	Ice tub, 4¾"	325.00
Bowl, 9¼", center-handled	275.00	**** Lamp, silver overlay	495.00
Bowl, 10¼", fruit	215.00	***** Mayonnaise, 6" diameter,	
Bowl, 10½", rolled edge	200.00	fits on 8" plate, spoon, 3 piece	210.00
Bowl, 11", console	200.00	******Plate, 10½"	150.00
Cake plate, 11¾"	200.00	Samovar	1,100.00
Cake stand, 2" high, footed	215.00	Saucer	25.00
* Candlestick, 5" wide, pair	245.00	Sugar, flat	175.00
Candy w/lid, footed, 5¼" high	395.00	Sugar, 4¼", footed	150.00
Candy w/lid, 3 part	295.00	Sugar, 5", footed	150.00
** Casserole, covered	595.00	Tray, 10¾", center-handled	215.00
*** Comport, 6¼"	195.00	Tray, 10⅞", oval-footed	250.00
Creamer, flat	175.00	Vase, 8¼", elliptical	695.00
Creamer, 4½", footed	150.00	Vase, fan-shaped	495.00
Creamer, 5", footed	150.00	Vase, 10"	335.00
Cup	75.00	Water bottle w/tumbler	600.00

* Blue $395.00   *** Blue $225.00   ***** Blue $295.00

** Black (silver overlay) $600.00   **** Possibly German   ****** Blue $225.00

DELLA ROBBIA #1058 WESTMORELAND GLASS COMPANY, Late 1920s – 1940s

Colors: Crystal, crystal w/applied lustre colors, milk glass, pink, and opaque blue.

My Della Robbia listing is just a start from the sparse catalog information that I possess. Let me know if you have additional pieces or of other information to which you may have access. The popularity of Della Robbia is extending to new collectors and supplies of many pieces are beginning to be severely limited.

You will find Della Robbia in crystal, pink, opaque blue, milk glass, and crystal with applied lustre colors. Notice that the fruits on each piece are apples, pears, and grapes. Two dissimilar color variations in the fruit decorations occur. All apples are red; pears, yellow; and grapes, purple; but the brilliance of the colors applied is diverse. Look at the pictures on page 60 and compare them to the punch set at the bottom of page 59. The darker colored fruits on page 60 are the variation that is most in demand. The dilemma with this darker color is that the applied lustre scuffs easily. Scratches show very distinctly on the darker hue. However, most collectors prefer not to mix the two. I have never seen a punch set in the darker stain, so you may have to settle for the lighter color if you want a punch set.

There are a couple of other patterns similar to Della Robbia, but both include a banana in the design. I have pictured this design with banana on the bottom of page 60. This is not Della Robbia, but shown for comparison.

If you have ever tried to carry around an 18" plate for that punch set, you will understand why you see so few of them for sale at shows. Special boxes have to be adapted to hold it. I was supposed to borrow some pieces of the lighter shade from one of my former customers in Kentucky, but my schedule didn't work out to go get it this time. Living in Florida does have a few disadvantages for photography, but not enough to convince me to move back.

There are two one-handled nappies on the top photo of page 60. The one on the left is heart shaped and more desired. The bowl on the right can also be found with the edge flatter than the one shown. Dinner plates now top $150.00, if you can find one at any price. All serving pieces need to be carefully examined for wear. Remember the prices listed are for mint condition pieces and not ones that are worn or scuffed.

Della Robbia pitcher and tumbler moulds were used to make some carnival colored water sets. These were made for Levay just as were pieces of red English Hobnail. They were made in light blue and amethyst carnival and maybe other colors I have not seen. I'm told that Westmoreland collectors seek them, but no collector of Della Robbia has ever questioned me about them.

Note that Della Robbia is pattern #1058. I previously have shown catalog pages that had some other lines shown alongside Della Robbia items. If not shown as #1058, then it is not Della Robbia.

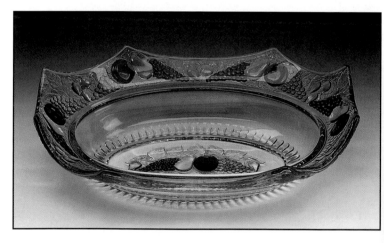

Basket, 9"	215.00	Plate, 6⅛", bread & butter	15.00
Basket, 12"	325.00	Plate, 7¼", salad	25.00
Bowl, 4½", nappy	30.00	Plate, 9", luncheon	40.00
Bowl, 5", finger	35.00	Plate, 10½", dinner	150.00
Bowl, 6", nappy, bell	35.00	*Plate, 14", torte	135.00
Bowl, 6½", one handle nappy	35.00	Plate, 18"	225.00
Bowl, 7½", nappy	45.00	Plate, 18", upturned edge, punch bowl liner	200.00
Bowl, 8", nappy, bell	55.00	Platter, 14", oval	195.00
Bowl, 8", bell, handle	75.00	Punch bowl set, 15 piece	895.00
Bowl, 8", heart, handle	125.00	Salt and pepper, pair	75.00
Bowl, 9", nappy	115.00	Salver, 14", footed, cake	150.00
Bowl, 12", footed	150.00	Saucer	10.00
Bowl, 13", rolled edge	150.00	Stem, 3 ounce, wine	30.00
Bowl, 14", oval, flange	275.00	Stem, 3¼ ounce, cocktail	28.00
Bowl, 14", punch	300.00	Stem, 5 ounce, 4¾", sherbet, high foot	25.00
Bowl, 15", bell	225.00	Stem, 5 ounce, sherbet, low foot	22.00
Candle, 4"	35.00	Stem, 6 ounce, champagne	28.00
Candle, 4", 2-lite	150.00	Stem, 8 ounce, 6", water	35.00
Candy jar w/cover, scalloped edge	125.00	Sugar, footed	25.00
Candy, round, flat, chocolate	110.00	Tumbler, 5 ounce, ginger ale	25.00
Comport, 6½", 3⅝" high, mint, footed	40.00	Tumbler, 8 ounce, footed	30.00
Comport, 8", sweetmeat, bell	115.00	Tumbler, 8 ounce, water	25.00
Comport, 12", footed, bell	135.00	Tumbler 11 ounce, iced tea, footed	35.00
Comport, 13", flanged	135.00	Tumbler 12 ounce, iced tea, bell	38.00
Creamer, footed	25.00	Tumbler 12 ounce, iced tea, bell, footed	38.00
Cup, coffee	20.00	Tumbler 12 ounce, 5³⁄₁₆", iced tea, straight	40.00
Cup, punch	15.00		
Pitcher, 32 ounce	265.00	*Pink $150.00	
Plate, 6", finger liner	12.00		

59

Westmoreland's Handmade,
Hand=Decorated Crystal

WESTMORELAND GLASS COMPANY

GRAPEVILLE, PENNSYLVANIA

Handmade Glassware of Quality

SINCE 1889

DIAMOND QUILTED, "FLAT DIAMOND" IMPERIAL GLASS COMPANY, Late 1920s – Early 1930s

Colors: Pink, blue, green, crystal, black; some red and amber.

With time and patience, pink or green Diamond Quilted can be collected in sets. More pieces are available in these than other colors. Occasionally, items in blue can be located, but it will take more than a stroke of luck to acquire very much. Few pieces are found in the other colors such as red and amber Diamond Quilted. Red is purchased more by collectors of red glass than by Diamond Quilted collectors. Black Diamond Quilted will take a long time to accumulate a luncheon set. Flat black pieces have the design on the bottom. Thus, the design on the plate can only be seen if it is turned over. Most black items have the pattern on the inside.

There are some Fenton pieces (pictured in earlier editions) that can be mixed with this pattern quite well. The color matches well, affording a resource for additional pieces.

Punch bowls sets remain elusive. I have only seen one for sale in the last 10 years of traveling; and it was missing some cups. Those punch bowls in green are a different shade of green than most other pieces. Therefore finding cups to match is a problem. Since the regular cup mold was also used to make the punch cup, that creates some havoc in finding green cups and saucers in matching hues. I saw some cups at a recent show that cried out for a punch bowl; they were the wrong color for the saucers on which they were displayed.

There is no dinner-sized plate in Diamond Quilted. Lack of a dinner plate used to stop a few admirers who planned on entertaining with their collection. I have always stated that you should collect what you like. If you like this pattern and wish to serve guests with it, then improvise and use something else for dinner plates — or just use it for desserts or appetizers.

Hazel Atlas made a quilted diamond pitcher and tumbler set in pink, green, cobalt blue, and a light blue similar to the one shown here. They are often confused with Imperial's Diamond Quilted. The quilting on Hazel Atlas pieces ends in a straight line around the top of each piece. Notice Imperial's Diamond Quilted pattern ends unevenly in points. You may also notice that the diamond designs on Hazel Atlas pieces are flat as opposed to those Imperial ones that are curved. The Hazel Atlas pitcher is flat and shaped like the straight-sided pitcher so commonly seen in Royal Lace.

Note the original sales catalog picture below. Console sets at 65¢ and a dozen candy dishes in assorted colors for $6.95 would be quite a bargain today. No, I do not have any for sale at that price. This ad is from a 1930s catalog. I mention that since I continue to receive letters every year from people trying to order glass from these old catalog ads placed throughout the book. One lady wrote three times. I am still not sure she ever understood that these were 69-year-old advertisements.

	Pink, Green	Blue, Black
Bowl, 4¾", cream soup	15.00	25.00
Bowl, 5", cereal	7.50	15.00
Bowl, 5½", one handle	7.50	22.00
Bowl, 7", crimped edge	9.00	22.00
Bowl, 7", straight	16.00	22.00
Bowl, 10½", rolled edge console	20.00	60.00
Cake salver, tall, 10" diameter	60.00	
Candlesticks (2 styles), pair	28.00	40.00
Candy jar and cover, footed	65.00	
Compote, 6" tall, 7¼" wide	45.00	
Compote and cover, 11½"	95.00	
Creamer	12.00	15.00

	Pink, Green	Blue, Black
Cup	9.50	17.50
Goblet, 1 ounce, cordial	12.00	
Goblet, 2 ounce, wine	12.00	
Goblet, 3 ounce, wine	12.00	
Goblet, 6", 9 ounce, champagne	11.00	
Ice bucket	55.00	85.00
Mayonnaise set:		
ladle, plate, comport	36.00	56.00
Pitcher, 64 ounce	50.00	
Plate, 6", sherbet	4.00	8.00
Plate, 7", salad	6.00	11.00
Plate, 8", luncheon	10.00	15.00
Punch bowl and stand	500.00	
Plate, 14", sandwich	15.00	
Sandwich server, center handle	25.00	50.00
Saucer	4.00	6.00
Sherbet	10.00	16.00
Sugar	12.00	15.00
Tumbler, 9 ounce, water	9.00	
Tumbler, 12 ounce, iced tea	9.00	
Tumbler, 6 ounce, footed	8.50	
Tumbler, 9 ounce, footed	12.50	
Tumbler, 12 ounce, footed	15.00	
Vase, fan, dolphin handles	55.00	75.00
Whiskey, 1½ ounce	8.00	

Covered Bowl—6¾ in. diam., deep round shape with 3 artistic feet, dome cover, fine quality brilliant finish **pot glass,** allover block diamond design, transparent RoseMarie and emerald green.
1C5603—Asstd. ½ doz. in carton, 20 lbs.
Doz $6.95

1C989—3 piece set, 2 transparent colors (rose and green), good quality, 10½ in. rolled rim bowl. TWO 3½ in. wide base candlesticks. Asstd. 6 sets in case, 30 lbs. . . . . **SET (3 pcs) 65c**

DIANA FEDERAL GLASS COMPANY, 1937 – 1941

Colors: Pink, amber, and crystal.

Pink Diana remains elusive but a few prices have declined in the past two years due to lack of new collectors. Price advances are not as frenzied as they were five or six years ago when many new collectors started buying this pattern about the same time. For a couple of years the prices doubled on some items. Now, there has been a price correction for several Depression patterns in the market, albeit not as bad as stocks of late.

Crystal Diana is not as available as it once was, and collectors have been paying more to finish sets they started. Amber and crystal Diana are not as desirable to collectors as the pink, a good thing since there is a true paucity of these colors. Diana is one of the used-to-be less expensive patterns. I have seen pictures of one collector's rainbow Diana collection — a mixture of the colors. It was charming, as she'd arranged it. Creativity is always a plus. This mixture of colors seems to be the collecting trend of the future.

Collectors of crystal Diana have now discovered what collectors of other colors noticed years ago. There are a small number of tumblers available. Tumblers, demitasse sets, candy dishes, shakers, sherbets, and even platters are seldom found in any Diana colors. There are fewer demitasse sets being marketed than in the past. Sets in crystal are more plentiful, as are the sprayed-on cranberry pink or red sets. Flashed red demitasses are selling for $10.00 to $12.00 each. Pink demitasse cup and saucer sets are being found occasionally, but the demand for these has slowed. This has caused prices to slip about $25.00 on a set of six.

Prices listed are actual selling prices for Diana and not advertised prices. There is a major difference between an advertised price for an item and the price being accepted by both buyer and seller. Rarely have I heard of something selling for more when advertised, but often I have heard of less. Today, dealers coast to coast are sharing information on prices. That's been a tremendous help to me as I work to keep pricing current in these books. The Internet, though a new tool with pricing, has to be approached carefully and not taken too literally. I attend as many Depression glass shows as possible and spend many hours checking prices and talking to dealers about what is, and what is not selling — and for what price.

Frosted or satinized pieces of Diana that have shown up in crystal and pink have a few admirers. Some of the larger bowls were frosted and drilled for lamp globes. Some crystal frosted pieces have been trimmed in colors, predominantly red, but you might spot green, yellow, or blue. A set of crystal frosted items with different colored trims is not as bizarre looking as you might surmise. However, achieving any of these specialty sets is a major undertaking unless you spy a complete set to start.

Some new collectors tend to mistake Diana with other swirled patterns such as Swirl and Twisted Optic. The centers of Diana pieces are swirled where the centers of other swirled patterns are plain. That elusive and somewhat odd Diana sherbet is shown in amber and in pink. The spirals on this sherbet are often mistaken for Hocking's Spiral and there is understandable debate as to its authenticity since it hardly resembles the finer lines of the remaining pieces of the pattern. It is shown in an original Federal advertisement for Diana. Pieces advertised by the company with a particular pattern are often accepted as that pattern. Another excellent example of this is the Moderntone tumbler.

	Crystal	Pink	Amber
* Ashtray, 3½"	2.50	3.50	
Bowl, 5", cereal	6.00	10.00	14.00
Bowl, 5½", cream soup	12.00	30.00	20.00
Bowl, 9", salad	12.00	20.00	18.00
Bowl, 11", console fruit	16.00	35.00	15.00
Bowl, 12", scalloped edge	16.00	30.00	20.00
Candy jar and cover, round	16.00	50.00	40.00
Coaster, 3½"	2.50	8.00	10.00
Creamer, oval	9.00	15.00	9.00
Cup	6.00	20.00	9.00
Cup, 2 ounce demitasse and 4½" saucer set	13.00	40.00	
Plate, 6", bread & butter	2.00	5.00	2.00
Plate, 9½"	6.00	20.00	9.00
Plate, 11¾", sandwich	9.00	25.00	10.00
Platter, 12", oval	12.00	33.00	15.00
Salt and pepper, pair	30.00	85.00	110.00
Saucer	1.50	5.00	2.00
Sherbet	3.00	10.00	10.00
Sugar, open oval	9.00	15.00	8.00
Tumbler, 4⅛", 9 ounce	30.00	50.00	30.00
Junior set: 6 demitasse cups & saucers with round rack	100.00	275.00	

* Green $3.00

DOGWOOD, "APPLE BLOSSOM," "WILD ROSE" MacBETH-EVANS GLASS COMPANY, 1929 – 1932

Colors: Pink, green, some crystal, Monax, Cremax, and yellow.

Dogwood is a beloved Depression pattern. Pink is the color in demand, which is excellent, since green is found only sporadically. Pink luncheon plates are abundant; I saw a stack of 35 recently. Larger, rimmed dinner plates are less easily found; and the large fruit bowl and platter are a nemesis for today's collectors. They were rarely found 20 years ago and usually enter the market, now, only through a collection being sold. The reason the large fruit bowls are so difficult to find is that these were sold to someone who frosted the bowls, drilled a hole in the center, and made ceiling globes out of them. These globes sell in the $125.00 range. There is a growing trend among collectors to own Depression glass shades and vintage light fixtures.

Pitchers and most tumbler sizes can occasionally be found; but they are pricey. Only the pink juice tumbler is truly rare; that price has escalated so that few collectors buy more than one. A cache of 12 turned up in the west not so long ago.

A tumbler that has the same shape as those of Dogwood, but is missing the Dogwood silk screening, is not Dogwood. There are pitchers shaped like Dogwood that do not have the silk screen design of Dogwood. These pitchers are not Dogwood either. They are merely the blanks made by MacBeth-Evans to go with the plain, no design tumblers that they made and sold separately with *various* pink sets. The pattern (Dogwood) has to be silk screened onto the pitcher for it to be considered Dogwood and to command those prices shown below. Some collectors buy these blanks to use with their sets, and that's perfectly fine as long as they understand that they are not the costly Dogwood. It is also easier on the pocketbook to replace a $10.00 tumbler than one that costs $50.00. However, I've gotten letters from irate collectors who have paid Dogwood prices for plain tumblers. Don't.

Some yellow (cereal bowl or luncheon plate) is found. It is a rarely seen color in Dogwood, but there is not much demand for it.

Cremax (beige) and Monax (white) are also rare colors of Dogwood that do not thrill many collectors. See a description and photo of these MacBeth-Evans colors under American Sweetheart. The Monax salver (12" plate) was once considered rare; but, over the years, it has turned out more common than thought and more of a novelty with collectors than a desired item. You can buy them for less, now, than you could 15 years ago.

There is a rolled edge cereal bowl being found that is different from the regular cereal. The flattened edge turns outward making it not as tall nor would it hold as much as the normally found cereal (shown as insert on page 67). These are being priced in a wide range, but will sell for $20.00 to $25.00 more than the regular cereal. How rare these are is undetermined.

The thick, footed style Dogwood sugar and creamer are illustrated in pink. There is a thin, flat style creamer and sugar also. Pink sugar/creamer sets are found in both styles, but green is only found in the thin variety. Thin creamers were made by adding a spout to thin cups and some of these have very indefinite spouts. There are thick and thin pink cups, but saucers for both styles are the same. Green cups come only in thin.

Pink grill plates come in two styles. Some have the Dogwood pattern all over the plate as the pink one pictured does, and others have the pattern only around the rim. Sherbets, grill plates (rim pattern only), and the large fruit bowls are difficult to acquire in green Dogwood. (Globes were made from the large green bowls, also.)

Dogwood sherbets are found with a Dogwood blossom etched on the bottom or plain. It makes no difference in price since they are only from different moulds.

Very Rare Glassware of the Depression Years, Second Series has a picture of the only known Dogwood coaster. Can you be the lucky one to find another? There is a Dogwood-like Tiffin pattern called Sylvan that came with stemmed pieces. Some collectors blend these with their Dogwood pattern.

	Pink	Green	Monax Cremax			Pink	Green	Monax Cremax
* Bowl, 5½", cereal	35.00	35.00	5.00		Plate, 9¼", dinner	36.00		
Bowl, 8½", berry	65.00	135.00	40.00		Plate, 10½", grill, AOP or			
** Bowl, 10¼", fruit	575.00	275.00	125.00		border design only	25.00	28.00	
Cake plate, 11", heavy					Plate, 12", salver	38.00		15.00
solid foot	1,200.00				Platter, 12", oval	750.00		
Cake plate, 13", heavy					Saucer	5.00	8.00	20.00
solid foot	165.00	150.00	225.00		Sherbet, low footed	35.00	115.00	
Coaster, 3¼"	595.00				Sugar, 2½", thin, flat	18.00	45.00	
Creamer, 2½", thin, flat	20.00	47.50			Sugar, 3¼", thick, footed	18.00		
Creamer, 3¼", thick, footed	25.00				Tumbler, 3½", 5 ounce,			
Cup, thick	18.00		45.00		decorated	250.00		
Cup, thin	15.00	40.00			Tumbler, 4", 10 ounce, decorated	50.00	100.00	
Pitcher, 8", 80 ounce, decorated	250.00	550.00			Tumbler, 4¾", 11 ounce,			
Pitcher, 8", 80 ounce (American					decorated	50.00	105.00	
Sweetheart Style)	625.00				Tumbler, 5", 12 ounce, decorated	75.00	125.00	
Plate, 6", bread and butter	9.00	12.00	22.00		Tumbler, moulded band	25.00		
* Plate, 8", luncheon	7.00	10.00						

* Yellow $75.00
** Lampshade $150.00

DORIC JEANNETTE GLASS COMPANY, 1935 – 1938

Colors: Pink, green, some Delphite, Ultra Marine, and yellow.

Collecting Doric is a treasure hunt many collectors relish, but it probably will not drain your checking account since it may require years to complete a set. I met someone at a show recently who had just finished her set, a 20-year quest. She was wondering aloud "which pattern to start next?" Collectors tell me they do not care how difficult a pattern is because the hunt enthralls them almost as much as the glass itself. Besides, some collectors aren't even trying for complete sets in today's market. They're blending patterns and colors they like into rainbow settings.

Collectors of green Doric have long been dismayed by the lack of pitchers and cream soups. The green 48 ounce pitcher, with or without ice lip, is nearly nonexistent for everyone today. Cereal bowls and all tumblers are only being spotted occasionally. Those pieces in pink are not regularly seen either, but they can all be located with persistent searching, save for the cream soup, never yet seen in pink. Cream soups, or consommés as some companies called them, are two handled. Cereal bowls have no handles but are often advertised as cream soups.

There is mould seam roughness on most pieces of Doric, especially on those elusive footed tumblers and cereals. This disheartens precise collectors who look for flawlessness. I, personally, would not let a little roughness stop me from owning these pieces if I saw them for sale. Remember that Depression glass was inexpensive, give-away glass. Mint condition, though desirable in glass collecting, can be carried to extremes. Magnifying glasses to look for flaws and black (ultraviolet) lights to check for repairs are seen at shows today. The light shows items that fluoresce, too, a property in some glass that is becoming a collectible factor. This does *not* mean an item is old, however, as I often hear.

Green Doric turns up in Florida, but is often cloudy ("sick") glass. Evidently, well water created mineral deposits that react with the glass. You could make a fortune if you could figure out a way to easily remove these deposits. I know I have heard of everything from Tidy Bowl to Efferdent tablets. As far as I know, this cloudiness cannot be removed short of polishing it out over a period of time. People with the proper equipment are now doing that, but it is expensive. Do not be duped into buying cloudy glass unless it is inexpensive, you plan on using it in your dishwasher anyway or you have that magic cure.

A yellow Doric pitcher is still the only one known; but it is doubtful that the factory made only one. I've been told by former workers that even experimental color runs generally consisted of 30 to 50 items. Large footed Doric pitchers come with or without an ice lip as shown in pink. Oddly, candy and sugar lids in this Jeannette pattern are not interchangeable. The candy lid is taller and more domed.

Sherbet and cloverleaf candies are commonly found in Delphite. All other Delphite pieces are rare in Doric and the price is still reasonable for so rare a color. Only the Delphite pitcher creates much of a pricing stir. Jeannette made mostly kitchenware items in Delphite, rather than dinnerware.

An iridescent, three-part candy was made in the 1970s and sold for 79¢ in our local dish barn. Sometimes an Ultra Marine candy is found within a piece of hammered aluminum.

I have included a photo of a boxed set. Some collectors find boxed sets to their liking and are willing to pay a small fortune for them, although these old boxes are usually dirty and not very colorful. Since they do lend a certain veracity to the product, don't pitch them away if you find one. The boxes are treasures to some.

	Pink	Green	Delphite		Pink	Green	Delphite
Bowl, 4½", berry	12.00	12.00	55.00	Plate, 6", sherbet	6.00	7.00	
Bowl, 5", cream soup		450.00		Plate, 7", salad	20.00	25.00	
Bowl, 5½", cereal	80.00	90.00		Plate, 9", dinner,			
Bowl, 8¼", large berry	30.00	35.00	150.00	serrated 175.00	20.00	20.00	
Bowl, 9", 2-handled	35.00	40.00		Plate, 9", grill	25.00	25.00	
Bowl, 9", oval vegetable	45.00	50.00		Platter, 12", oval	33.00	30.00	
Butter dish and cover	80.00	97.50		Relish tray, 4" x 4"	15.00	12.00	
Butter dish bottom	25.00	32.50		Relish tray, 4" x 8"	25.00	20.00	
Butter dish top	55.00	65.00		Salt and pepper, pair	35.00	37.50	
Cake plate, 10", 3 legs	30.00	35.00		Saucer	3.50	4.50	
Candy dish and cover, 8"	42.00	42.00		Sherbet, footed	16.00	18.00	10.00
*Candy dish, 3-part	10.00	10.00	12.00	Sugar	15.00	15.00	
Coaster, 3"	20.00	20.00		Sugar cover	20.00	30.00	
Creamer, 4"	20.00	14.00		Tray, 10", handled	28.00	30.00	
Cup	12.00	14.00		Tray, 8" x 8", serving	40.00	40.00	
Pitcher, 5½", 32 ounce, flat	50.00	55.00	1,200.00	Tumbler, 4½", 9 ounce	80.00	120.00	
Pitcher, 7½", 48 ounce,				Tumbler, 4", 10 ounce, footed	75.00	100.00	
footed, yellow at $2,000.00	750.00	1,250.00		Tumbler, 5", 12 ounce, footed	90.00	135.00	

*Candy in metal holder $40.00. Iridescent made in the 70s. Ultra Marine $18.00.

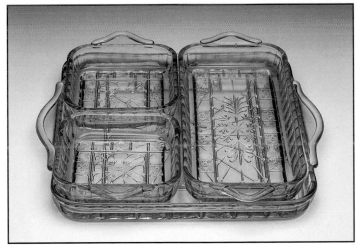

DORIC AND PANSY JEANNETTE GLASS COMPANY, 1937 – 1938

Colors: Ultra Marine; some crystal and pink.

Rare items in Ultra Marine Doric and Pansy keep coming into America from England and Canada, where they were sold as parts of a tea set. No wonder we thought the teal butter, sugar, creamer, and salt and pepper were rare in the early collecting days. They were, but apparently only in the continental United States. We were not looking outside our boundaries where we now know that much Depression era glassware was sold. (I just talked to a collector from Australia who informed me there's quite a bit of Depression ware to be found there, though few know what it is.)

The price of the Doric and Pansy butter dish remains steady, although you cannot presently visit a glass show without seeing at least one for sale.

Neither tumblers nor berry bowls are being found in the accumulations abroad. There are two tumblers pictured on the right. The common one (shaped like the flat Doric tumbler) is shown in front of the scarcely found one. Only two of the straight sided, 4¼", ten ounce tumblers have been discovered. Both turned up on the West Coast. Beware of weakly patterned shakers. These should be priced less (say 25%). If color and shape are the only clues to the shaker's pattern, then leave it alone unless it is seriously low priced. Weak patterns and cloudiness befall many shakers. Cloudy shakers are not worth mint prices. Cloudiness was caused by a chemical reaction between the glass and its contents either salt or pepper. Salt often corroded original metal shaker tops and while those are desirable, new lids are acceptable and available to collectors.

Color variations face every collector buying Jeannette's Ultra Marine. Some pieces have a distinctly green hue instead of blue. Notice differences in my picture. Few collectors presently buy the green shade of Ultra Marine, but who is to know how it may be treasured down the collecting road.

Berry bowls and children's sets are found in pink. Peculiarly, there have been no reports of children's sets or pink Doric and Pansy found in England or Canada.

Luncheon sets in crystal can be accumulated, albeit, with difficulty. Sets of sugars and creamer in crystal are usually bought by collectors of sugar and creamers, rather than Doric and Pansy collectors. Someday, these crystal pieces may be equally appealing to collectors.

	Green, Teal	Pink, Crystal		Green, Teal	Pink, Crystal
Bowl, 4½", berry	24.00	12.00	Plate, 7", salad	40.00	
Bowl, 8", large berry	95.00	33.00	Plate, 9", dinner	40.00	15.00
Bowl, 9", handled	45.00	25.00	Salt and pepper, pr.	425.00	
Butter dish and cover	495.00		Saucer	5.00	4.00
Butter dish bottom	70.00		Sugar, open	110.00	85.00
Butter dish top	425.00		Tray, 10", handled	38.00	
Cup	16.00	12.00	Tumbler, 4½", 9 ounce	120.00	
Creamer	115.00	85.00	Tumbler, 4¼", 10 ounce	595.00	
Plate, 6", sherbet	11.00	7.50			

DORIC AND PANSY
"PRETTY POLLY PARTY DISHES"

	Teal	Pink		Teal	Pink
Cup	50.00	35.00	Creamer	55.00	35.00
Saucer	9.00	7.00	Sugar	55.00	35.00
Plate	11.00	8.00	14-piece set	390.00	275.00

ENGLISH HOBNAIL, LINE #555 WESTMORELAND GLASS COMPANY, 1917 – 1940s; few items through 1980s

Colors: Pink, turquoise/ice blue, cobalt blue, green, lilac, red, opal trimmed blue, red flashed, black, blue, amber, and milk.

Some items of Early American/English Hobnail in various colors and trims were manufactured by Westmoreland, off and on, for over 70 years. It was first called Early American and was by far Westmoreland's most prolific line, having hundreds of items. The major production years ranged from 1926 through the early 1940s; and somewhere along the way, it became English Hobnail in their ads. Two distinct shapes occur in the pattern, round and square based items. Black footed (c.1929), flashed red, and gold trimmed items are sporadically found, today, but are mostly considered to be novelties by collectors.

New collectors need to learn to distinguish English Hobnail from Hocking's Miss America, which was the competitive line. The centers of English Hobnail pieces have rays of varying distances. Notice the upright pieces in the photographs for this six-point star effect. In Miss America, shown on page 135, the center rays all end equidistant from the center. The hobs on English Hobnail are more rounded and feel smoother to the touch; goblets flare and the hobs go directly into a plain rim area. Miss America's hobs are sharper to touch and the goblets do not flare at the rim. All goblets and tumblers of Miss America have three sets of rings above the hobs before entering a plain glass rim. If you have a candy jar that measures more or less than Miss America's 11½" including the cover, then it is probably English Hobnail which comes in several sizes.

Due to space limitations, I have arbitrarily grouped crystal, amber, Westmoreland's 1960s "Golden Sunset" color, and others into the *Collectible Glassware of the 40s, 50s, 60s...* and am pricing only the major collected colors in this book. I am aware crystal was made from the early teens and some amber in the late 1920s; but crystal experienced a major push by the company in the W.W.II years, when chemicals for color production were hard to get. There are several catalog pages from Westmoreland's later years shown in the fifth edition of the 40s, 50s, 60s book. Refer to those for individual identification of pieces.

Two price arrangements are here. Pink and green make up one column and turquoise/ice blue makes up the other. A piece in the very scarce cobalt blue or black will bring 40% to 50% more than the turquoise blue prices listed. Very little cobalt English Hobnail is being unveiled and even fewer pieces in black. You can see one of each of the four pieces that were found on the bottom of page 74. More English Hobnail color collectors seek turquoise/ice blue by virtue of its unique beauty. I have been able to gather enough items for a decent photo on page 74. Bear in mind, that it took four years to accumulate what is shown. Milk glass items have little following to date, although some of the rarer pieces are found in that 40s, 50s, 60s color; and only a few collectors are found for red items, made in the 1970s for LeVay.

A few pieces of turquoise were produced in the 1970s. These later items appear to be a different quality and have a deeper color when compared to the older pieces. A few years ago, some of us were treated to the sight of a large collection of turquoise/ice blue English Hobnail being marketed at a show. It was captivating to us who had never seen so much at one time. Several new collectors were started with that set; I'm sure they all wish they had bought the entire set, instead of trying to find it now.

Note the flat, pink shaker in the photograph at top of page 73. This is also a late discovery. Reports of a turquoise flat shaker have now been confirmed. Surprises still turn up in patterns that have been collected for years. That is part of the collecting allure.

Sets of pink or green English Hobnail can be assembled with time and perseverance. This pattern does have color inconsistencies, doubtless due to its various periods of manufacture. Pink is the simplest color to find, but it is found in two distinct shades. There are three different greens, from a light, yellow-green to a deep, dark green. Some collectors mix shades of color, but others aren't so inclined. This mixing is being termed rainbow collecting and is currently in vogue.

	Pink/ Green	Turquoise/ *Ice Blue		Pink/ Green	Turquoise/ *Ice Blue
Ashtray, 3"	20.00		Bowl, 8", footed	55.00	
Ashtray, 4½"		22.50	Bowl, 8", hexagonal footed, 2-handled	95.00	150.00
Ashtray, 4½", square	25.00		Bowl, 8", pickle	30.00	
Bonbon, 6½", handled	25.00	40.00	Bowl, 8", round nappy	35.00	
Bottle, toilet, 5 ounce	35.00	50.00	Bowl, 9", celery	32.00	
Bowl, 3", cranberry	17.00		Bowl, 10", flared	40.00	
Bowl, 4", rose	50.00		Bowl, 11", rolled edge	45.00	80.00
Bowl, 4½", finger	15.00		Bowl, 12", celery	35.00	
Bowl, 4½", round nappy	13.00	30.00	Bowl, 12", flange or console	50.00	
Bowl, 4½", square footed, finger	15.00	35.00	Candlestick, 3½", round base	25.00	35.00
Bowl, 5", round nappy	15.00	40.00	Candlestick, 9", round base	40.00	50.00
Bowl, 6", crimped dish	18.00		Candy dish, 3 footed	60.00	
Bowl, 6", round nappy	16.00		Candy, ½ lb. and cover, cone shaped	55.00	100.00
Bowl, 6", square nappy	16.00		Cigarette box and cover, 4½" x 2½"	27.50	55.00
Bowl, 6½", grapefruit	22.00		Cigarette jar w/cover, round	50.00	60.00
Bowl, 6½", round nappy	20.00		Compote, 5", round, footed	25.00	
Bowl, 7", round nappy	22.00		Compote, 6", honey, round footed	30.00	
Bowl, 8", cupped, nappy	30.00		Compote, 8", ball stem, sweetmeat	60.00	

*Cobalt blue – 40 to 50 percent higher

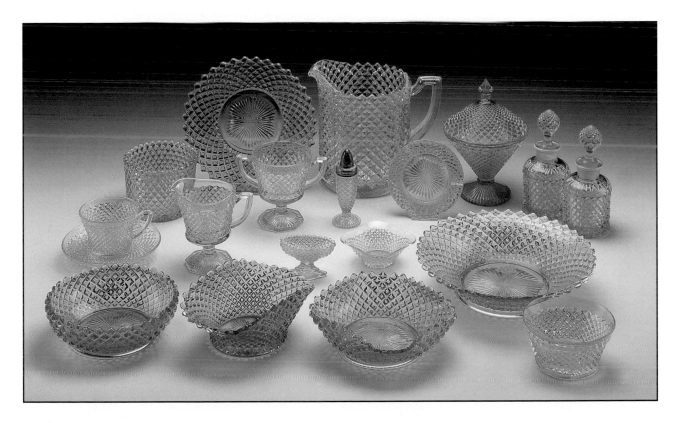

ENGLISH HOBNAIL

	Pink/ Green	Turquoise/ *Ice Blue		Pink/ Green	Turquoise/ *Ice Blue
Creamer, hexagonal, footed	22.50	45.00	Saucer, demitasse, round	15.00	
Creamer, square footed	42.50		Saucer, round	4.00	5.00
Cup	18.00	25.00	Shaker, pair, flat	150.00	250.00
Cup, demitasse	55.00		Shaker, pair, round footed	77.50	
Ice tub, 4"	47.50	90.00	Stem, 2 ounce, square footed, wine	30.00	60.00
Ice tub, 5½"	65.00	120.00	Stem, 3 ounce, round footed, cocktail	20.00	35.00
Lamp, 6¼", electric	65.00		Stem, 5 oz., sq. footed, oyster cocktail	16.00	
Lamp, 9¼", electric	135.00		Stem, 8 oz., sq. footed, water goblet	30.00	50.00
Marmalade w/cover	60.00	85.00	Stem, sherbet, round foot, low		12.00
Mayonnaise, 6"	20.00		Stem, sherbet, square footed, low	12.00	
Nut, individual, footed	20.00		Stem, sherbet, round high, foot	1500	
Pitcher, 23 ounce, rounded	150.00		Stem, sherbet, square footed, high	15.00	35.00
Pitcher, 32 ounce, straight side	185.00		Sugar, hexagonal, footed	22.50	45.00
Pitcher, 38 ounce, rounded	225.00		Sugar, square footed	45.00	
Pitcher, 60 ounce, rounded	295.00		Tidbit, 2 tier	45.00	85.00
Pitcher, 64 ounce, straight side	300.00		Tumbler, 5 ounce, ginger ale	18.00	
Plate, 5½", round	9.50		Tumbler, 8 ounce, water	22.00	
Plate, 6", square finger bowl liner	9.00		Tumbler, 10 ounce, ice tea	25.00	
Plate, 6½", round	10.00		Tumbler, 12 ounce, ice tea	30.00	
Plate, 6½, round finger bowl liner	9.50		Urn, 11", w/cover (15")	395.00	
Plate, 8", round	12.50		Vase, 7½", flip	85.00	
Plate, 8½", round	15.00	25.00	Vase, 7½", flip jar w/cover	135.00	
Plate, 10", round	45.00	85.00	Vase, 8½", flared top	135.00	250.00
Plate, 14", round, torte	60.00		Vase, 10" (straw jar)	110.00	
Puff box, w/ cover, 6", round	50.00	77.50			

*Cobalt blue 40 to 50% higher

FANCY COLONIAL #582 IMPERIAL GLASS COMPANY c. 1914

Colors: Crystal, pink, green, teal, some iridized Rubigold and Ice (rainbow washed crystal).

When I think of how many pieces of this pattern I've had in my shop and sold over the years, never thinking I would want to include it in a book, it's mind blowing. I could have had five times the number of table glass pieces shown here. Fancy Colonial was one of the most prolific, open stock patterns that Imperial ever made. When I first began looking for glass 30 years ago, this pattern was everywhere, probably due to some reintroduction of the time. I remember Cathy asking me if I wanted to gather this line, which people in the field were calling "Button and Flute" and "Pillar & Optic" and I told her, "No way. People aren't interested in stuff they're still making." They weren't, *then*, but now Imperial is out of business and I'm being asked for it at shows. Hence, the catching up I'm being forced to do. Again, it was in production, off and on, throughout the company's history, a few items being made in whatever colors and for whatever promotions they were running at the time. Moulds were expensive to make. Sheer economics behooved companies to use them for as long as they possibly could. I met a man from Hocking's work force whose sole job was to rework the worn molds into reusable forms. Reissues by the company themselves should not be treated to the same feelings of anathema that con artist's greedy reproductions engender in collectors.

In doing my homework, I saw figures bandied about saying there were "more than 80," "around 100," "over 150" pieces supposedly made in Fancy Colonial. The list below includes what I could document. Cathy thinks she's seen a punch bowl in this. Have you? I'm very certain this isn't all there was; let me hear from you regarding what you see or have that is not included. Measurements are helpful for collectors — and authors.

	All colors*		All colors*		All colors*
Bonbon, 5½", handle	25.00	Cup, custard, flare edge	17.50	Stem, 3 ounce, port, deep	30.00
Bottle, water, no stop	75.00	Cup, punch, straight edge	15.00	Stem, 4½ ounce, cocktail, shallow	20.00
Bowl, 3½", nappy	12.00	Goblet, egg cup, low foot deep	30.00	Stem, 4 ounce, burgundy, deep	30.00
Bowl, 4½", nappy	15.00	Goblet, low foot, café parfait	25.00	Stem, 5 ounce, claret, deep	30.00
Bowl, 4½", rim foot berry	15.00	Mayo w/liner, flat	55.00	Stem, 6 ounce, champagne, deep	21.00
Bowl, 5", nappy or olive	15.00	Oil bottle w/stopper, 6¼ ounce	65.00	Stem, 6 ounce, saucer/champagne,	
Bowl, 5", footed, 2 handle	20.00	Oil bottle, 5½ ounce, bulbous, w/stopper	75.00	shallow	20.00
Bowl, 5", nut or lily (cupped rim)	20.00	Pickle, 8", oval	30.00	Stem, 8 ounce, goblet, deep	25.00
Bowl, 5", rim foot berry	17.50	Pitcher, 3 pint	150.00	Stem, 10 ounce, goblet, deep	25.00
Bowl, 6", nappy	20.00	Plate, 5¾"	12.00	Sugar w/lid	30.00
Bowl, 7", nappy or rim foot berry	35.00	Plate, 7½", salad	25.00	Tumbler, 2 ounce, whiskey	20.00
Bowl, 7", lily	40.00	Plate, 10½", cake	45.00	Tumbler, 4 ounce	15.00
Bowl, 8", 2-handle berry	65.00	Plate, mayonnaise liner	15.00	Tumbler, 5 ounce, belled rim or not	15.00
Bowl, 8", nappy or salad	35.00	Salt & Pepper, pair	75.00	Tumbler, 6 ounce	15.00
Bowl, 8", spoon tray (hump edge)	35.00	Salt, table or footed almond, handle	22.00	Tumbler, 8 ounce	18.00
Bowl, 8", lily (cupped)	45.00	Saucer	8.00	Tumbler, 10 ounce	18.00
Bowl, 8", rim foot berry	35.00	Sherbet, 3¼", low ft. flare rim or not	22.50	Tumbler, 12 ounce, iced tea	20.00
Bowl, 9", rim foot berry	40.00	Sherbet, 4¼", low foot	22.50	Tumbler, 14 ounce, iced tea	22.00
Butter & cover	75.00	Sherbet, 4¾", footed Jelly	25.00	Vase, 8", low foot, flare	65.00
Celery, 12", oval	50.00	Spoon (flat open sugar)	20.00	Vase, 10" flat, bead base, ruffled	
Comport, 4", footed	25.00	Stem, 1 ounce, cordial, deep	40.00	rim	85.00
Comport, 5½", footed	30.00	Stem, 2 ounce, wine, deep	30.00	Vase, 12" flat, bead base, rufffled	
Comport, 6¼", footed	35.00	Stem, 3 ounce, cocktail, shallow	20.00	rim	110.00
Creamer, footed	25.00				

* Crystal subtract 25%; teal add 25%

75

FIRE-KING DINNERWARE "PHILBE" HOCKING GLASS COMPANY, 1937–1938

Colors: Blue, green, pink, and crystal.

Fire-King Dinnerware is attracting more attention after its inclusion in my *Anchor Hocking's Fire-King & More, Book II*. It's a wonderful pattern that would have many collectors if more of it were presently available. However, that isn't the case. The most frequently asked question is where do I find a piece. Finding it is like mining gold with pick and shovel. If you're very lucky, you might see a piece. If more were available, prices would be even higher than they are due to the number of collectors wanting "just one piece." On a wish list received from a cup and saucer collector who needs only four or five sets to represent every pattern in my books is this "Philbe" pattern in any color. Why put it in the book? People need to recognize it should they find a piece. Everybody gets lucky sometime. You wouldn't want to miss your opportunity.

A high sherbet/champagne is now in the listing, along with a non-stemmed sherbet, which is pictured in the Fire-King book. Usually, Fire-King Dinnerware is found on Cameo shaped blanks; but some pieces, including footed tumblers, nine ounce water goblets, and the high sherbets are on a Mayfair shaped blank. Additional stems could be found. Watch for them.

The crystal cup and saucer set found in Michigan has a platinum band that was also on the blue set shown in a previous edition.

Somebody turned up a complete green candy. I have owned two green candy bottoms and one complete blue, but I have never found the green top. I once had a lid brought to me that was supposed to fit the candy, but it turned out to be the lid for the cookie. The cookie lid is a tad larger.

The blue of Fire-King Dinnerware is very similar to Mayfair's blue. Many pieces have that platinum trim that can be seen in the photograph. All the platinum banded blue pieces in the picture, except the pitcher, turned up in 1975 at a flea market in Ohio. I have never seen any blue Mayfair trimmed in platinum. This seems strange since these patterns were made about the same time. Mayfair was finishing up as Fire-King was being introduced. Was this a special order production, which would account for its scarcity? As many different pieces as were made, there should be a supply just waiting to be retrieved. Keep looking.

Many pieces shown here are the only ones ever found. Of the four pitchers shown, only three other pitchers (two pink juices and a blue water without platinum band) have been unearthed. The easiest to find blue items are the footed tumblers which are rare in other colors. The tea seems twice as available as the water.

Usually found pieces of pink include oval vegetable bowls and the 10½" salver. That oval bowl is also available in green and crystal. I have only bought those two items in the two years since the last book was published. Next easiest to obtain would be green grill or luncheon plates. Any color 6" saucer/sherbet plate is rarer than larger plates. Why should you care if you don't collect this pattern? Should you actually find one, it's guaranteed someone wants it. Sell or trade it for something you want.

	Crystal	Pink, Green	Blue		Crystal	Pink, Green	Blue
Bowl, 5½", cereal	20.00	45.00	75.00	Plate, 10½", salver	65.00	95.00	110.00
Bowl, 7¼", salad	50.00	80.00	115.00	Plate, 10½", grill	40.00	75.00	95.00
Bowl, 10", oval				Plate, 11⅝", salver	50.00	62.50	95.00
vegetable	75.00	90.00	165.00	Platter, 12", closed			
Candy jar, 4", low,				handles	60.00	125.00	175.00
with cover	215.00	725.00	795.00	Saucer, 6", (same as			
Cookie jar with cover	600.00	950.00	1,500.00	sherbet plate)	40.00	65.00	95.00
Creamer, 3¼", footed	75.00	135.00	150.00	Sherbet, 3¾", no stem	75.00		550.00
Cup	60.00	110.00	175.00	Sherbet, 4¾", stemmed		450.00	
Goblet, 7¼", 9 ounce,				Sugar, 3¼", footed	75.00	135.00	150.00
thin	95.00	185.00	235.00	Tumbler, 4", 9 ounce,			
Pitcher, 6", 36 ounce,				flat water	40.00	105.00	130.00
juice	295.00	625.00	895.00	Tumbler, 3½", footed,			
Pitcher, 8½", 56 ounce	395.00	925.00	1,175.00	juice	40.00	150.00	175.00
Plate, 6", sherbet	40.00	65.00	95.00	Tumbler, 5¼", 10 ounce,			
Plate, 8", luncheon	20.00	37.50	47.50	footed	40.00	80.00	100.00
Plate, 10", heavy				Tumbler, 6½", 15 ounce,			
sandwich	40.00	95.00	125.00	footed, iced tea	50.00	85.00	90.00

FLORAL, "POINSETTIA" JEANNETTE GLASS COMPANY, 1931 – 1935

Colors: Pink, green, Delphite, Jadite, crystal, amber, red, black, custard, and yellow.

A botanist wrote that this is a Passion Flower (Passiflora), not a Poinsettia — and not a hemp plant as another supposed it to be. After 30 years of collectors calling it "Floral," the name probably isn't going to change at this point.

Notice, on page 81, the rare, ruffled top, pink Floral comport. The known straight top comport is on the bottom row of page 79. Both are rarely seen. Pink comports are harder to find than green, but there are more collectors seeking green ones. Study the listing of unusual items found at the end of the writing for rare items.

Some green Floral pieces, rarely found in the United States, are being uncovered in England and Canada. Slight variations of color and design exist in these items. They are frequently a lighter green color, slightly paneled, and have ground bottoms. A ground bottom oftentimes indicates an early production run of the pattern. The green cup without a saucer has a ground bottom and is slightly footed. The base of the cup is larger than the normally found saucer indentation. Today, some dealers have representatives in England hunting for American-made glassware along with those fine European antiques. I ship more and more books to England as well as Australia and New Zealand.

Prices remain steady on green Floral, flat-bottomed pitchers and tumblers. Northwestern (Washington, Oregon) dealers tell me that lemonade pitchers are disappearing from that market. Pink lemonade pitchers substantially outnumber green.

Two varieties of pink Floral platters exist. One has a normal flat edge; the other, higher priced and more rarely seen, has a sharp, inner rim like the platter in Cherry Blossom. This price has some Floral collectors settling for the more inexpensive one.

Be sure to read about the similarly made Floral lamp in Adam pattern on page 6.

On a sour note, the smaller, footed Floral shakers have now been reproduced in pink, cobalt blue, red, and a very dark green color, the last four colors of little concern since they originally were never made. The darker green will not glow under a black (ultraviolet) light as will the old. The new pink shakers, however, are a reasonably good copy of pattern and color. A quick way to tell the Floral reproduction is to look at the threads where the lid screws onto the shaker. On the old, there are two parallel threads that end right before the side mould seams. The new Floral has one continuous line thread that starts on one side and continues around the shaker until it ends above the beginning line on the other side. There is approximately one inch of overlapped thread making two lines for that inch; but the whole thread is one continuous line and not two separate ones as on the old. To my knowledge, no other Floral reproductions have been made as of May 2001.

Floral sugar and candy lids are interchangeable, as are most such Jeannette lids.

Floral designs can be found on the under side of lids and on the bottom of square Jadite kitchenware/refrigerator storage containers made by Jeannette in the mid-1930s.

Rare and unusual items in Floral (so far) include the following:

a) a set of Delphite blue;
b) a yellow, two-part relish dish;
c) an amberina (red/yellow) plate, cup, and saucer;
d) green and crystal juice pitchers w/ground, flat bottoms;
e) 3-footed vases (rose bowls) in green and crystal, flared at the rim; some hold flower frogs with the Floral pattern on the frogs;
f) crystal lemonade pitcher;
g) lamps;
h) green grill plate;
i) an octagonal vase with Floral patterned, octagonal foot, in crystal and green;
j) ruffled edge berry and master berry bowl;
k) pink and green Floral ice tubs;
l) oval vegetable with cover;

m) 2 styles (straight or ruffled edge) of 9" comports in pink and green;
n) 9 ounce flat tumblers in green;
o) 3 ounce footed tumblers in green;
p) beige (custard) and opaque red 8" round bowl;
q) caramel colored dinner plate;
r) cream soups;
s) beige (custard) creamer and sugar;
t) green dresser set;
u) beige (custard), 8½" bowl (like Cherry Blossom);
v) footed, black water tumbler;
w) round vegetable w/o handles w/cover;
x) round based 6" flat shaker, pictured in the *Very Rare Glassware of the Depression Years 6th Edition*.

FLORAL

	Pink	Green	Delphite	Jadite
Bowl, 4", berry, ruffled $65.00	20.00	23.00	50.00	
Bowl, 5½", cream soup	750.00	750.00		
* Bowl, 7½", salad, ruffled $150.00	32.00	32.00	60.00	
Bowl, 8", covered vegetable	50.00	65.00	75.00 (no cover)	
Bowl, 9", oval vegetable	25.00	28.00		
Butter dish and cover	105.00	95.00		
Butter dish bottom	30.00	30.00		
Butter dish top	75.00	65.00		
Canister set: coffee, tea, cereal, sugar, 5¼" tall, each				95.00
Candlesticks, 4", pair	90.00	95.00		
Candy jar and cover	40.00	42.50		
Creamer, flat, Cremax $160.00	18.00	20.00	77.50	
Coaster, 3¼"	12.00	12.00		
Comport, 9"	950.00	995.00		
*** Cup	15.00	15.00		
Dresser set		1,250.00		
Frog for vase, also crystal $500.00		725.00		
Ice tub, 3½", high, oval	895.00	975.00		
Lamp	295.00	295.00		
Pitcher, 5½", 23 or 24 ounce		550.00		
Pitcher, 8", 32 ounce, footed, cone	38.00	45.00		
Pitcher, 10¼", 48 ounce, lemonade	250.00	275.00		
Plate, 6", sherbet	8.00	9.00		
Plate, 8", salad	15.00	16.00		
** Plate, 9", dinner	20.00	22.00	150.00	
Plate, 9", grill		295.00		
Platter, 10¾", oval	25.00	27.50	150.00	
Platter, 11" (like Cherry Blossom)	85.00			
Refrigerator dish and cover, 5" square		75.00	95.00	50.00
*** Relish dish, 2-part oval	22.00	24.00	160.00	
**** Salt and pepper, 4", footed, pair	50.00	55.00		
Salt and pepper, 6", flat	55.00			
*** Saucer	12.00	12.00		
Sherbet	20.00	20.00	85.00	
Sugar, Cremax $160.00	10.00	12.00	72.50 (open)	
Sugar/candy cover	17.50	20.00		
Tray, 6", square, closed handles	20.00	20.00		
Tray, 9¼", oval for dresser set		195.00		
Tumbler, 3½", 3 ounce, footed		175.00		
Tumbler, 4", 5 ounce, footed, juice	20.00	25.00		
Tumbler, 4½", 9 ounce, flat		185.00		
Tumbler, 4¾", 7 ounce, footed, water	25.00	25.00	195.00	
Tumbler, 5¼", 9 ounce, footed, lemonade	52.50	60.00		
Vase, 3 legged rose bowl		525.00		
Vase, 3 legged flared (also in crystal)		495.00		
Vase, 6⅞" tall (8 sided)		*****450.00		

* Cremax $125.00

** These have now been found in amber and red.

*** This has been found in yellow.

**** Beware reproductions.

***** Crystal $275.00

FLORAL AND DIAMOND BAND U.S. GLASS COMPANY, Late 1920s

Colors: Pink, green; some iridescent, black, and crystal.

In a 1928 catalog, you could buy a Floral and Diamond Band jelly compote for 35 cents. It was also advertised in Sear's catalogs of that same time. Notice that half the ad for the berry set pictured below says Diamond Band and Floral and not vice versa. There is not enough Floral and Diamond Band available now to provide a huge number of collectors with sets, but it can still be collected. I see pieces for sale, though they often show use marks.

Rough mould lines on many Floral and Diamond Band pieces are typical of all U.S. Glass Company patterns of this era. This heavy, seamed pattern was not finished as well as many of the later patterns. This is normal for Floral and Diamond Band and not considered an impairment by long-time collectors who have come to ignore some roughness. Another difficulty in gathering Floral and Diamond Band is finding varying shades of green. Some green has a blue tint. You need to decide how flexible you are about color matching

Floral and Diamond Band luncheon plates, sugar lids, pitchers, and iced tea tumblers (in both pink and green) are hard to acquire. Cathy has a lucky friend who inherited a complete pitcher set in green. Six tumblers were advertised in that '28 catalog mentioned above for 85 cents. Many Floral and Diamond Band butter bottoms have been "borrowed" to be used on more expensive U.S. Glass patterns such as Strawberry and Cherryberry. This has taken place because these U.S. Glass butter bottoms are plain and, thus, compatible, since the patterns are located on the top only. Floral and Diamond Band butter dishes used to be low priced in comparison to Strawberry and Cherryberry; so, collectors bought the bargain Floral and Diamond Band butter dishes to use the bottoms for those more costly patterns. These past collecting proclivities have now produced a dearth of butter bottoms for Floral and Diamond Band.

The small Floral and Diamond Band creamer and sugar have been found in black with ground bottoms; but no other pieces have been spotted in that color. That same sugar and creamer, in various colors, is often found with a cut flower over the top of the customary moulded flower.

Crystal pitchers and butter dishes are rare in Floral and Diamond Band. Notice the crystal pitcher in the bottom photograph on page 83. It has a yellow hue, typical of this crystal.

Floral and Diamond Band pitchers with exceptional iridescent color bring premium prices from carnival glass collectors as a pattern called "Mayflower." Unfortunately, most of these iridescent pitchers are generally weakly colored and unacceptable to carnival buyers. Several of these types have surfaced lately at shows. Dealers who sell both Depression and carnival glass have been buying the good colored pitchers at Depression glass shows and reselling them at carnival glass conventions and auctions for years. Sometimes glassware overlaps categories of collecting, as does Floral and Diamond Band; and, occasionally, it receives more respect from one group of collectors than it does the other.

	Pink	Green		Pink	Green
Bowl, 4½", berry	10.00	12.00	Sugar, small	10.00	12.00
Bowl, 5¾", handled, nappy	15.00	15.00	Sugar, 5¼"	18.00	18.00
Bowl, 8", large berry	20.00	20.00	Sugar lid	55.00	65.00
* Butter dish and cover	140.00	130.00	Tumbler, 4", water	25.00	25.00
Butter dish bottom	100.00	100.00	Tumbler, 5", iced tea	45.00	50.00
Butter dish top	40.00	30.00			
Compote, 5½", tall	20.00	25.00			
Creamer, small	10.00	12.00			
Creamer, 4¾"	18.00	20.00			
* Pitcher, 8", 42 ounce	125.00	135.00			
Plate, 8" luncheon	45.00	45.00			
Sherbet	7.00	8.00			

* Iridescent $275.00; Crystal $125.00

Seven-Piece Berry Set
You'll really be most satisfied with the purchase of this set. It's very attractive, and affords a fitting and stylish addition to your present pieces. In green pressed glass, with diamond and floral design. Large bowl, 8 inches in diameter, and six sauce dishes to match, 4½ inches in diameter.
35N6838—Weight, packed, 7 pounds. Per set......**68c**

Seven-Piece Water Set
Made from green pressed glass, with a floral and diamond design. You'll find that the sparkling scintillating pitcher and glasses are a set you'll be mighty proud to own when serving cold drinks. 3-pint pitcher. Six 8-ounce tumblers.
35N6837—Weight, packed, 12 pounds. Per set. **$1.18**

FLORENTINE NO. 1, OLD FLORENTINE, "POPPY NO. 1"
HAZEL ATLAS GLASS COMPANY, 1932 – 1935

Colors: Pink, green, crystal, yellow, and cobalt blue. (See Reproduction Section.)

The first thing novices to Florentine need to do is learn how to distinguish between Florentine No. 1 and Florentine No. 2. Study the outline shapes. The serrated edge pieces are hexagonal (six sided); this edging occurs on all flat pieces of Florentine No. 1. All footed pieces (such as tumblers, shakers, or pitchers) have the serrated edge on that foot. In Florentine No. 2, all pieces have a plain edge as can be seen in the photographs on page 87. Florentine No. 1 was once advertised as hexagonal and Florentine No. 2 was advertised as round. However, both patterns were advertised and sold together in mix/matched sets. Today, some collectors follow that lead.

The 48 ounce, flat-bottomed pitcher was sold with both Florentine No. 1 and No. 2 sets. It was listed as 54 ounces in catalogs, but usually measures six ounces less. It depends upon the lip as to how many ounces it will hold before liquid runs out. My inclination is to only list this pitcher with Florentine No. 1 using the handle shape as my criterion. In defiance of that logic, this pitcher is frequently found with flat-bottomed Florentine No. 2 tumblers, forcing me to list it with both.

Many flat tumblers with paneled interiors are being found in sets with Florentine No. 1 pitchers. These paneled tumblers should be considered Florentine No. 1 rather than Florentine No. 2. That recommendation is for die-hard collectors only. Paneled flat tumblers are tough to find; but few collectors care.

Today, pink Florentine No. 1 is the most difficult color to find. Pink footed tumblers, covered oval vegetable bowl, and ruffled creamers and sugars are all but unavailable at any price. Sets can be collected in green, crystal, or yellow with time and effort. Those irregular edges are easily damaged; look there, underneath and top, when you pick up a piece to buy.

Fired-on colors have surfaced in luncheon sets, but there is little collector fervor for these at the moment. You can find all sorts of colors and colored bands on crystal. A primary disadvantage to these banded colors is finding enough to put a set together.

Many 5½" yellow ashtrays have VFW (Veterans of Foreign Wars) embossed in the bottom. I have seen more with this imprint than without it. I have not seen an embossed design on any color other than yellow.

A legitimate, second cobalt blue Florentine No. 1 pitcher has turned up in the West. Do not mistake one of these for the cone shaped, reproduction cobalt No. 2 pitcher found everywhere.

Florentine No. 1 shakers have been reproduced in pink and cobalt blue. Other colors normally follow. No original cobalt blue Florentine No. 1 shakers have ever been found; so those are easy to ignore. The reproduction pink shaker is somewhat more difficult to differentiate. When comparing a reproduction shaker to several old pairs from my inventory, the old shakers have a major open flower on each side. There is a top circle on this blossom with three smaller circles down each side. The seven circles form the outside of the blossom. The reproduction blossom looks more like a strawberry with no circles forming the outside of the blossom. Do not use the threading test mentioned under Floral for the Florentine No. 1 shakers, however. It will not work for Florentine although the same importing company out of Georgia makes these. The threads are correct on this reproduction pattern. The reproductions I have seen as of May 2001 have been badly moulded, but that is not to say that it cannot be corrected.

	Crystal, Green	Yellow	Pink	Cobalt Blue
Ashtray, 5½"	22.00	30.00	30.00	
Bowl, 5", berry	12.00	15.00	15.00	22.50
Bowl, 5", cream soup or ruffled nut	25.00		20.00	60.00
Bowl, 6", cereal	25.00	30.00	35.00	
Bowl, 8½", large berry	30.00	35.00	40.00	
Bowl, 9½", oval vegetable and cover	55.00	75.00	75.00	
Butter dish and cover	125.00	180.00	160.00	
Butter dish bottom	50.00	85.00	85.00	
Butter dish top	75.00	95.00	75.00	
Coaster/ashtray, 3¾"	18.00	20.00	28.00	
Comport, 3½", ruffled	*40.00		18.00	65.00
Creamer	11.00	22.00	20.00	
Creamer, ruffled	45.00		50.00	70.00
Cup	9.00	13.00	12.00	85.00
Pitcher, 6½", 36 oz., footed	40.00	45.00	45.00	850.00
Pitcher, 7½", 48 ounce, flat, ice lip or none	75.00	195.00	135.00	
Plate, 6", sherbet	6.00	7.00	6.00	

	Crystal, Green	Yellow	Pink	Cobalt Blue
Plate, 8½", salad	8.00	12.00	11.00	
Plate, 10", dinner	18.00	25.00	25.00	
Plate, 10", grill	12.00	15.00	20.00	
Platter, 11½", oval	20.00	25.00	25.00	
**Salt and pepper, footed	37.50	55.00	55.00	
Saucer	3.00	4.00	4.00	17.00
Sherbet, 3 ounce, footed	11.00	14.00	14.00	
Sugar	9.50	12.00	12.00	
Sugar cover	18.00	30.00	30.00	
Sugar, ruffled	40.00		50.00	70.00
Tumbler, 3¼", 4 oz., footed	16.00			
Tumbler, 3¾", 5 ounce, footed, juice	16.00	25.00	25.00	
Tumbler, 4", 9 oz., ribbed	16.00		22.00	
Tumbler, 4¾", 10 ounce, footed, water	22.00	24.00	24.00	
Tumbler, 5¼", 12 ounce, footed, iced tea	28.00	30.00	30.00	
Tumbler, 5¼", 9 ounce, lemonade (like Floral)			125.00	

*Crystal $15.00   ** Beware reproductions

FLORENTINE NO. 2, "POPPY NO. 2" HAZEL ATLAS GLASS COMPANY 1932 – 1935

Colors: Pink, green, yellow, crystal, some cobalt, amber, and ice blue. (See Reproduction Section.)

Read about the differences between the two Florentines in the first paragraph of the preceding Florentine No. 1 pattern. If you are a new or advanced collector running out of pieces to find, try mixing the Florentines together, a practice the company itself employed, since boxed sets have turned up over the years containing both patterns.

A conundrum of this pattern is shown via the green ruffled nut or cream soup, left of the regularly found cream soup. This piece qualifies as Florentine No. 1 because it matches the other ruffled pieces (comport, creamer, and sugar) in that pattern. The frustration here is the shape of the handles on the bowl, which only match items in Florentine No. 2. Thus, we have an overlapping piece that can be used with either pattern. A pink one is pictured with Florentine No. 1.

The more expensive, seldom seen, footed, 6¼", twenty-four ounce, cone-shaped pitcher is shown on the right in the top photograph. The more frequently found footed pitcher stands 7½" tall and is shown on the left. Measure height from the base to the top of the spout. There is over an inch difference and this will not vary as greatly as ounce capacities.

That 7½" pitcher and footed water tumbler have been reproduced in a lack luster cobalt blue, amber, pink, and a dark green. This pitcher was never originally made in those colors; therefore, no one should assume these reproductions to be old.

Custard cups remain the most elusive piece in Florentine No. 2; a crystal one is pictured on a yellow, 6¼" indented plate. The saucer curves up on the edges while the custard plate is flat with a larger indentation.

The bulbous, 76 ounce pitcher has eluded many collectors, particularly in yellow. The 10" relish dish comes in three styles. The most commonly found "Y" style is pictured in green and yellow. The unusual style has two curved, separate divisions, one on each side. The undivided is the most difficult to acquire.

Grill plates with a round indent for the cream soup have been found in green, crystal and, now, yellow. Since the last book, a gentleman has turned up a batch of six or eight in yellow. They are quite rare.

Green Florentine is more requested than crystal, but crystal is scarce; hence, prices are similar. Some amber, shown in earlier editions, is the rarest Florentine color; but only a few items have been discovered. Most sizes of flat tumblers have been found in amber, but no old pitcher.

Both lids to the butter dishes and the oval vegetables are interchangeable in the two Florentine patterns. Candy lids and butter lids are similar in size. The candy lid measures 4¾" in diameter, but the butter dish lid measures 5" exactly. Those measurements are from outside edge to outside edge.

Luncheon sets of red, orange, green, and blue have surfaced, with the fired-on colors being sprayed over crystal.

	Crystal, Green	Pink	Yellow	Cobalt Blue
Bowl, 4½", berry	15.00	17.00	22.00	
Bowl, 4¾", cream soup	18.00	16.00	22.00	
Bowl, 5½"	33.00		42.00	
Bowl, 6", cereal	33.00		42.00	
Bowl, 7½", shallow			95.00	
Bowl, 8", large berry	28.00	32.00	38.00	
Bowl, 9", oval vegetable and cover	65.00		90.00	
Bowl, 9", flat	27.50			
Butter dish and cover	110.00		165.00	
Butter dish bottom	25.00		70.00	
Butter dish top	75.00		95.00	
Candlesticks, 2¾", pair	50.00		70.00	
Candy dish and cover	100.00	145.00	155.00	
Coaster, 3¼"	13.00	16.00	22.00	
Coaster/ashtray, 3¾"	17.50		30.00	
Coaster/ashtray, 5½"	20.00		38.00	
* Comport, 3½", ruffled	40.00	15.00		65.00
Creamer	9.00		12.00	
Cup, amber 50.00	9.00		10.00	
Custard cup or jello	60.00		85.00	
Gravy boat			65.00	
Pitcher, 6¼", 24 ounce, cone-footed			175.00	
** Pitcher, 7½", 28 ounce, cone-footed	38.00		35.00	
Pitcher, 7½", 48 ounce	75.00	135.00	265.00	
Pitcher, 8¼", 76 ounce	110.00	225.00	450.00	

	Crystal, Green	Pink	Yellow	Cobalt Blue
Plate, 6", sherbet	4.00		6.00	
Plate, 6¼", with indent	22.00		32.00	
Plate, 8½", salad	8.50	8.50	10.00	
Plate, 10", dinner	16.00		16.00	
Plate, 10¼", grill	14.00		18.00	
Plate, 10¼", grill w/cream soup ring	40.00			
Platter, 11", oval	16.00	16.00	25.00	
Platter, 11½", for gravy boat			55.00	
Relish dish, 10", 3-part or plain	22.00	28.00	32.00	
*** Salt and pepper, pair	42.50		50.00	
Saucer, amber $15.00	4.00		5.00	
Sherbet, ftd., amber $40.00	10.00		12.00	
Sugar	10.00		12.00	
Sugar cover	15.00		28.00	
Tray, round, condiment for shakers, creamer/sugar			80.00	
Tumbler, 3⅜", 5 oz., juice	14.00	12.00	22.00	
Tumbler, 3⁹⁄₁₆", 6 oz., blown	18.00			
**** Tumbler, 4", 9 oz., water	14.00	16.00	21.00	70.00
Tumbler, 5", 12 oz., blown	20.00			
**** Tumbler, 5", 12 oz., tea	35.00		55.00	
Tumbler, 3¼", 5 oz., footed	15.00		18.00	
Tumbler, 4", 5 oz., footed	15.00		17.00	
Tumbler, 5", 9 oz., footed	30.00		35.00	
Vase or parfait, 6"	30.00		65.00	

*Crystal – $15.00   ** Ice Blue – $500.00   ***Fired-on Red, Orange, or Blue, Pr. – $42.50   **** Amber – $75.00

FLOWER GARDEN WITH BUTTERFLIES, "BUTTERFLIES AND ROSES"
U.S. GLASS COMPANY, FACTORY "R," TIFFIN PLANT, c. 1924

Colors: Pink, green, blue-green, canary yellow, crystal, amber, and black.

As more old catalog pages are unearthed throughout the country, we're privileged to learn things about older glassware that our pioneer authors didn't know when they named patterns. The original appellation for this was Brocade, after the wonderful brocaded etching decorating the surface. It is believed to have been in production for approximately a 10 year period, though obviously not continuously judging from the dearth of items available. Flower Garden with Butterflies was one pattern we enjoyed collecting for 20 years. After letting it go, I have had a troublesome time buying enough to photograph for the book. I should have kept more pieces; but hindsight is always 20-20. Earlier editions will show a much larger display. This pattern is found so rarely that few new collectors are attempting it. Over the years, collections have been assembled and today, some patterns only appear on the market when sets are sold. Yet, this is one pattern that lends itself extremely well to one piece display.

I have seen a black candlestick that only had the end of a butterfly antenna on it. You really had to search to find that little piece of butterfly. The other candlestick of the pair had half a butterfly. Perhaps some item will turn up where the butterfly flew away entirely.

A crystal cologne with black stopper turned up after I had previously photographed a black cologne sans stopper. I missed my opportunity to photograph them both whole. Be sure to check out the dauber in the perfumes. Many of them are broken off or ground down to hide the broken end. Daubers are much harder to find than the bottles themselves; take that into consideration if buying only the bottle. That goes for any perfume/cologne in any pattern. The piece handled most often usually suffered the damage and was tossed away.

A collector desired, heart-shaped candy is shown.

Flower Garden with Butterflies has three styles of powder jars, which probably explains why so many oval and rectangular dresser trays are found. Dresser trays and luncheon plates are the only routinely found items in the pattern. Indubitably, more powder jars than trays were broken through years of use. Two different footed powders exist with the smaller, 6¼", shown in amber and green. The taller, not shown, stands 7½" high. Thankfully, the lids for these footed powders are the same. The flat powder jar has a 3½" diameter. We never found a blue, flat powder.

I have already discussed the so-called "Shari" perfume or cologne set in earlier books, but I frequently get letters about it as an unlisted piece of Flower Garden. It's a semi-circular, footed glass dresser box that holds five wedge (pie shaped) bottles. This container is often confused with Flower Garden because it has flower designs on it. Labels found intact on bottles promoted the New York/Paris affiliation of "Charme Volupte" but nowhere was the word "Shari" mentioned on the labels. One bottle had contained cold cream, another vanishing cream, and three others once held parfumes. There are dancing girls at either end of the box, and flowers abound on the semi-circle. There are no dancing girls on Flower Garden. Other not-to-be-mistaken-for Flower Garden pieces include the 7" and 10" trivets with flowers all over them made by U.S. Glass. They were mixing bowl covers and they do not have butterflies.

	Amber Crystal	Pink Green Blue-Green	Blue Canary Yellow
Ashtray, match-pack holders	165.00	190.00	225.00
Candlesticks, 4", pair	42.50	55.00	95.00
Candlesticks, 8", pair	77.50	135.00	130.00
Candy w/cover, 6", flat	130.00	155.00	
Candy w/cover, 7½", cone-shaped	80.00	130.00	175.00
Candy w/cover, heart-shaped		1,250.00	1,300.00
* Cologne bottle w/stopper, 7½"		210.00	350.00
Comport, 2⅞" h.		23.00	28.00
Comport, 3" h., fits 10" plate	20.00	23.00	28.00
Comport, 4¼" h. x 4¾" w.			50.00
Comport, 4¾" h. x 10¼" w.	48.00	65.00	85.00
Comport, 5⅞" h. x 11" w.	55.00		95.00
Comport, 7¼" h. x 8¼" w.	60.00	80.00	
Creamer		75.00	
Cup		75.00	

	Amber Crystal	Pink Green Blue-Green	Blue Canary Yellow
Mayonnaise, footed, 4¾" h. x 6¼" w., w/7" plate & spoon	75.00	95.00	135.00
Plate, 7"	16.00	21.00	30.00
Plate, 8", two styles	15.00	17.50	25.00
Plate, 10"		42.50	48.00
Plate, 10", indent for 3" comport	32.00	40.00	45.00
Powder jar, 3½", flat		80.00	
Powder jar, footed, 6¼" h.	80.00	145.00	185.00
Powder jar, footed, 7½" h.	80.00	145.00	195.00
Sandwich server, center handle	60.00	75.00	110.00
Saucer		25.00	
Sugar		75.00	
Tray, 5½" x 10", oval	55.00	60.00	
Tray, 11¾" x 7¾", rectangular	60.00	75.00	90.00
Tumbler, 7½"	175.00		
Vase, 6¼"	75.00	100.00	175.00
Vase, 10½"		135.00	235.00

* Stopper, if not broken off, ½ price of bottle

PRICE LIST FOR BLACK ITEMS ONLY

Bonbon w/cover, 6⅝" diameter	250.00
Bowl, 7¼", w/cover, "flying saucer"	395.00
Bowl, 8½", console, w/base	150.00
Bowl, 9", rolled edge, w/base	200.00
Bowl, 11", footed orange	225.00
Bowl, 12", rolled edge console w/base	200.00
Candlestick 6" w/6½" candle, pair	495.00
Candlestick, 8", pair	325.00
Cheese and cracker, footed, 5⅜" h. x 10" w.	325.00
Comport and cover, 2¾" h. (fits 10" indented plate)	200.00
Cigarette box & cover, 4⅜" long	165.00
Comport, tureen, 4¼" h. x 10" w.	250.00
Comport, footed, 5⅝" h. x 10" w.	225.00
Comport, footed, 7" h.	175.00
Plate, 10", indented	100.00
Sandwich server, center-handled	135.00
Vase, 6¼", Dahlia, cupped	155.00
Vase, 8", Dahlia, cupped	210.00
Vase, 9", wallhanging	350.00
Vase, 10", 2-handled	225.00
Vase, 10½", Dahlia, cupped	265.00

"FLUTE & CANE," "SUNBURST & CANE," "CANE," "HUCKABEE," SEMI-COLONIAL
NO. 666 & 666½ IMPERIAL GLASS COMPANY, c. 1921

Colors: Crystal, pink, green, Rubigold (marigold), Caramel slag.

First of all, let me be frank. My wife talked me into including this pattern with the unfortunate "Devil's" line number. She finds the cane look intriguing. In an aside, we were standing in line at a license bureau in officialdom once, when a lady came in and pitched a license at the clerk and said very loudly for all to hear, "I'm not having this Devil's number on my car." Everybody strained to see what the number was. Sure enough, she'd been issued "666" something. Bible belt people know this association. It appears whomever assigned the numbers at Imperial did not. (Neither did the state.) I was told that the half number beside Imperial's line numbers indicated the less expensively made glassware sold in places like F.W. Woolworth, Sears, Montgomery Wards, et. al.

I doubt this listing is complete and I suspect there are early pieces out there in blue, which was being run in this time frame; but I can't confirm that right now. I'm fairly certain I've seen some; but since I wasn't paying specific attention to this pattern.... I do, however, remember seeing a sugar and creamer in slag when I was at the factory in the 80s, though it is not in any of the catalogs they presented me then. As was Imperial's (and other) glass companies' wont, they reintroduced a few pieces from older moulds into their lines from time to time, and in whatever colors they were running then. Since my catalog information doesn't encompass their entire history, I can't be certain what other colors you'll find in "Flute and Cane." If you'll be kind enough to let me know what you turn up, I'd be most appreciative and will endeavor to pass it along to collectors.

Many of the Rubigold pieces are quite rare and highly prized by carnival glass collectors. The tall, slender pitcher, tumblers, cups, 6" plates, and goblets are considered very desirable items to own. However, various bowls are what are generally seen, today. The 6" plate was marketed with the sherbet as an ice cream set, with the molasses as an underliner and with the custard cup as a saucer. There ought to be quite a few of those available; but, alas, not so. Sorry, but there is a very cane appearing candle in the picture that officially belongs with the Amelia #671 line, shown on page 10. You can't always trust what you see.

	Crystal*		Crystal*		Crystal*
Bowl, 4½", fruit	10.00	Compote, 6½", oval, ftd., 2-handle	30.00	Salt & pepper	45.00
Bowl, 6½", oval, pickle	18.00	Compote, 7½", stem w/bowl	25.00	Sherbet, 3½", stem	12.00
Bowl, 6½", square	15.00	Compote, 7½", stem, flat	25.00	Spooner (open sm. sug)	15.00
Bowl, 7½", salad	25.00	Creamer	15.00	Stem, 1 ounce, cordial	25.00
Bowl, 8½", large. fruit	30.00	Cup, custard	12.00	Stem, 3 ounce, wine	18.00
Bowl, crème soup, 5½"	20.00	Molasses, nickel top	65.00	Stem, 6 ounce, champagne	15.00
Butter w/lid, small		Oil bottle w/stopper, 6 ounce	45.00	Stem, 9 ounce, water	18.00
(powder box look)	35.00	Pitcher, 22 ounce, 5¼"	45.00	Sugar w/lid	25.00
Butter, dome lid	55.00	Pitcher, 51 ounce	65.00	Tumbler, 9 ounce	30.00
Celery, 8½", oval	25.00	Pitcher, tall/slender	75.00	Vase, 6"	37.50
Celery, tall, 2 handle	40.00	Plate, 6"	20.00	*Add 50% for colors	

FORTUNE HOCKING GLASS COMPANY, 1937 – 1938

Colors: Pink and crystal.

An expenditure of time and a little fortune can still assemble a set of Fortune, a small pattern where luncheon plates are costly and you customarily find them only one at a time. In the past, both Fortune tumblers have been bought by collectors of Queen Mary and Old Colony to use with those sets because they were inexpensive and looked fine. Now the prices of Fortune tumblers have come into their own and it is not as feasible to use them with other sets. I generally see tumblers and small berry bowls when I encounter Fortune.

A few pitchers whose patterns are similar to Fortune are turning up and some collectors are buying them for use with their sets. These "go-with" pitchers are selling in the $25.00 to $30.00 range. So far, no actual Fortune pitcher has turned up; but never say never.

The covered candy is a useful display item.

	Pink, Crystal		Pink, Crystal
Bowl, 4", berry	10.00	Cup	12.00
Bowl, 4½", dessert	12.00	Plate, 6", sherbet	8.00
Bowl, 4½", handled	12.00	Plate, 8", luncheon	28.00
Bowl, 5¼", rolled edge	22.00	Saucer	5.00
Bowl, 7¾", salad or large berry	25.00	Tumbler, 3½", 5 ounce, juice	12.00
Candy dish and cover, flat	28.00	Tumbler, 4", 9 ounce, water	15.00

FRUITS HAZEL ATLAS AND OTHER GLASS COMPANIES, 1931 – 1935

Colors: Pink, green, some crystal, and iridized.

Fruits patterned water tumblers (4") in all colors are the pieces usually seen. Iridescent "Pears" tumblers are abundant. Federal Glass Company probably made these iridescent tumblers while they were making iridescent Normandie and a few pieces in Madrid. Water tumblers with cherries or other fruits are found in pink, but locating any green tumbler is a problem.

Fruits collectors have several pieces, now, that are almost impossible to find in this scarce 1930s pattern. The 3½" (5 ounce) juice and 5" (12 ounce) ice tea tumblers have joined the large and small berry bowls as the pieces of green to own. Few of the berry bowls are being found but even fewer tumblers. I own one iced tea; two juice tumblers promised to me turned out to be Cherry Blossom. Fruits tumblers have only cherries and no blossoms.

Since so many collectors are searching for green iced teas, juice tumblers, and bowls, their prices continue upward. I have never seen pink juice or tea tumblers, though I did list them once, as did the person who appears to have plagiarized all my mistakes in a competing Depression book presented as theirs. Originally, I only listed one price for all Fruits colors. As more collectors bought the green, the price of green rose faster than pink; so, I split prices into two listings, not catching the nonexistence of those particular sizes of pink tumblers which had been masked under that "all colors" label. Most collectors pursue available green water tumblers to go with the pitcher. Pink water tumblers have no pitcher.

Fruits berry bowls in both sizes are among the hardest to obtain in all Depression glass patterns. Since this is not one of the major collected patterns and does not have thousands of admirers, the paucity of both sizes of bowls has only lately been noticed.

Fruits pitchers have only cherries in the pattern. Sometimes they are mislabeled as Cherry Blossom, flat-bottomed pitchers. Notice that the handle is shaped like that of flat Florentine pitchers (Hazel Atlas Company) and not like Cherry Blossom (Jeannette Glass Company) flat pitchers. Crystal Fruits pitchers sell for less than half the price of green and other crystal pieces are hardly collected. They are available should you want an economically priced beverage set.

	Green	Pink
Bowl, 4½", berry	35.00	28.00
Bowl, 8", berry	90.00	50.00
Cup	8.00	9.00
Pitcher, 7", flat bottom	95.00	
Plate, 8", luncheon	12.00	12.00
Saucer	5.50	4.00

	Green	Pink
Sherbet	12.00	12.00
Tumbler, 3½", juice	65.00	
* Tumbler, 4" (1 fruit)	20.00	18.00
Tumbler, 4" (combination of fruits)	30.00	22.00
Tumbler, 5", 12 ounce	165.00	

* Iridized $8.00

GEORGIAN, "LOVEBIRDS" FEDERAL GLASS COMPANY, 1931 – 1936

Colors: Green, crystal, and amber.

Two lovebirds (or parakeets, as one reader corrected) perched side by side help to easily identify most pieces of Federal Glass Company's Georgian. Pieces without the birds include both sizes of tumblers, the hot plate, and a few dinner plates. Few collectors seek dinner plates without birds; that style plate sells for less. Baskets customarily alternate with birds in the design on all other pieces. The tumblers only have baskets; you can sometimes find a bargain on tumblers if the seller does not know about the missing birds. There once was a great flurry of activity among the buying public toward this pattern. In the mid-1970s, a set was donated to the Smithsonian by the Peach State Depression Glass Club in the name of President Jimmy Carter. Those pieces were engraved and numbered. Some extras were sold or given as prizes. Thus, if you run into such an item, it has added history.

Basic pieces in Georgian are easily found. Berry bowls, cups, saucers, sherbets, sherbet plates, and luncheon plates can be accumulated. Georgian tumblers, however, are difficult to find. Several boxed sets of 36 water tumblers have turned up in the Chicago area, where a newspaper gave the tumblers away to subscribers in the 1930s. I've even been told that these were found stored in Al Capone's vault, albeit by a notorious leg puller. Prices for iced teas have more than doubled the price of water tumblers. I have owned at least a dozen Georgian waters for every iced tea to give you an idea of how difficult teas are to find.

Many of the Georgian serving pieces were heavily utilized; be wary of mint pricing for pieces that are scratched and worn from usage. You pay a premium for mint condition. Remember that all prices listed in this book are for mint condition pieces. Damaged or scratched and worn pieces should go for less depending upon the extent of damage and wear. If you are gathering this glass to use, some imperfections may not make as much difference as collecting for eventual selling. Mint condition glass will sell more readily and for a much better price if you ever decide to part with your collection.

Georgian Lazy Susans (cold cuts servers) are more rarely seen than the Madrid ones that turn up, sporadically, at best. You can see one pictured below. A walnut tray turned up in Ohio with an original decal label that read "Kalter Aufschain Cold Cuts Server Schirmer Cincy." Most of these servers have been found in Kentucky and southern Ohio. These wooden Lazy Susans made of walnut are 18½" across with seven 5" openings for holding the so-called hot plates. Somehow, I believe these 5" hot plates are mislabeled since they are found on a cold cuts server. These cold cuts (hot) plates have only the center motif design.

Reports of a Georgian mug have been exaggerated. Someone found a creamer without a spout and called it a mug. There are other patterns known that have creamers or pitchers without a spout; and one other Federal pattern, Sharon, has at least one two-spouted creamer known. Spouts were applied by hand at most glass factories using a wooden tool. Quality control of this glass was not as demanding as today. Most actual mugs from the period have flat bottoms or are larger in capacity or decidedly taller.

There's a round, thin plate made by Indiana Glass having two large parakeets as its center design, covering nearly the whole plate. This is not Georgian.

GEORGIAN

	Green			Green
Bowl, 4½", berry	9.00		* Hot Plate, 5", center design	60.00
Bowl, 5¾", cereal	25.00		** Plate, 6", sherbet	7.00
Bowl, 6½", deep	68.00		Plate, 8", luncheon	11.00
Bowl, 7½", large berry	62.00		Plate, 9¼", dinner	25.00
Bowl, 9", oval vegetable	65.00		Plate, 9¼", center design only	22.00
Butter dish and cover	85.00		Platter, 11½", closed-handled	68.00
Butter dish bottom	50.00		Saucer	3.00
Butter dish top	35.00		Sherbet	11.00
Cold cuts server, 18½", wood with			Sugar, 3", footed	10.00
seven 5" openings for 5" coasters	900.00		Sugar, 4", footed	17.00
Creamer, 3", footed	12.00		Sugar cover for 3"	45.00
Creamer, 4", footed	17.00		Tumbler, 4", 9 ounce, flat	70.00
Cup	10.00		Tumbler, 5¼", 12 ounce, flat	135.00

* Crystal $25.00   ** Amber $40.00.

GOTHIC GARDEN PADEN CITY GLASS COMPANY, 1930s

Colors: Pink, green, black, yellow, and crystal.

Gothic Garden is Paden City's etch containing nearly all the favorite elements of 1930s ware, birds, flowers, scrolls, garlands, and urns. It ought to be the hottest etch ever made in that time frame. The bird's body faces outward on either side of the design medallion, but their heads turn backward toward the center floral motif. Gothic Garden is found mostly on Paden City's Line #411 (square shapes with the corners cut off), but you may find it on other Paden City blanks. Other colors than those I have listed may occur; let me know what you find, so I can add to the listings. Measurements may vary up to an inch due to the turned up edges on bowls; do not take these as absolute gospel.

I bought a black bowl like the one pictured in pink and saw a flat, yellow candy like the one pictured in "Peacock Reverse." Since it was prized more highly by the owner than by me, he still owns it.

Gothic Garden does have a creamer and sugar which lends credence to the thought that there may be a luncheon set available; lack of cups and saucers hasn't hurt the collecting of other Paden City patterns. Cups and saucers are rare in all etched patterns of this company. Did the etching department not like to work on smaller pieces? For the time being I am only listing one price; add 25% for black and subtract 25% for crystal. What little crystal I have seen has been gold trimmed which, with good gold, will fetch nearly the price of colored ware. I see quite a bit of this at formal shows, some pieces with astronomical prices. However, since I keep seeing those same pieces, I think for some reason Gothic Garden hasn't caught on with collectors just yet.

	All colors		All colors
Bowl, 9", tab handle	65.00	Creamer	45.00
Bowl, 10", footed	85.00	Plate, 11", tab handle	65.00
Bowl, 10⅛", handle	95.00	Server, 9¾", center handled	85.00
Bowl, 10½", oval, handle	100.00	Sugar	45.00
Cake plate, 10½", footed	80.00	Vase, 6½"	125.00
Candy, flat	125.00	Vase, 8"	165.00
Comport, tall, deep top	65.00	Vase, 9½"	110.00

95

HEX OPTIC, "HONEYCOMB" JEANNETTE GLASS COMPANY, 1928 – 1932

Colors: Pink, green, Ultra Marine (late 1930s), and iridescent in 1950s.

Jeannette's Hexagon Optic doesn't command the respect in Depression glass circles that its rich history demands. It was an historic glass design, manufactured in one of the first fully automated systems of the time and presented in those new brilliant green and wild rose colors that were impressing the buying public. In addition, it came in both tableware and kitchenware items so that milady's entire glass needs could be met in matching ware. It was innovative and impressive in a trade just moving from hand making glass into an age of automation.

Today, Hex Optic is more noticed by kitchenware collectors than any other pattern of Depression glass because of the myriad, matching kitchenware pieces available. Sugar shakers, bucket reamers, mixing bowls, stacking sets, and butter dishes were designed in green and pink. In fact, were it not for kitchenware collectors becoming addicted to Hex Optic, it might still be inconspicuous and unnoticed in the glass collecting realm.

There are two styles of pitchers in Hexagon Optic, one being footed and having the Deco age cone shape and the other, a flat bottomed, cylindrical shape. This 8 inch tall, 70 ounce, flat-bottomed version has now turned up in green. Five or six people have written to say they are being found in Minnesota and Wisconsin. The footed pitcher is hardly seen, now, having quietly disappeared into collections. Jeannette's Hex Optic pitcher is thick. Other companies' honeycomb pitchers are out there that are thin.

Iridescent oil lamps, both style pitchers, and tumblers were all made during Jeannette's iridized craze of the 1950s. The Ultra Marine tumblers were probably a product of the late 1930s when the company was making Doric and Pansy.

The sugar and creamer in this pattern have ear shaped, "wing" handles. Early pieces of Jeannette's glass carried a J in a triangle trademark.

	Pink, Green
Bowl, 4¼", ruffled berry	9.00
Bowl, 7½", large berry	15.00
Bowl, 7¼", mixing	15.00
Bowl, 8¼", mixing	20.00
Bowl, 9", mixing	25.00
Bowl, 10", mixing	28.00
Bucket reamer	65.00
Butter dish and cover, rectangular 1 pound size	90.00
Creamer, 2 style handles	7.00
Cup, 2 style handles	10.00
Ice bucket, metal handle	30.00
Pitcher, 5", 32 ounce, sunflower motif in bottom	25.00
Pitcher, 9", 48 ounce, footed	50.00
Pitcher, 8", 70 ounce, flat	195.00
Plate, 6", sherbet	2.50

	Pink, Green
Plate, 8", luncheon	5.50
Platter, 11", round	15.00
Refrigerator dish, 4" x 4"	18.00
Refrigerator stack set, 4 piece	75.00
Salt and pepper, pair	30.00
Saucer	3.00
Sugar, 2 styles of handles	7.00
Sugar shaker	235.00
Sherbet, 5 ounce, footed	7.00
Tumbler, 3¾", 9 ounce	4.50
Tumbler, 5", 12 ounce	7.00
Tumbler, 4¾", 7 ounce, footed	7.50
Tumbler, 5¾" footed	10.00
Tumbler, 7", footed	12.00
Whiskey, 2", 1 ounce	8.00

HOBNAIL HOCKING GLASS COMPANY, 1934 – 1936

Colors: Crystal, crystal w/red trim, and pink.

A majority of Depression era glass companies made hobnailed patterns, but Hocking's Hobnail is readily recognized by seasoned collectors due to its pieces being shaped like those found in Miss America or Moonstone. In truth, the 1940s Moonstone pattern is actually Hocking's Hobnail design with an added white accent to the hobs and edges. Hobnail serving pieces are difficult to find, but beverage sets are abundant.

The light amethyst color pictured below was Lilac according to Anchor Hocking labels on most of the pieces shown. The other color is Ivory that was made mostly for ovenware usage. I believe the Lilac would have sold well, but appears to have never been marketed. These pieces are shown compliments of Anchor Hocking. They have been extremely helpful in allowing me to photograph pieces that you would never get a chance to experience otherwise.

Notice how red-trimmed crystal Hobnail stands out on page 98. Collectors have been captivated by this red trim which is found principally on the West Coast. The decanter and footed juices are the only red-trimmed pieces I see with any regularity in my travels in the Eastern half of the country. We bought a small set with red decoration and all pieces sold at the first glass show we displayed them.

Footed juice tumblers were sold to accompany the decanter as a wine set; thus, it was also a wineglass unless the preacher stopped by. Timing had a lot to do with tumblers and stems during this era. During Prohibition wineglasses were sold as juices and the champagnes as high sherbets. Wineglasses during that era routinely held approximately three ounces. Today, people consider the eight to ten ounce water goblets from the Depression era as wine goblets; twenty-first century wine connoisseurs want larger glasses. Dealers should verify size with customers when they ask for wines since they may really want water goblets.

Hocking made only four pieces in pink. Another pink Hobnail pattern, such as one made by MacBeth-Evans, can coexist with this Hocking pattern; that way, you can add a pitcher and tumblers, something unavailable in Hocking's ware. Many other companies' Hobnail patterns will mingle with Hocking's Hobnail.

	Pink	*Crystal		Pink	*Crystal
Bowl, 5½", cereal		4.00	Plate, 8½", luncheon	7.50	4.00
Bowl, 7", salad		4.50	Saucer/sherbet plate	4.00	1.50
Cup	6.00	4.50	Sherbet	5.00	3.00
Creamer, footed		6.00	Sugar, footed		6.00
Decanter and stopper, 32 ounce		32.00	Tumbler, 5 ounce, juice		4.00
Goblet, 10 ounce, water		8.00	Tumbler, 9 ounce, 10 ounce, water		5.50
Goblet, 13 ounce, iced tea		10.00	Tumbler, 5¼",15 ounce, iced tea		15.00
Pitcher, 18 ounce, milk		22.00	Tumbler, 3 ounce, footed, wine/juice		5.50
Pitcher, 67 ounce		28.00	Tumbler, 5 ounce, footed, cordial		6.00
Plate, 6", sherbet	4.00	1.50	Whiskey, 1½ ounce		6.00

*Add 20 – 25% for red trimmed pieces

97

HOMESPUN, "FINE RIB" JEANNETTE GLASS COMPANY, 1939 – 1949

Colors: Pink and crystal.

There are nine Homespun tumblers pictured below. Amazingly, there is no actual Homespun pitcher. A large Fine Rib pitcher, also made by Hazel-Atlas was originally packaged by the company for use with Homespun. It has similar narrow bands and matches in color, but has no waffling design. Band at top tumblers are harder to find; but most collectors seek the ribbed.

Pictured on the right are the flat, 13½ ounce (band at top) tea and the 12½ ounce (no band) tea. In front of them is the nine ounce (band above ribs, waffle bottomed) tumbler. Confusion reigns with the three tumblers in the middle. There is little difference in height; but the seven ounce (ribs to top, straight, concentric ring bottom) is on the left, next to the nine ounce (ribs to top, straight, waffle bottomed). Even though there is a two ounce difference in capacity, there is only ³⁄₁₆" difference in height. Notice the small eight ounce (ribs to top, flared, plain bottomed) tumbler on the right of those. This style is difficult to find. The two footed teas are often confused because they both hold 15 ounces and there is only ⅛" difference in height. Collectors sometimes refer to them as skinny and fat bottomed. There is a slight stem on the taller one and no stem on the other. It only makes a difference when ordering by mail or off the Internet.

There is no Homespun sugar lid. The lid sometimes displayed on the sugar is a Fine Rib powder jar top.

Homespun bowls have tab handles. Sherbets suffer from inner rim roughness (irr), but are elusive. Buy them when you see them.

There is no child's teapot in crystal and there are no sugar and creamers in this tea set. You can see the pink child's teapot in the center below.

	Pink, Crystal		Pink, Crystal
Bowl, 4½", closed handles	18.00	Sherbet, low flat	17.50
Bowl, 5", cereal, closed handles	30.00	Sugar, footed	12.50
Bowl, 8¼", large berry	30.00	Tumbler, 3⅞", 7 ounce, straight	24.00
Butter dish and cover	62.00	Tumbler, 4⅛", 8 ounce, water, flared top	24.00
Coaster/ashtray	6.50	Tumbler, 4¼", 9 ounce, band at top	24.00
Creamer, footed	12.50	Tumbler, 4⁵⁄₁₆", 9 ounce, no band	24.00
Cup	14.00	Tumbler, 5⅜", 12½ ounce, iced tea	35.00
Plate, 6", sherbet	8.00	Tumbler, 5⅞", 13½ ounce, iced tea, banded at top	35.00
Plate, 9¼", dinner	22.00	Tumbler, 4", 5 ounce, footed	8.00
Platter, 13", closed handles	22.00	Tumbler, 6¼", 15 ounce, footed	35.00
Saucer	5.00	Tumbler, 6⅜", 15 ounce, footed	35.00

HOMESPUN CHILD'S TEA SET

	Pink	Crystal		Pink	Crystal
Cup	35.00	25.00	Teapot cover	80.00	
Saucer	11.00	8.00	Set: 14-pieces	375.00	
Plate	14.00	10.00	Set: 12-pieces		175.00
Teapot	55.00				

INDIANA CUSTARD, "FLOWER AND LEAF BAND" INDIANA GLASS COMPANY, 1930s; 1950s

Colors: Ivory or custard, early 1930s; white, 1950s.

Indiana Custard bewitches a few new collectors every year, but most cannot find ample pieces unless they live near Indiana. I went to a show over the weekend where a dealer from Maine had a rather large set missing sherbets and some bowls. She did have cup and saucers although they were of varying shades, the other small problem with Indiana Custard. Some of the pieces are more yellow and translucent than others. These cups were translucent, but the supposedly matching saucers were very beige. Note my cup, saucer, sherbet, and creamer in the photograph. They look more yellow due to the translucency. Most collectors don't mix these two hues. I talked to the dealer for a while and discovered the set had been bought at auction in Maine. She didn't know the previous owners, but I'd bet they were from the Midwest. Quantities of this pattern have been uncovered in Ohio and Indiana in the past, but even those areas are beginning to be depleted. This is the region to visit if you are seriously pursuing any Indiana glassware pattern.

Indiana Custard is the only Depression era pattern where cups and sherbets are the most aggravating items to find. Some collectors consider the sherbet overvalued; but those who have searched for years without owning one, would repudiate that point. In all honesty, they are probably a good buy at today's price. Cups have been more difficult for me to find than the sherbets, but I usually have found the sherbets in groups of six or eight and the cups one or two at a time. Both sell, even at these prices.

Indiana made this pattern in white in the 1950s under the name Orange Blossom. So far, there is only minor demand for this color, though it's a lovely, pristine white. Orange Blossom can be found in my *Collectible Glassware from the 40s, 50s, 60s....*

I have been unable to establish if there is a full set of yellow floral decorated pieces available. I have seen a set of Indiana Custard decorated like the saucer with the colored flowers in the center. After 60 years, a problem with collecting the florals might be that the decorations flake. (Any dealer knows something about dealing with "flakes".) Granted, obtaining an entire set a piece or two at a time would be a formidable task. However, most people enjoy chasing glass patterns. They tell me over and over at shows how much fun they've had doing it.

	French Ivory		French Ivory
Bowl, 5½", berry	12.00	Plate, 7½", salad	20.00
Bowl, 6½", cereal	30.00	Plate, 8⅞", luncheon	20.00
Bowl, 7½", flat soup	35.00	Plate, 9¾", dinner	32.00
Bowl, 9", 1¾" deep, large berry	35.00	Platter, 11½", oval	40.00
Bowl, 9½", oval vegetable	35.00	Saucer	8.00
Butter dish and cover	65.00	Sherbet	100.00
Cup	37.50	Sugar	12.00
Creamer	16.00	Sugar cover	25.00
Plate, 5¾", bread and butter	7.00		

IRIS, "IRIS AND HERRINGBONE" JEANNETTE GLASS COMPANY, 1928 – 1932; 1950s; 1970s

Colors: Crystal, iridescent; some pink and green; recently bi-colored red/yellow and blue/green combinations, and white.
(See Reproduction Section.)

Unfortunately, reproduced Iris dinner plates, coasters, and iced teas from Taiwan have hit the market. Turn to page 247 for details. Right now, there are constant reports of cereal and soup bowls turning up. I have not been able to confirm either of those. Yet, with the sheer number of reports, it is very likely they are being made, also. All the new crystal is very clear. If you place old crystal Iris on a white paper, it will look gray or slightly yellow. The new just looks crystal without any tinge of color.

Prices for crystal Iris have stabilized or even softened a bit, especially for iced teas and dinner plates. We have been through this with other patterns over the years and it will just take a while for collectors to adjust and know differences to look for in old and new. Price cycles occur even in patterns without reproduction hassles. Prices reach a plateau or drop slightly for a while, and then they start an upward march again. In the immediate past, fervent collectors helped inflate prices by buying harder-to-find pieces no matter what the expense. Now, some dealers are stocked with the harder to find items that are not selling as well in the new price zone created by the recent buying fever.

The Internet has opened up a world that has both good and bad aspects to collecting. Bad news is that there are people selling who misrepresent their wares. Reproduced items get on there first as "old" and people pay high prices before word gets out in the collecting world. The other side of that coin is that once known, word is flashed worldwide. An Internet address where merchandise is furnished by reputable dealers is www.glassshow.com.

Iris used to be a plentiful pattern; now, there is so much sitting in collections that only a few pieces are plentiful. There are enough pitchers, water tumblers, butter dishes, ruffled bowls, and wines to satisfy everyone wanting them. Demitasse cups are available; saucers are not. Many of these cups were originally sold on copper saucers instead of glass.

Iridescent candy bottoms are a product of the 1970s when Jeannette made crystal bottoms and flashed them with two-tone colors such as red/yellow or blue/green. Many of these were sold as vases; and, over time, the colors have peeled off or been purposely stripped to make them, again, crystal candy bottoms. These later pieces can be distinguished by the lack of rays on the foot. Similarly, white vases were made and sprayed outside with green, red, and blue. White vases sell in the area of $15.00 – 18.00. These are not rare. I have seen a pink painted over white vase in an antique mall for $90.00 marked rare pink Iris. I hope that no one believes that. The rare vase is transparent pink.

The decorated red and gold Iris that keeps turning up was called Corsage and styled by Century in 1946. This information was on a card attached to a 1946 wedding gift. A number of collectors are seeking this.

The 5¾", 4 ounce and 8 ounce water goblet, 4" sherbet, and the demitasse cup and saucer are the most difficult pieces to find in iridescent.

IRIS

	Crystal	Iridescent	Transparent Green/Pink
Bowl, 4½", berry, beaded edge	45.00	9.00	
Bowl, 5", ruffled, sauce	10.00	25.00	
Bowl, 5", cereal	115.00		
Bowl, 7½", soup	165.00	60.00	
Bowl, 8", berry, beaded edge	85.00	28.00	
Bowl, 9½", ruffled, salad	14.00	13.00	195.00
Bowl, 11½", ruffled, fruit	15.00	14.00	
Bowl, 11", fruit, straight edge	65.00		
Butter dish and cover	47.50	45.00	
Butter dish bottom	12.50	12.50	
Butter dish top	35.00	32.50	
Candlesticks, pair	42.50	45.00	
Candy jar and cover	195.00		
*** Coaster	100.00		
Creamer, footed	13.00	13.00	150.00
Cup	15.00	14.00	
* Demitasse cup	45.00	150.00	
* Demitasse saucer	145.00	250.00	
Fruit or nut set	110.00	150.00	
Goblet, 4", wine		28.00	

	Crystal	Iridescent	Transparent Green/Pink
Goblet, 4½", 4 ounce, cocktail	24.00		
Goblet, 4½", 3 ounce, wine	16.00		
Goblet, 5½", 4 ounce	25.00	225.00	
Goblet, 5½", 8 ounce	26.00	225.00	
** Lamp shade, 11½"	97.50		
Pitcher, 9½", footed	40.00	42.50	
Plate, 5½", sherbet	15.00	12.00	
Plate, 8", luncheon	110.00		
*** Plate, 9", dinner	55.00	45.00	
Plate, 11¾", sandwich	35.00	30.00	
Saucer	10.00	9.00	
Sherbet, 2½", footed	27.00	15.00	
Sherbet, 4", footed	25.00	225.00	
Sugar	11.00	11.00	150.00
Sugar cover	12.00	12.00	
Tumbler, 4", flat	150.00		
Tumbler, 6", footed	20.00	20.00	
*** Tumbler, 6½", footed	30.00		
Vase, 9"	30.00	25.00	225.00

* Ruby, Blue, Amethyst priced as iridescent

** Colors, $85.00

*** Has been reproduced

102

JUBILEE LANCASTER GLASS COMPANY, Early 1930s

Colors: Yellow, crystal, and pink.

I decided to try and untangle this Jubilee knot we've been in over the years. The accepted cut (#1200) considered to be the Jubilee pattern is a piece having a 12 petal, open centered flower. (I clarify that for readers who wrote thinking *any* ware with an open center, 12-petal flower is Jubilee. No, it is not. I also need to point out that the cut design has to be on the piece. Plain, uncut blanks are not Jubilee.) The confusion with Jubilee occurs when you find Standard Glass Company's paneled blanks with a #1200 cut. A pioneer author gave these the name "Tat"; but people finding these pieces over the years said, "Ah! Jubilee!" and placed them with their pattern. This practice became so common that the Standard items are now accepted as "Jubilee" pattern. Further confusion arises when people find Standard Glass Company's closed center, 12-petal flower cut (#89) on paneled blanks, which Standard sold as Martha Washington pattern. Basic pieces of Lancaster's Jubilee were presented on smooth blanks (no optic panels). Standard's #1200 was presented on optic paneled blanks. Martha Washington came on optic paneled blanks, with rayed foot tumblers and fancy handled cups. Both of these sister companies showed companion-serving wares for these patterns using the same petal edged, fancy handled blanks. To further confuse things, Standard had a #200 and a #28 cut, very like #1200, which had the same flower with more cut branches, which were presented on those same type serving pieces, with some petal blank, three-toed bowls and trays thrown in for good measure. Other like cuts include a mayo bowl with 16 petals and a cutting with 12 petals, but having a smaller petal in between the larger ones. Quite frankly, *most* collectors are happy to buy *any* of these pieces as Jubilee pattern to enhance their sets.

Notice the four pink pieces pictured. The petal blank, three-toed bowl is Standard's #200 cut. The cup, saucer, and plate are Lancaster #1200. Probably all the pulled (no ball) stems are Standard lines; but there are ball stemmed, optic panel goblets like the smooth ones found in Jubilee. So, these ball types can't only belong to Lancaster.

The 3", eight ounce, non-stemmed sherbet has 11 petals, as does the three-footed covered candy. You can see that sherbet and the oyster cocktail in the *Very Rare Glassware of the Depression Years, Fourth Series*. Having only 11 petals on the candy and sherbet apparently came from cutting problems experienced when using the standard 6" cutting wheel. The foot of the sherbet and the knob on the candy were in the way when a petal of the design was cut directly up and down. The glasscutter had to move over to the side in order to cut a petal. Because of this placement, only an 11 petal flower resulted on these pieces. Yes. Those two 11 petal pieces are Jubilee and both are hard to find. The 12" vase has a 4" top, 3½" base, and a bulbous 6" middle. This vase is one piece of Jubilee that not all collectors want.

The #889 liner plate for the #890 mayo does have a raised rim, making that liner plate even more rare than the mayo. I've been wrong about that in the past. When I got my magnifying glass out to read the catalog numbers, the plates do *not* have the same number as I first believed. Sorry. Some mayonnaise sets have 16 petals on bowl and plate.

New collectors can be assured that Jubilee luncheon sets are plentiful. However, there is a decided lack of serving pieces for #1200 Jubilee. Prices on these seldom-found items are high.

Crystal items are turning up in small batches; I have shown a few in the photograph below. At this time, crystal appears more scarce than the seldom-found pink.

JUBILEE

	Pink	Yellow
Bowl, 8", 3-footed, 5⅛" high	250.00	200.00
Bowl, 9", handled fruit		125.00
Bowl, 11½", flat fruit	195.00	160.00
Bowl, 11½", 3-footed	250.00	250.00
Bowl, 11½", 3-footed, curved in		225.00
Bowl, 13", 3-footed	250.00	225.00
Candlestick, pair	185.00	185.00
Candy jar, w/lid, 3-footed	325.00	325.00
Cheese & cracker set	255.00	265.00
Creamer	35.00	20.00
Cup	40.00	14.00
Mayonnaise & plate	295.00	250.00
w/original ladle	320.00	270.00
Plate, 7", salad	22.50	14.00
Plate, 8¾", luncheon	27.50	14.00
Plate, 13½", sandwich, handled	85.00	50.00
Plate, 14", 3-footed		200.00
Saucer, two styles	12.00	4.00
Sherbet, 3", 8 ounce		70.00
Stem, 4", 1 ounce, cordial		250.00
Stem, 4¾", 4 ounce, oyster cocktail		75.00
Stem, 4⅞", 3 ounce, cocktail		150.00
Stem, 5½", 7 ounce, sherbet/champagne		95.00
Stem, 7½", 11 ounce		175.00
Sugar	35.00	18.00
Tray, 11", 2-handled cake	65.00	45.00
Tumbler, 5", 6 ounce, footed, juice		95.00

	Pink	Yellow
Tumbler, 6", 10 ounce, water	75.00	35.00
Tumbler, 6⅛", 12½ ounce, iced tea		150.00
Tray, 11", center-handled sandwich	195.00	210.00
Vase, 12"	350.00	350.00

"KALEIDOSCOPE" Believed to be HOCKING GLASS COMPANY, c. 1930s

Colors: "Mayfair" blue, green, and pink.

"Kaleidoscope" is our given name for this ware. Cathy said it reminded her of the patterns that use to appear at the end of her toy one. We've searched our older Hocking catalogs and Depression era ads and have had no luck finding anything official regarding this line. We're fairly certain Hocking made it because of the Mayfair blue coloring and the fact that what you see here was purchased from a collection of a former employee. I keep finding "Kaleidoscope" items in my travels through Ohio and Pennsylvania, further suggesting a manufacturer in that region. It is not a plentiful pattern, but there are enough basic pieces to gather a nice table setting if you wish.

Blue seems to be the most plentiful color; but pieces in pink, green, and perhaps even crystal can be unearthed. I didn't put crystal in the color listing because I'm relying on memory thinking I saw a sugar and creamer at one time. As a younger man, I would have known for certain. Now, memory is not as reliably photographic as it once was. I saw several sets of blue years ago when I wasn't looking for photography items.

You will probably locate things that I have not listed; kindly let me know what you find. Hunting the glass and researching new patterns takes eons of time. I can certainly use all the help I can get. Your input is valuable to us all and I'm *trying* to be responsible and get the things you tell, write, and show me into the computer so I can remember to include them two years down the road when I'm rewriting the pattern heading. My wife has gotten very exasperated with my "mislaying" some information given in the past.

	Blue	Green/Pink		Blue	Green/Pink
Bowl, 5", berry	15.00	12.50	Plate, 9½", dinner	25.00	20.00
Bowl, flat soup	30.00	25.00	Plate, 9½", grill	22.50	17.50
Bowl, oval vegetable w/tab handles	45.00	35.00	Platter, oval w/tab handles	45.00	35.00
Celery, tab handles	50.00	40.00	Saucer	5.00	4.00
Creamer	25.00	20.00	Stem, 6 ounce, sherbet	15.00	12.50
Cup	20.00	15.00	Stem, 9 ounce, water	30.00	20.00
Plate, 6", bread	10.00	8.00	Sugar	25.00	20.00

Colors: Blue w/opalescent edge and green w/opalescent edge, et al.

Imperial's Laced Edge pattern was manufactured in some pieces in an array of colors; only the large dinnerware opalescent blue and green offerings are being priced in this book since that is where collector demand lies. Most of the colors without the white edge were made into the 1950s and later; so, they creep out of the time parameter (pre-1940) for this book. Imperial called this white edging "Sea Foam." Sea Foam treatment varies from barely covering the edge of pieces to others having a ½" of prominent, opalescent edging.

Its long-time collectors commonly call opalescent blue "Katy Blue." Wasn't there an old 30s tune about Katy with the blue eyes? Blue and green pieces without the white edge sell for about half of the prices listed. There does not appear to be much demand for crystal. I have never seen crystal pieces with Sea Foam. Have you?

Creamers have several different appearances on the lips because their spouts were individually made using a wooden tool. Cereal bowls vary from 4⅞" to 5⅝", soup bowls from 6⅞" to 7¼", and berry bowls from 4⅜" to 4¾". Turning out the edge of the bowl caused size differences. Some edges go straight up while others are flattened. Collectors will accept differences in order to have enough bowls.

Some collectors do not accept the 12" cake plate (luncheon plate in Imperial catalog) or the 9" vegetable bowl (salad in ad) as Laced Edge because the edges are more open than those of the other items are. Thanks go to a Laced Edge collector from Illinois for sharing an original ad (page 108) showing an inflated retail price along with the cost in coupons for Laced Edge pieces. Notice the bowl and cake plate are both shown with this pattern. Originally, you could obtain six tumblers for fewer coupons than the platter or divided, oval bowl. Maybe that is why they are so difficult to find today. Not many would exchange their costly coupons for them.

The rarely discovered, undivided, oval vegetable bowl is absent from this ad and most collections today. It was the most expensive piece in this pattern to obtain with coupons.

The vase in the second row of page 107 is Sea Foam blue but not officially Laced Edge.

	Opalescent			Opalescent
Basket bowl	225.00	Mayonnaise, 3-piece		135.00
Bowl, 4⅜"– 4¾", fruit	30.00	Plate, 6½", bread & butter		18.00
Bowl, 5"	37.50	Plate, 8", salad		35.00
Bowl, 5½"	37.50	Plate, 10", dinner		85.00
Bowl, 5⅞"	37.50	Plate, 12", luncheon		
Bowl, 7", soup	90.00	(per catalog description)		80.00
Bowl, 9", vegetable	110.00	Platter, 13"		185.00
Bowl, 11", divided oval	115.00	Saucer		15.00
Bowl, 11", oval	160.00	Sugar		40.00
Candlestick, double, pair	175.00	Tidbit, 2-tiered, 8" & 10" plates		110.00
Cup	35.00	Tumbler, 9 ounce		55.00
Creamer	40.00			

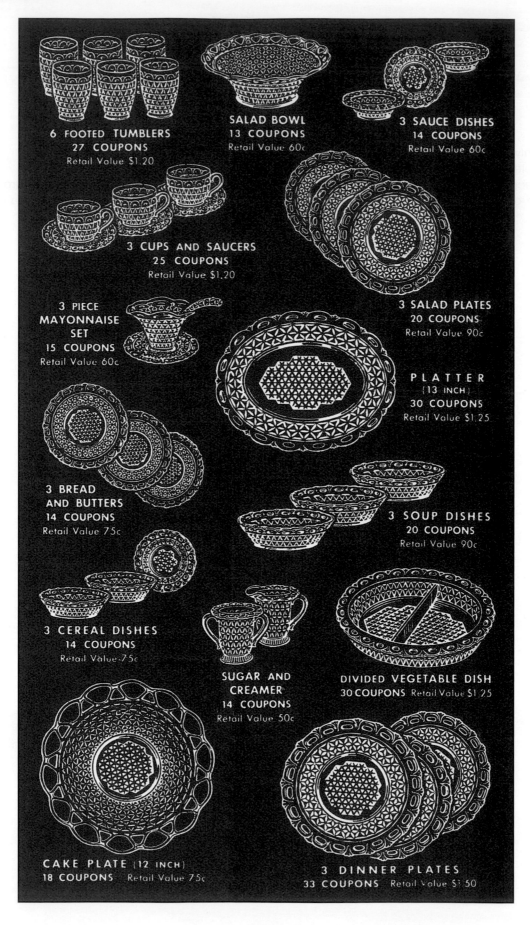

6 FOOTED TUMBLERS
27 COUPONS
Retail Value $1.20

SALAD BOWL
13 COUPONS
Retail Value 60c

3 SAUCE DISHES
14 COUPONS
Retail Value 60c

3 CUPS AND SAUCERS
25 COUPONS
Retail Value $1.20

3 SALAD PLATES
20 COUPONS
Retail Value 90c

3 PIECE
MAYONNAISE
SET
15 COUPONS
Retail Value 60c

PLATTER
(13 INCH)
30 COUPONS
Retail Value $1.25

3 BREAD
AND BUTTERS
14 COUPONS
Retail Value 75c

3 SOUP DISHES
20 COUPONS
Retail Value 90c

3 CEREAL DISHES
14 COUPONS
Retail Value 75c

SUGAR AND
CREAMER
14 COUPONS
Retail Value 50c

DIVIDED VEGETABLE DISH
30 COUPONS   Retail Value $1.25

CAKE PLATE (12 INCH)
18 COUPONS   Retail Value 75c

3 DINNER PLATES
33 COUPONS   Retail Value $1.50

LAKE COMO HOCKING GLASS COMPANY, 1934 – 1937

Color: White with blue scene; some with red scene

Lake Como is so elusive that some collectors report they never see it. I find it now and then, but usually pieces in the sets I have bought have been worn. One young couple told me that they were buying less than mint glass in order to have some of the harder-to-find pieces. When offered for sale, "like new" Lake Como sells very briskly. Note the just discovered red on the right!

There are only 13 different pieces of Lake Como and all are pictured below. Nevertheless, only the sugar, creamer, and shakers are customarily found. Other pieces are seen very infrequently. A majority of pieces found today are worn or faded from use. Evidently this blue design did not hold up to 60 years of washings. Prices below are for mint condition Lake Como (full bright pattern). You should be able to buy worn Lake Como at 50% to 80% of the prices listed depending upon the amount of wear.

The cereal bowl is pictured standing up next to the sugar in the top row so you can see the pattern. It is not a smaller plate that is unlisted. The camera loses the depth when you present them this way.

The flat soup is standing up on the right of the middle row. The floral decoration on the edge is embossed (like the normally found Vitrock soup) instead of painted in blue. You will find platters almost as difficult to find as soup bowls; but most collectors are looking for several soups, which creates a greater problem than finding only one platter. There has been a small supply of vegetable bowls found in the last few years; thus, the price has softened on them somewhat. Finding either style cup will be a headache.

Bowl, 6", cereal	28.00	Plate, 9¼", dinner	35.00
Bowl, 9¾", vegetable	50.00	Platter, 11"	75.00
Bowl, flat soup	105.00	Salt & pepper, pair	45.00
Creamer, footed	32.50	Saucer	12.00
Cup, regular	30.00	Saucer, St. Denis	12.00
Cup, St. Denis	30.00	Sugar, footed	32.50
Plate, 7¼", salad	22.50		

LARGO LINE #220 PADEN CITY GLASS COMPANY, Late 1937 – 1951; CANTON GLASS COMPANY, 1950s

Colors: Amber, crystal, crystal w/ruby flash, light blue, red.

I have split Paden City's Largo (#220) and Maya (#221) into separate patterns as promised. Hopefully, we can get the listings correctly separated. So if you find a listing wrong or missing, just let me know.

Collectors for Cambridge may be more aware of this pattern than others since there is a tendency of dealers to misidentify the light blue Largo as Cambridge's Caprice pattern. Largo was not as widely distributed as was Cambridge glass; hence our looking high and low for it today. We have been buying both Largo and Maya for several years in order to display them in this book. That experience leads us to believe that the flat candy dish and the two-lipped comport are relatively scarce. We have found several divided candy bottoms in our travels, but never a top in Largo. That 5" bowl in the foreground on the bottom of page 111 may take a lid of some kind.

Collectors find the delightful, four-footed sugar and creamer appealing. Item collectors for those help to put a dent in the sparse supply. Notice the Ruby flashed creamer and sugar on the right on page 111. These were probably souvenir items since they have two names and a 1943 date inscribed in the red. Paden City etchings occur on both light blue and crystal. I have never yet found etched designs on red.

Blue cups turned up on several occasions with the non-indented 6⅝" plates. I was beginning to think there was no saucer until we found an amber one; alas, no amber cup though.

Please note that Largo pieces can be distinguished from Maya by the thistle (ball) design found on Maya. You have to be observant to notice the Largo pattern line on the candle. A red one is pictured below.

Since this is a relatively new pattern to the book, I would greatly appreciate your sharing any further information you might have regarding other pieces.

	Amber/Crystal	Blue/Red		Amber/Crystal	Blue/Red
Ashtray, 3", rectangle	16.00	30.00	Comport, double spout, pedestal	35.00	75.00
Bowl, 5"	15.00	25.00	Comport, fluted rim, pedestal	35.00	75.00
Bowl, 6", deep	8.00	35.00	Comport, 6½" x 10", plain rim,		
Bowl, 7½"	20.00	37.50	pedestal	32.50	70.00
Bowl, 7½", crimped	22.50	45.00	Creamer, footed	22.00	45.00
Bowl, 9", tab-handled	30.00	70.00	Cup	15.00	30.00
Bowl, 11⅝", 3½" deep, tri-footed,			Mayonnaise, toed	25.00	55.00
flared rim	35.00	80.00	Plate, 6⅝"	8.00	15.00
Bowl, 12¾", 4¾" deep, tri-footed,			Plate, 8"	10.00	20.00
flat rim	35.00	80.00	Plate, 10¾", cheese w/indent	20.00	40.00
Cake plate, pedestal	35.00	95.00	Saucer	5.00	10.00
Candleholder	30.00	55.00	Sugar, footed	22.00	45.00
Candy, flat w/lid, 3-part	30.00	95.00	Tray, 13¾", tri-footed, serving	25.00	70.00
Cigarette box, 4" x 3¼" x 1½"	30.00	65.00	Tray, 14", five-part, relish	40.00	95.00
Comport, cracker	15.00	28.00			

LAUREL McKEE GLASS COMPANY, 1930s

Colors: French Ivory, Jade Green, White Opal, Poudre Blue, and various colors of decorated rims.

Poudre Blue Laurel has traditionally been the color most favored by collectors. The surge in demand for Anchor Hocking's Jade-ite wares has segued into McKee's Jade Green Laurel ware, rapidly elevating prices in that color. Happily, Jade Laurel is the color most often found, followed closely by French Ivory (beige) and then Poudre Blue, erroneously called Delphite blue by collectors. French Ivory excites few collectors at this time; prices there have remained stable. I have moved the White Opal pricing into the same column as French Ivory since those prices are more representative of it's worth, now, than the Jade.

Soup bowls in any color are rarely seen, but demand for Jade ones has surged. You can see a Poudre Blue soup pictured in *Very Rare Glassware of the Depression Years, Fifth Series*. Laurel shakers are hard to find with bold patterns. Many Laurel shaker designs are indistinct. Jade Green Laurel shakers are quite rare as some of those searching for them have found.

Serving pieces in all colors are inadequately supplied. That trend has reared its ugly head in many patterns from this era. Evidently serving pieces were either broken or considered too expensive and were not purchased to go with basic sets.

Beloved children's Laurel tea sets are swallowed into collections. The Scottie dog decal sets were made in Jade Green or French Ivory colors. Collectors of Scottie items have advanced the prices on these sets to levels where few collectors try to buy full sets. They are delighted just to possess one piece. Laurel children's sets are also found with border trims of red, green, or orange. Orange borders appear to be the most difficult to locate, though all trims are scarce. Watch for wear on these colored trims; it appears many children did, in fact, play with these dishes.

I have included a pattern shot of a dinnerware piece trimmed in black, a heretofore unheard of trim. While I was at the show in Chicago last weekend, Cathy, on a whim, decided to take in the local flea market and ran into four black trimmed pieces of Laurel, a plate, dessert, saucer, and berry bowl. There was no cup. Upon questioning the owner, she was told there were six sets found in a Pennsylvania farmhouse. Though it was nearly noon when she visited, no other dealer had been interested enough in these unusual items to purchase them; she was excited to find something new to show in Laurel. Enjoy!

	Jade or Decorated Rims	White Opal, French Ivory	Poudre Blue		Jade or Decorated Rims	White Opal, French Ivory	Poudre Blue
Bowl, 4¾", berry	15.00	10.00	15.00	Plate, 6", sherbet	16.00	10.00	10.00
Bowl, 6", cereal	25.00	12.00	28.00	Plate, 7½", salad	20.00	10.00	16.00
Bowl, 6", three legs	25.00	15.00		Plate, 9⅛", dinner	25.00	15.00	30.00
Bowl, 7⅞", soup	40.00	35.00	85.00	Plate, 9⅛", grill, round or scalloped	25.00	15.00	
Bowl, 9", large berry	40.00	30.00	55.00	Platter, 10¾", oval	50.00	30.00	50.00
Bowl, 9¾", oval vegetable	50.00	30.00	55.00	Salt and pepper	85.00	50.00	
Bowl, 10½", three legs	60.00	40.00	70.00	Saucer	4.50	3.00	7.50
Bowl, 11"	60.00	40.00	85.00	Sherbet	20.00	12.00	
Candlestick, 4", pair	65.00	35.00		Sherbet/champagne, 5"	75.00	50.00	
Candlestick, 3 footed	95.00			Sugar, short	25.00	10.00	
Cheese dish and cover	95.00	60.00		Sugar, tall	25.00	11.00	35.00
Creamer, short	25.00	62.00		Tumbler, 4½", 9 ounce, flat	65.00	40.00	
Creamer, tall	25.00	15.00	40.00	Tumbler, 5", 12 ounce, flat		55.00	
Cup	15.00	9.00	22.00				

CHILDREN'S LAUREL TEA SET

	French Ivory	Jade or Decorated Rims	Scottie Dog Jade	Scottie Dog Ivory
Creamer	30.00	100.00	250.00	125.00
Cup	25.00	50.00	100.00	50.00
Plate	10.00	20.00	75.00	37.50
Saucer	8.00	12.50	75.00	37.50
Sugar	30.00	100.00	250.00	125.00
14-piece set	235.00	530.00	1,500.00	750.00

LINCOLN INN FENTON GLASS COMPANY, Late 1920s

Colors: Red, cobalt, light blue, amethyst, black, green, green opalescent, pink, crystal, amber, and jade (opaque).

Lincoln Inn stems appear to be the only pieces you spot while seeking this pattern. If someone asks me for Lincoln Inn, it is usually prefaced with, "I don't need stems, but what else do you have?" Stemware was sold to be used with china. With so many colors, Lincoln Inn must have filled color demands quite well. At the moment, you might possibly collect a complete setting in crystal, but other colors I doubt that you could, in spite of the fact that tableware was advertised in at least eight of the above listed colors in 1929. Red and the several shades of blue remain the most desirable colors for collectors. Fortunately those are the colors that are most often encountered. Depicted on page 115 are some of the diverse colors you could collect if you are willing to buy a piece or two at a time. This pattern perfectly fits rainbow-collecting trends beginning to flourish in the coterie of glass.

Champagne/sherbets in every color are bountiful. A small collection could be made of just these pieces. Tumblers and other stems are a little more difficult; but acquiring a pitcher or serving pieces in any color is a burden. Fenton remade an iridized, dark carnival colored pitcher and tumblers in the 1980s. Any other iridescent piece you might see in this pattern is of recent production. All light blue pitchers have turned up in the South; so look for them.

A 1930s catalog shows Lincoln Inn plates with a fruit design (intaglio) in the center. I have a shown some crystal ones in the bottom row on page 115. We saw a 9" crystal bowl with the fruit center at an antique mall in Florida, but the owner thought it to be really rare, so he still owns it.

Lincoln Inn shakers are seen infrequently. Even crystal shakers are adept at hiding. Collectors gathering only shakers tell me these Lincoln Inn ones may not be the highest priced in the book, but they are among the most difficult to find. Red and black shakers are the favored colors; but do not pass any color in your travels even crystal. I once found a red pair sitting with Royal Ruby in a dark corner of a shop. They were priced as red shakers. You need to check in every nook and cranny in shops that do not cherish Depression glass as we do.

Many red Lincoln Inn pieces are amberina in color. For novices, amberina is red glass that has some yellow hues in it. Reheating yellow glass made it change to red; irregular heating caused some parts to remain yellow. Some dealers have told collectors this is a rare color in order to sell it. In a certain sense, that may have a trace of truth. Actually, it was a blunder; and the inconsistent amounts of yellow on each piece make it hard to match colors. Some old timers in glass collecting reject amberina pieces for their collections. However, there are some actually searching for amberina glass. There is a growing attraction for all two-toned glassware.

	Cobalt Blue, Red	**All Other Colors		Cobalt Blue, Red	**All Other Colors
Ashtray	17.50	12.00	Plate, 8"	15.00	10.00
Bonbon, handled, square	15.00	12.00	Plate, 9¼"	45.00	11.50
Bonbon, handled, oval	16.00	12.00	Plate, 12"	65.00	15.50
Bowl, 5", fruit	11.50	8.50	* Salt/pepper, pair	275.00	175.00
Bowl, 6", cereal	15.00	9.00	Sandwich server, center handle	175.00	110.00
Bowl, 6", crimped	15.00	8.50	Saucer	5.00	3.50
Bowl, handled olive	15.00	9.50	Sherbet, 4½", cone shape	17.00	11.50
Bowl, finger	20.00	12.50	Sherbet, 4¾"	20.00	12.50
Bowl, 9", shallow		23.00	Sugar	20.00	14.00
Bowl, 9¼", footed	85.00	30.00	Tumbler, 4 ounce, flat, juice	30.00	9.50
Bowl, 10½", footed	85.00	35.00	Tumbler, 9 ounce, flat, water		19.50
Candy dish, footed, oval	45.00	20.00	Tumbler, 5 ounce, footed	30.00	11.00
Comport	30.00	14.50	Tumbler, 9 ounce, footed	30.00	14.00
Creamer	22.50	14.50	Tumbler, 12 ounce, footed	50.00	19.00
Cup	12.00	12.00	Vase, 9¾"	165.00	85.00
Goblet, water	30.00	15.50	Vase, 12", footed	225.00	100.00
Goblet, wine	30.00	16.50			
Nut dish, footed	25.00	12.00	* Black $300.00		
Pitcher, 7¼", 46 ounce	800.00	700.00	** w/fruits, add 20 – 25%		
Plate, 6"	9.00	4.50			

LINE #555 PADEN CITY GLASS COMPANY, Late 1930s – 1951; CANTON GLASS COMPANY, 1950s

Colors: Crystal, light blue, red.

Paden City's Line #555 blank was used for several different Paden City etches and cuttings. Most notable is the Gazebo pattern illustrated in my *Elegant Glassware of the Depression Era*. Additional pieces of Line #555 are pictured there. The heart-shaped candy bottoms are divided into three sections and the lids were placed along the back for height in the photo There is a stylized tulip etch on the right side and a Floral etch on left. There is a single candle here. You can see the double pictured with the Gazebo pattern.

The tray on the left was for the creamer and sugar, but was also listed separately. Canton Glass bought Paden City moulds and continued many of the pieces of line #555 during the early 1950s.

	*Crystal		*Crystal
Bowl, 6", 2-part nappy	12.00	Plate, 8"	10.00
Bowl, 6", nappy	12.00	Plate, 12½", 2-handled	22.50
Bowl, 9", 2-handled	20.00	Plate, 16", salad or punch liner	45.00
Bowl, 14", shallow	25.00	Punch bowl	65.00
Cake stand, pedestal foot	25.00	Punch cup	8.00
Candlestick, 1-light	17.50	Relish, 11", round, 3-part	25.00
Candlestick, 2-light	25.00	Relish, 7½", square, 2-part	14.00
Candy, w/lid, "heart"	45.00	Relish, 9¾", rectangular, 3-part	20.00
Candy, w/lid, 10¼", pedestal foot	35.00	Saucer	4.00
Candy, w/lid, 11", pedestal foot	40.00	Relish, 10½", round, 5-part	25.00
Creamer	10.00	Sugar	10.00
Cup	8.00	Tray, 9"	12.00
Mayonnaise liner	7.50	Tray, 11", center handle	30.00
Mayonnaise	15.00		
Plate, 6"	5.00	* Double price for colors	

"LITTLE JEWEL" DIAMOND BLOCK LINE #330 IMPERIAL GLASS COMPANY, Late 1920s – Early 1930s

Colors: Black, crystal, green, iridescent, pink, white, yellow.

Several pieces of this pattern were advertised for sale in a 1920s catalog under the "Little Jewel" appellation. This name stuck rather than the Diamond Block one given at Imperial. "Little Jewel" is a diminutive Imperial pattern that is attracting people to its design. Seldom do these customers recognize it as Depression era glass. They are only buying it because it appeals to them. Colored items are the most popular, but not a lot of color is being found. Yet, even crystal with this delightful design can make an excellent display. This "Little Jewel" won't cause you price tag trauma, another appealing aspect.

The blue handled jelly on the second row and the vase on the left in the bottom row almost disappeared into the dark blue background, but that color is found in small quantities. I suggest if you find blue items, you snatch them up.

	Crystal	Colors		Crystal	Colors
Bowl, 5½", square, honey dish	10.00	15.00	Jelly, 4½", handle	8.00	12.00
Bowl, 5", lily	10.00	12.00	Jelly, 5", footed	10.00	15.00
Bowl, 6½"	10.00	15.00	Jug, pint tankard	22.50	45.00
Bowl, 7½", berry	15.00	18.00	Pickle dish, 6½"	12.50	20.00
Celery, 8½", tray	18.00	22.50	Sugar	8.00	15.00
Creamer	8.00	15.00	Vase, 6", bouquet	12.00	18.00

"LOIS" LINE #345, et al. UNITED STATES GLASS COMPANY c. 1920s

Colors: Crystal, green, and pink.

"Lois" was etched mostly on Line #345, which is composed of octagon (eight sided) shapes. As was the custom with early factory lines, these pieces were offered to merchants as an assortment package. Assortments were generally comprised of six to 12 or 15 items; and in the case of etchings, the etchings could cross several line number wares. It may have been a way of getting rid of remaining product, a gathering of "all those pink items left and put thus and so etch on all of them and offer them as assortment #12." Sometimes assortment packages were assembled around a theme, such as table setting or luncheon set or serving items; but, often as not, they were just various wares put in a grouping. Sometimes assortments came as numbers 1, 2, or 3, so that to get a complete line, the merchant had to buy all the various assortments. These were early marketing ploys used by companies to sell their wares; and we know this ware was thus marketed.

I'm very certain you will find other items than those in the listing; and some of them will be on other than octagon shape #345. I'd very much appreciate a postcard telling me of any other items you find; and measurements are always helpful.

	All colors		All colors
Bowl, 10", fruit, pedestal foot	50.00	Mayo or whipped cream w/ladle	45.00
Bowl, 10", salad, flat rim	40.00	Pitcher, milk	45.00
Bowl, 12", console, rolled edge	50.00	Plate, cheese liner	25.00
Cake, salver, pedestal foot	55.00	Plate, dinner	35.00
Candle, short, single	30.00	Server, center handled	45.00
Candy box, octagonal lid	65.00	Sugar, footed	25.00
Candy jar w/lid, cone shape	55.00	Tumbler, footed	35.00
Comport, cheese	20.00	Vase, 10"	65.00
Creamer, footed	25.00		

LORAIN, "BASKET," NO. 615 INDIANA GLASS COMPANY, 1929 – 1932

Colors: Green, yellow, and some crystal.

Indiana's yellow Lorain, adored by early collectors, is rather scarce in today's marketplace. When you do find it, you may have to deal with mould roughness on the seams of the pieces. If you are inflexible about absolutely mint condition glassware, then you should focus on some other pattern.

After buying and selling numerous collections of Lorain and discussing varied ideas with collectors who have pursued Lorain for years, certain conclusions emerge. First, you should buy any cereal bowls you can find. Check inner rims closely; they damage. The 8" deep berry is the most difficult piece to unearth. Most collectors only want one, but they often wait years to find it. Dinner plates are almost as scarce as cereals, but scratches are the norm for these. There are a few people who know how to polish these lines away, now; so, if the plates are reasonable enough, you might gamble that in the future this service will be more available. Oval vegetable bowls are few and far between in both colors. Saucers are harder to dredge up than cups because of mould roughness and wear and tear on them over the years. Collecting has turned upside-down. Dealers used to decline to buy saucers unless there were cups with them. Today, many of these once ignored saucers are eagerly bought even if there are no cups available. There are more than a dozen patterns of Depression glass where saucers are more difficult to find than cups, and this is one of them. Since Lorain is limited, you might be tempted to buy pieces that are less than mint when you come across them; just try to pay less than the mint prices listed.

Sporadically, rarer pieces of Lorain escalate in price. Usually that means several collectors all need the same piece at about the same time. Collectors are starting to buy green Lorain because of price and availability. Green is less expensive and more easily found. A few pieces are found in crystal, but I'm not sure a set is possible. A few items could complement your colored wares, however.

Some crystal is found with colored borders of red, yellow, green, and blue. For those who have written to ask about the snack tray, one with yellow trim is pictured below. It was made from the platter mould that had a ring added for a cup. In talking to several collectors recently, I have been advised that the snack plates trimmed in yellow or green do not seem to be offered, lately, at any price. Collectors of yellow used to find these for incorporation into their sets. Crystal cups are found trimmed in the four colors to match the snack trays; but just as often, they were crystal, lacking the trim.

New collectors, please note that the white and green avocado-colored sherbets (which have an open lace border) are a mid-1950s (or later) issue made by Anchor Hocking. They were used regularly by florists for small floral arrangements and many are found with a tacky, clay-like substance in the bottom that was used to secure flowers. Not long ago, they were also acclaimed as an Indiana product, which is likely. The more research I do, the more I find out about wares starting with one company and being successively made by others. We know it was a practice to farm moulds out from one company to another for special product runs. However, several of these have been found with Anchor Hocking paper stickers, a practice of theirs in the late 1950s and early 1960s.

I've had a couple of letters regarding goblets with a basket design like that of Lorain. These are probably an early Tiffin product. If you want to use them with Lorain, do so. There is also a heavy Hazel-Atlas green goblet similar in shape to Colonial Block that has a basket etching. Basket designs were prolific in the 1920s and 1930s.

LORAIN

	Crystal, Green	Yellow
Bowl, 6", cereal	50.00	70.00
Bowl, 7¼", salad	50.00	70.00
Bowl, 8", deep berry	125.00	185.00
Bowl, 9¾", oval vegetable	60.00	75.00
Creamer, footed	20.00	27.50
Cup	12.00	15.00
Plate, 5½", sherbet	10.00	12.50
Plate, 7¾", salad	13.00	14.00
Plate, 8⅜", luncheon	20.00	28.00
Plate, 10¼", dinner	60.00	63.00
Platter, 11½"	30.00	45.00
Relish, 8", 4-part	25.00	40.00
Saucer	4.50	6.00
Sherbet, footed	26.00	30.00
Snack tray, crystal/trim	35.00	
Sugar, footed	20.00	27.50
Tumbler, 4¾", 9 ounce, footed	25.00	30.00

LOTUS PATTERN #1921 WESTMORELAND GLASS COMPANY, 1921 – 1980

Colors: Amber, amethyst, black, blue, crystal, green, milk, pink, red, and various applied color trims; satinized colors.

Lotus, pattern #1921, was in production over 60 years, off and on; and thanks to Chas West Wilson's *Westmoreland Glass*, we know it to have been designed by Gustav Horn. My wife, Cathy began buying Lotus because she enjoys flowers but her allergies decree that we sacrifice real ones. So, she makes up for that with glass or silk varieties. She first bought the green, petal bottomed candles to decorate our dining room table. Next, she bought the tall, twist stem compote that joined the candles as a centerpiece. Then, I noticed different colors of little bowls clustered about like water lilies on a pond. I got the message; I began to pick up a piece every so often to her delight. Pictured are various items we've accumulated. In the satinized items pictured below, the green on the right and the domed blue candle are later issues. There is a wonderful variety of later issued colors available.

The amethyst and domed amber candle are more recent colors as is the red. Notice the flattened foot on the green candle. This mashed version indicates it is from an older mould. That green candy in the back needs a lid, which is flat, not domed, and rests below the petal rim. Only some of the colors are illustrated.

There are several rare pieces of Lotus including a lamp, tumbler, cologne bottle, and puff box, although most colognes found are of later manufacture. They are still desirable. The elusive tumbler is crystal with a green petal foot. All opalescent-edged Lotus was made near the end of Westmoreland's production in the 1970s and 1980s.

	Satinized Colors					Satinized Colors		
	Amber Crystal White	Blue, Green Pink	*Cased Colors			Amber Crystal White	Blue, Green Pink	*Cased Colors
Bowl, 6", lily (flat mayonnaise)	15.00	25.00	40.00		Lamp	175.00	250.00	
Bowl, 9", cupped	55.00	85.00	110.00		Mayonnaise, 4", ftd., flared rim	15.00	25.00	30.00
Bowl, 11", belled	65.00	95.00	125.00		Mayonnaise, 5", footed, bell rim	27.50	52.50	72.50
Bowl, oval vegetable	55.00	85.00	110.00		Plate, 6", mayonnaise	8.00	12.00	15.00
Candle, 4", single	20.00	35.00	40.00		Plate, 8½", salad	10.00	35.00	40.00
Candle, 9" high, twist stem	50.00	70.00	90.00		Plate, 8¾", mayonnaise	12.50	17.50	22.50
Candy jar w/lid, ½ pound	65.00	95.00	125.00		Plate, 13", flared	35.00	50.00	65.00
Coaster	12.00	15.00	20.00		Puff box, 5", w/cover	100.00	125.00	
Cologne, ½ ounce	75.00	110.00	145.00		Salt, individual	12.00	20.00	20.00
Comport, 2½", mint, twist stem	35.00				Shaker	30.00	40.00	
Comport, 6½", honey	18.00	25.00	45.00		Sherbet, tulip bell	22.00	35.00	35.00
Comport, 5" high	30.00	40.00	50.00		Sugar	22.00	28.00	35.00
Comport, 8½" high, twist stem	50.00	85.00	110.00		Tray, lemon, 6", handle	22.50	30.00	40.00
Creamer	22.00	28.00	35.00		Tumbler, 10 ounce		45.00	

MADRID FEDERAL GLASS COMPANY, 1932 – 1939; INDIANA GLASS COMPANY, 1980s

Colors: Green, pink, amber, crystal, and "Madonna" blue. (See Reproduction Section.)

In early collecting days, blue Madrid was one of those Depression glass patterns that you loved. You couldn't visit a show without seeing it on dealers' tables. Today, you never see a piece of the old, soft "Madonna" blue Madrid. It's all vanished into collections.

Amber, however, is still very available in today's marketplace.

Madrid has been subject of controversy since 1976 when the Federal Glass Company remanufactured this pattern for the Bicentennial under a new name, "Recollection" glassware. Many companies resurrected wares from past lines during this time frame, not just Federal. Each piece of this reissued Federal ware was embossed '76 in the design. The flaw, here, was that it was remade in an amber color comparable to the original which caused concern with collectors of the older amber Madrid. Collectors were informed about the products, and many purchased these sets presuming they would someday be collectible as Bicentennial products. Unluckily, Indiana Glass bought the Madrid moulds when Federal went out of business, removed the '76 date and made crystal. The older crystal butter was selling for several hundred dollars and the new one sold for $2.99. Prices nose-dived! Next, they made pink; and even though it was a lighter pink than the original, prices dipped in the collectibles market for the old pink. Later, Indiana made blue; it was a brighter, harsher blue than the beautiful, soft blue of the original Madrid; still, it had a detrimental effect on the prices of the 1930s blue. All pieces made in pink have now been made in blue. Any blue piece found without a price below is new. After blue came teal, finally, a color not made in the 1930s. Wonderfully, today, that is all water under the bridge and learned collectors are, once again, requesting the beautiful older Madrid with confidence.

I keep noticing the later-made pink Madrid sugar and creamers with high prices at flea markets and antique malls. Originally, there were no pink sugar and creamers made. Check my list below for pieces made in pink. If no price is listed, then it was not made in the 1930s. (See the new pink in the Reproduction Section in the back.)

The rarely seen Madrid gravy boats and platters have almost always been found in Iowa. I was approached by a lady at the Chicago Depression glass show a couple of weeks ago who told me she bought a Madrid gravy boat without the platter for $8.00 at a yard sale in Iowa last summer. She thought the people used a book and priced it as a creamer as everything else was too high to buy. These two pieces are priced separately, but reflect a decided increase. Rare Depression glass is beginning to command higher and higher prices. I do not expect this trend to stop as more and more collectors enter the field and the rare pieces become even more scarce than they already are.

Mint condition sugar lids in any color Madrid are a treasure. Footed tumblers are harder to find than flat ones with juice tumblers making a surge in price. Amber footed shakers are harder to find than flat ones. Footed shakers are the only style you can find in blue. Any heavy, flat ones you spot are new.

Collectors of green Madrid have turned out to be almost as sparse as the pattern. Green is possibly as rare as blue, but with fewer collectors.

A wooden Lazy Susan is pictured in *Very Rare Glassware of the Depression Years, Second Series*. It is like the Georgian one pictured on page 93 only with Madrid inserts.

MADRID

	Amber	Pink	Green	Blue
Ashtray, 6", square	350.00		295.00	
Bowl, 4¾", cream soup	18.00			
Bowl, 5", sauce	7.00	8.00	7.00	30.00
Bowl, 7", soup	16.00		16.00	
Bowl, 8", salad	14.00		17.50	50.00
Bowl, 9⅜", large berry	20.00	20.00		
Bowl, 9½", deep salad	32.00			
Bowl, 10", oval veg.	18.00	15.00	22.50	40.00
* Bowl, 11", low console	14.00	11.00		
Butter dish w/lid	70.00		90.00	
Butter dish bottom	27.50		40.00	
Butter dish top	37.50		50.00	
* Candlesticks, pr., 2¼"	22.00	20.00		
Cookie jar w/lid	45.00	30.00		
Creamer, footed	9.00		12.50	20.00
Cup	7.00	7.50	8.50	16.00
Gravy boat	1,000.00			
Gravy platter	1,000.00			
Hot dish coaster	50.00		50.00	
Hot dish coaster w/indent	60.00		60.00	
Jam dish, 7"	27.50		20.00	40.00
Jello mold, 2⅛", tall	10.00			
Pitcher, 5½", 36 ounce juice	40.00			
** Pitcher, 8", sq., 60 oz.	50.00	35.00	125.00	175.00

	Amber	Pink	Green	Blue
Pitcher, 8½", 80 ounce	60.00		200.00	
Pitcher, 8½", 80 ounce, ice lip	60.00		225.00	
Plate, 6", sherbet	5.00	3.50	4.00	8.00
Plate, 7½", salad	10.00	9.00	9.00	22.00
Plate, 8⅞", luncheon	8.00	7.00	9.00	18.00
Plate, 10½", dinner	60.00		55.00	75.00
Plate, 10½", grill	9.50		20.00	
Plate, 10¼", relish	15.00	12.50	16.00	
Plate, 11¼", round cake	22.00	10.00		
Platter, 11½", oval	17.00	14.00	16.00	24.00
Salt/pepper, 3½", footed, pair	135.00		110.00	165.00
Salt/pepper, 3½", flat, pair	50.00		65.00	
Saucer	3.00	5.00	5.00	10.00
Sherbet, two styles	7.00		12.00	17.50
Sugar	7.00		14.00	15.00
Sugar cover	50.00		60.00	225.00
Tumbler, 3⅞", 5 ounce	13.00		32.00	40.00
Tumbler, 4¼", 9 ounce	15.00	15.00	20.00	35.00
Tumbler, 5½", 12 ounce, 2 styles	22.00		30.00	50.00
Tumbler, 4", 5 oz., footed	35.00		40.00	
Tumbler, 5½", 10 ounce, footed	33.00		45.00	
Wooden Lazy Susan, cold cuts coasters	995.00			

* Iridescent priced slightly higher   ** Crystal $150.00

MANHATTAN, "HORIZONTAL RIBBED" ANCHOR HOCKING GLASS COMPANY, 1938 – 1943

Colors: Crystal, pink; some green, ruby, and iridized.

If you find a piece of Manhattan that does not fit the measurements in the list below, then you may have a piece of Anchor Hocking's newer line, Park Avenue. You can see this recent pattern in my book *Anchor Hocking's Fire-King & More, Second Edition.*

Park Avenue was introduced by Anchor Hocking in 1987 to "re-create the Glamour Era of 1938 when Anchor Hocking first introduced a classic" according to the Inspiration '87 catalog issued by the company. Anchor Hocking went to the trouble to preserve the integrity of their older glassware, however. None of the pieces in this line are exactly like the old Manhattan. They are only similar and Manhattan was never made in blue as this line has been. Some collectors of Manhattan have bought this new pattern to augment Manhattan or for use. Manhattan's collectibility has not been affected by the making of Park Avenue; however, the new line has caused some chaos with Manhattan cereal bowls. The older 5¼" cereals are rarely seen, particularly in mint condition; Park Avenue line lists a small bowl at 6". All the original Manhattan bowls measure 1¹⁵⁄₁₆" high. If the bowl you have measures more than two inches, then you have a piece of Park Avenue. Be especially vigilant if the bowl is mint. Manhattan cereals do not have handles. The handled berry measures 5⅜". I mention the measurements because there is an immense price difference. In fact, the reason the 5⅜" handled berry has increased in price so much is from dealers selling them as cereals.

Manhattan comport price hikes can be directly attributed to margarita or martini drinkers. These were designed for candy or mints at the outset, but you cannot persuade a drinker that these were not designed for mixed drinks. Now we get a Park Avenue piece that is creating a problem. *A Park Avenue martini glass has been designed for the beverage market which is so similar to the old comport that it took me a while to figure out a difference. The old comport has four wafers on the stem while the new one has five. It has only been made in crystal.*

Manufacturers outside the factory made metal accessories. Anchor Hocking sold their wares to other companies who made these accoutrements with tongs or spoons hanging or otherwise attached to them. There is a distant possibility that metal pieces were sold to Hocking; but years ago employees told me that they never fabricated anything but glass at the factory.

Pink Manhattan cups, saucers, and dinner plates do exist, but are rarely seen. The saucer/sherbet plates of Manhattan are like many of Hocking's saucers; they have no cup ring. Both sizes of Manhattan Royal Ruby pitchers turn up occasionally. The real mind blower was the Jade-ite large Manhattan pitcher that has now been found.

Manhattan sherbets have a beaded bottom like the tumblers, but the center insert to the relish tray does not have these beads. These are often confused. Relish tray inserts can be found in crystal, pink, and Royal Ruby. The center insert is always crystal on these relish trays although a pink sherbet was put in the center of the pink relish at the photo session. Sorry. I just can't physically monitor everything at these sessions.

Manhattan is one pattern that is aided by the many look-alike pieces that can be added to it. Some collectors buy Hazel-Atlas shakers to use with Manhattan since they are round rather than the original squared ones that Hocking made. However, I have deliberately left out all the look-alike Manhattan in these photographs except the L.E. Smith double candle.

MANHATTAN

	Crystal	Pink			Crystal	Pink
* Ashtray, 4", round	12.00			Relish tray, 14", 5-part	30.00	
Ashtray, 4½", square	18.00			Relish tray, 14", with inserts	85.00	85.00
Bowl, 4½", sauce, handles	11.00		***	Relish tray insert	5.50	8.00
Bowl, 5⅜", berry w/handles	18.00	24.00	****	Pitcher, 24 ounce	40.00	75.00
Bowl, 5¼", cereal, no handles	100.00	175.00		Pitcher, 80 ounce, tilted	50.00	75.00
Bowl, 7½", large berry	22.00			Plate, 6", sherbet or saucer	8.00	75.00
Bowl, 8", closed handles	25.00	28.00		Plate, 8½", salad	17.00	
Bowl, 9", salad	30.00			Plate, 10¼", dinner	25.00	195.00
Bowl, 9½", fruit, open handle	35.00	45.00		Plate, 14", sandwich	28.00	
Candlesticks, 4½", square, pair	22.00			Salt & pepper, 2", square, pair	30.00	50.00
Candy dish, 3 legs, 6¼"		15.00		Saucer/sherbet plate	7.00	75.00
** Candy dish and cover	37.50			Sherbet	12.00	18.00
Coaster, 3½"	16.00			Sugar, oval	12.00	15.00
Comport, 5¾"	33.00	40.00	*****	Tumbler, 10 ounce, footed	20.00	24.00
Creamer, oval	12.00	15.00		Vase, 8"	25.00	
Cup	17.00	275.00	**	Wine, 3½"	6.00	

*Add for Hocking $15.00; add for others $12.50   **Look-Alike   ***Ruby $4.00   ****Ruby $400.00   *****Green or iridized $15.00

MAYA LINE #221 PADEN CITY GLASS COMPANY, Late 1930s – 1951; CANTON GLASS COMPANY, 1950s

Colors: Crystal, light blue, red.

I have split Paden City's Largo (#220) and Maya (#221) into separate patterns as promised for this book. Hopefully, we can get the listings separated correctly, but it will be entertaining, so if you find a listing under the wrong pattern, or one missing, just let me know. The cheese dish seems to be the most coveted piece of Maya

The sugar and creamer in Maya seem to be rarer than those of Largo. Sugar and creamer collectors also prize them, but they are flat and not footed. We found a pair, but they didn't make it into the Maya photography box by the time we needed them. We buy glass for two years for each of the major books and then have to sort all those purchases into the separate patterns. A major difficulty in that is living in Florida and photographing in Kentucky. You can't drive 800 miles to rectify mistakes in omission. I have done that when we lived in Kentucky and only 250 miles from the Paducah studio.

Etched patterns can be found on both light blue and crystal. Please note that Maya pieces can be distinguished from Largo by the thistle (ball) design.

Since this is a new pattern to the book, I would greatly appreciate your sharing any further information you might have regarding other pieces.

	Crystal	Colors		Crystal	Colors
Bowl, 7", flared rim	18.00	35.00	Comport, 6½" x 10", plain rim, pedestal	32.50	70.00
Bowl, 9½", non-flared	30.00	60.00	Creamer, flat.	22.00	45.00
Bowl, 11⅝", 3½" deep, tri-footed, flared rim	35.00	80.00	Mayonnaise, tri-footed	15.00	40.00
Bowl, 12¾", 4¾" deep, tri-footed, flat rim	35.00	80.00	Mayonnaise, tri-footed, crimped	20.00	45.00
Cake plate, pedestal	35.00	75.00	Plate, 6⅝"	8.00	15.00
Candleholder	30.00	55.00	Plate, 7", mayonnaise	10.00	20.00
Candy, footed w/lid, 3-part	40.00	95.00	Sugar, flat	22.00	45.00
Cheese dish w/lid	75.00	175.00	Tray, 13¾", tri-footed, serving	25.00	70.00
Comport, fluted rim, pedestal	35.00	75.00	Tray, tab-handled	25.00	60.00

MAYFAIR FEDERAL GLASS COMPANY, 1934

Colors: Crystal, amber, and green.

Federal redesigned their Mayfair glass moulds into what finally became known as the Rosemary pattern because Hocking had copyrighted the name *Mayfair* first. I have shown only the old Federal Mayfair pattern before it was altered.

You will have to refer to a previous book to see the transitional period glassware made between the old Federal Mayfair pattern and what was to become known as the Rosemary pattern. These transitional pieces have arching in the bottom of each piece rather than the waffle design, and there is no waffling between the top arches. If you turn to the Rosemary (page 201) for reference, you will see that the design under the arches is entirely plain. Collectors regard these transitional pieces a part of Federal Mayfair rather than Rosemary and that is why they are priced here. As of now, these sell for the price of Mayfair even though they are much more scarce. There does not seem to be enough available to make a set of this transitional ware, but it blends with Mayfair better than Rosemary because of the waffling in the design.

Federal's Mayfair was a very limited production (before limited productions were the mode of selling merchandise). Maybe that's a hint that you ought to start looking at it as another possible set to collect. Amber and crystal are the colors that can be collected (in the true pattern form). Amber cream soups have been found in small numbers and platters in even fewer numbers. Crystal Mayfair can be collected as a set. I had a letter about transitional crystal cream soups but no confirming picture. Green can only be bought in transitional form. Any of those comments can be rebutted should you have anything different than that in your collection.

I, personally, prefer the scalloped lines of Mayfair to those of the plainer Rosemary, but I also prefer the crystal color. Note the red decorated flowers in the second row. I couldn't pass them by, but I have not seen other pieces with that decoration. There may be sets like this or it could be some artist's addition. Mayfair is a challenging set to collect. Once you gather it, you will not be sorry. Mix the transitional with the regular pattern in amber. They go well together and only an experienced collector will recognize the difference.

The Mayfair sugar, like Rosemary, looks like a large sherbet since it does not have handles. There are no sherbets in this pattern. I once bought six sugar bowls from a flea market dealer who sold them as sherbets. I have also seen them labeled "spooners."

Generally, you will find several pieces of Mayfair together, rather than a piece here and there. You can get a brisk beginning to a collection that way.

	Amber	Crystal	Green		Amber	Crystal	Green
Bowl, 5", sauce	9.00	6.50	15.00	Plate, 9½", dinner	17.50	12.00	15.00
Bowl, 5", cream soup	25.00	15.00	25.00	Plate, 9½", grill	17.50	8.50	15.00
Bowl, 6", cereal	18.00	9.50	25.00	Platter, 12", oval	30.00	20.00	45.00
Bowl, 10", oval vegetable	35.00	18.00	45.00	Saucer	4.00	2.50	4.00
Creamer, footed	13.00	10.50	20.00	Sugar, footed	13.00	11.00	20.00
Cup	12.00	5.00	15.00	Tumbler, 4½", 9 ounce	35.00	15.00	45.00
Plate, 6¾", salad	7.00	4.50	9.00				

MAYFAIR, "OPEN ROSE" HOCKING GLASS COMPANY, 1931–1937

Colors: Ice blue, pink; some green, yellow, and crystal. (See Reproduction Section.)

In a 1937 distributors' catalog, ten items of No. 2000 line pink Mayfair "exquisitely etched with rose floral design" (painted) could be bought *by the dozen* for under $1.75. The least expensive item was the cereal bowl for 37 cents a dozen. The most expensive was the 80 ounce pitcher for $1.75. This illustrates how inexpensively a shop owner could obtain this ware to help sell his product or lure people to his store. Mayfair was possibly the most popular Depression glass pattern in the country, due in part to its major distribution throughout the states. Many families still have pieces left in their possession. This particular ware advertised above, was satinized using camphoric acid and hand painted. Few collectors cared about these satin pieces in the past; but that has changed, today. Collectors seek mint examples of this handworked pattern.

Rare colors found in Mayfair include yellow and green. Sets are possible. I've seen two with my own eyes; and I know of some others in the making. It takes money and patience. Pieces in these colors are rarely seen and very expensive in mint condition. I've been seeing a yellow square vegetable offered for four figures, for example. Be sure to note the blue cup with a pink trim. There were several of these rarities found, the first bi-colored Mayfair pieces known. You are as likely as anyone to find a rare piece at a sale.

The crystal creamer and covered sugar are rarely seen, but I have only met a few collectors for crystal Mayfair. Though these items are rare, with little demand, they do not yet command big prices. The juice pitcher, shakers, butter bottom (only), and the divided platter are commonly seen pieces in crystal. A reader wrote that the divided platter was given as a premium with the purchase of coffee or spices in late 1930s. This platter is often found in a metal holder.

Blue Mayfair is stunningly beautiful and unfortunately, nearly all gone from the market, today. In the early days of collecting, the supply for this seemed the same as the pink. Alas, not so! It commands goodly sums when found; however, its lack of availability is almost precluding its rise in price at this time. One new collector asked me if I had a piece available to just show her what it looked like. "I've been doing this for two years, and I've never seen a piece of blue!" she confided.

Pink Mayfair has a large selection of pieces and an equally large following. Various stems and tumblers enable you to approach collecting from several perspectives. A setting for four with all the pieces is expensive. However, if you try not to buy everything made, you can put a small set together for about the same money as most other patterns.

There are a few details about Mayfair that need to be pointed out. Some stems have a plain foot while others are rayed. The 10" celery measures 11½" handle to handle and the 9" one measures 10½" handle to handle. (The measurements in this book normally do not include handles unless so noted.) Footed iced teas vary in height. Some teas have a short stem above the foot and others have almost none. This causes the heights to vary to some extent. It is just a mould variation, which may account for capacity differences, too. Note under measurements on page 2 the listings of tumblers that I have taken from old Hocking catalogs. In two catalogs from 1935, these were listed as 13 ounce; but in 1936, both catalogs listed the tumbler as 15 ounces. I have never found a 13 ounce tumbler.

I spend hours answering questions and calls about rare and reproduction pieces in Mayfair. There was an inquiry on the Internet about reproduction shot glasses. It's uncomplicated. The originals have a split stem on the flower design while the reproductions have a single stem. That has never changed since they were first made at Mosser. I have updated the Reproduction Section in the back to take care of the odd colors of cookie jars and shakers now being found. Please read pages 249 and 250 if you are having problems.

You may see a price advertised or displayed at shows for more (and sometimes less) than my listed price. You must ultimately decide the worth of an item to you.

Attend a glass show; you'll be glad you did. At the recent show in Texas, two ladies said it was the most "fantastic, fun experience" they'd ever had.

	*Pink	Blue	Green	Yellow
Bowl, 5", cream soup	65.00			
Bowl, 5½", cereal	35.00	55.00	85.00	85.00
Bowl, 7", vegetable	30.00	60.00	175.00	175.00
Bowl, 9", 3⅛ high, 3-leg console	5,500.00		5,500.00	
Bowl, 9½", oval vegetable	35.00	80.00	125.00	135.00
Bowl, 10", vegetable	32.00	80.00		135.00
Bowl, 10", same covered	135.00	150.00		995.00
Bowl, 11¾", low flat	65.00	72.50	50.00	225.00
Bowl, 12", deep, scalloped fruit	65.00	110.00	50.00	255.00
Butter dish and cover or 7", covered vegetable	75.00	325.00	1,300.00	1,300.00

*Frosted or satin finish items slightly lower if paint is worn or missing

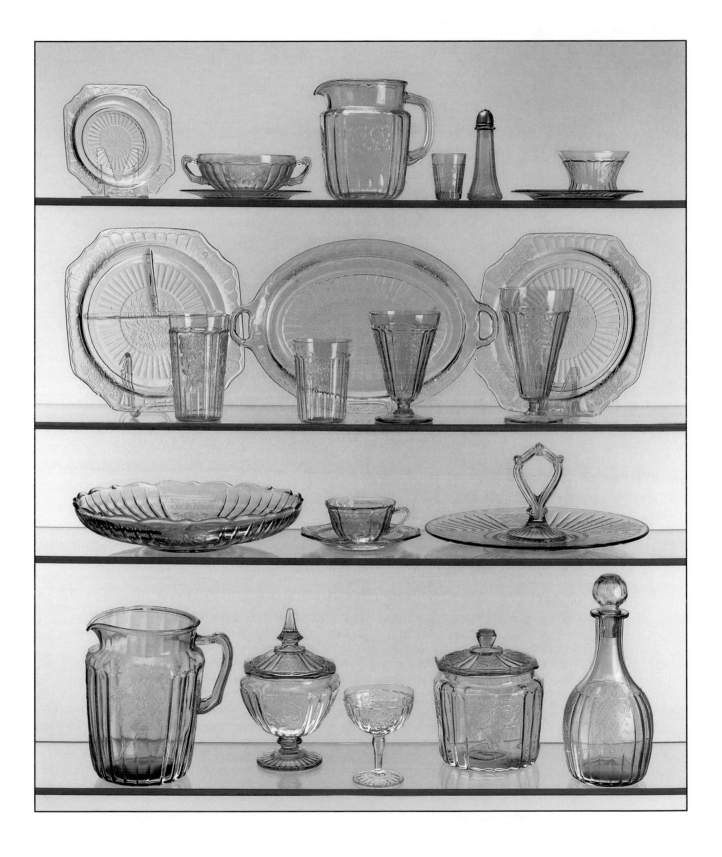

MAYFAIR

	*Pink	Blue	Green	Yellow
Butter bottom with indent				300.00
Butter dish top	45.00	265.00	1,150.00	1,150.00
Cake plate, 10", footed	32.00	75.00	150.00	
Candy dish and cover	60.00	325.00	595.00	495.00
Celery dish, 9", divided			195.00	195.00
Celery dish, 10"	48.00	75.00	125.00	125.00
Celery dish, 10", divided	285.00	80.00		
Cookie jar and lid	55.00	295.00	595.00	895.00
Creamer, footed	32.00	85.00	225.00	225.00
Cup	20.00	55.00	155.00	155.00
Cup, round	350.00			
Decanter and stopper, 32 ounce	225.00			
Goblet, 3¾", 1 ounce cordial	1,200.00		995.00	
Goblet, 4⅛", 2½ ounce	995.00		950.00	
Goblet, 4", 3 ounce cocktail	110.00		395.00	
Goblet, 4½", 3 ounce, wine	110.00		450.00	
Goblet, 5¼", 4½ ounce, claret	1,000.00		950.00	
Goblet, 5¾", 9 ounce, water	80.00		495.00	
Goblet, 7¼", 9 ounce, thin	265.00	250.00		
** Pitcher, 6", 37 ounce	70.00	165.00	600.00	600.00
Pitcher, 8", 60 ounce	85.00	195.00	650.00	500.00
Pitcher, 8½", 80 ounce	125.00	225.00	800.00	850.00
Plate, 5¾" (often substituted as saucer)	15.00	25.00	90.00	90.00
Plate, 6½", round sherbet	16.00			
Plate, 6½", round, off-center indent	25.00	30.00	135.00	135.00
Plate, 8½", luncheon	33.00	55.00	85.00	85.00
Plate, 9½", dinner	60.00	80.00	150.00	150.00
Plate, 9½", grill	50.00	60.00	85.00	125.00
Plate, 11½", handled grill				125.00
Plate, 12", cake w/handles	55.00	75.00	40.00	
*** Platter, 12", oval, open handles	35.00	75.00		
Platter, 12½", oval, 8" wide, closed handles			235.00	235.00
Relish, 8⅜", 4-part	40.00	75.00	165.00	165.00
Relish, 8⅜", non-partitioned	225.00		295.00	295.00
**** Salt and pepper, flat, pair	65.00	325.00	1,100.00	875.00
Salt and pepper, footed	10,000.00			
Sandwich server, center handle	55.00	85.00	40.00	135.00
Saucer (cup ring)	40.00			150.00
Saucer (same as 5¾"plate)	15.00	25.00	90.00	90.00
Sherbet, 2¼", flat	195.00	165.00		
Sherbet, 3", footed	17.50			
Sherbet, 4¾", footed	90.00	85.00	165.00	165.00
Sugar, footed	30.00	85.00	210.00	210.00
Sugar lid	1,650.00		1,100.00	1,100.00
Tumbler, 3½", 5 ounce, juice	45.00	125.00		
Tumbler, 4¼", 9 ounce, water	36.00	110.00		
Tumbler, 4¾", 11 ounce, water	225.00	150.00	225.00	225.00
Tumbler, 5¼", 13½ ounce, iced tea	65.00	275.00		
Tumbler, 3¼", 3 ounce, footed, juice	85.00			
Tumbler, 5¼", 10 ounce, footed	48.00	195.00		225.00
Tumbler, 6½", 15 ounce, footed, iced tea	45.00	325.00	300.00	
Vase (sweet pea)	145.00	135.00	325.00	
Whiskey, 2¼", 1½ ounce	80.00			

*Frosted or satin finish items slightly lower if paint is worn or missing
***Divided Crystal $12.50

** Crystal $15.00
**** Crystal $17.50 pair — Beware reproductions.

Colors: Crystal, pink; some green, ice blue, Jade-ite, and Royal Ruby. (See Reproduction Section.)

This beloved 1930s Depression pattern continues to be requested at shows and turns up at markets. I bought several items at a chance roadside stop this past summer for bargain rates. Novices need to know to carefully check the points on the items, particularly the plate edges. Often parts of these points are missing, or chipped, especially underneath; and peruse candy jar knobs to make certain they haven't been glued back on.

Miss America tumblers and stems have three parallel lines before leading into a plain glass rim. Westmoreland's English Hobnail pattern, which made its appearance and sold well first, is often mistaken for Miss America. Check the differences by reading the comparison of the two under that pattern. Because of wonderful marketing schemes promoting Hocking's wares, Miss America eventually exceeded English Hobnail's popularity with the public. I suspect it was made available to suppliers more economically.

Newcomers should stop and view the five-part relish pictured in the top of page 136. This piece is rare in pink but not in crystal. Pink ones turn up from time to time; you should learn to recognize this piece so you do not miss one.

A set of rare Royal Ruby (c. 1938) Miss America is pictured on page 136. A former employee of the company originally owned it. There were two styles of water goblets, footed juices, and sherbets in this group. Notice how one of the water goblets and one of the footed juices flare at the top. The sherbets do the same; but only one style was photographed. This set contained the first Miss America cups, sherbets, and footed and flat juices I had seen in Royal Ruby. It was originally a basic set for eight. A few other pieces turn up occasionally in the market. An individual reproduced butter dishes in red in the late 1970s; but they were an amberina red. No original red butter has been seen.

Some pieces of Miss America are found with metal lids. The relish (four-part dish) and cereal bowl are often found that way. These pieces were sold to some company who made lids to fit. They are not original factory lids.

Any time a glass pattern was made for several years, it will be possible to find pieces that deviate in size. In talking to former mould makers, I learned that moulds were "cut down" when they wore. Therefore, some pieces were made a little smaller each time the moulds were reworked.

Reproductions have appeared in a few pieces of Miss America pattern since the early 1970s. Please refer to page 251 for a listing and facts regarding these nuisances. Shakers that are fatter toward the foot are the best ones to buy, since that style has not been reproduced. Narrow, thinner bottomed reproduction shakers are like flies at stockyards now, everywhere.

A few odd-colored or flashed pieces of Miss America surface occasionally. I have shown some of these in previous editions. Flashed-on red, green, or amethyst are not plentiful enough to collect a set. However, there may be more interest in odd colors now that rainbow collections are in vogue.

	Crystal	Pink	Green	Royal Ruby
Bowl, 4½", berry			15.00	
Bowl, 6¼", cereal	10.00	30.00	20.00	
Bowl, 8", curved in at top	40.00	95.00		600.00
Bowl, 8¾", straight, deep fruit	35.00	85.00		
Bowl, 10", oval vegetable	15.00	45.00		
Bowl, 11", shallow				900.00
*Butter dish and cover	210.00	695.00		
Butter dish bottom	10.00	30.00		
Butter dish top	200.00	665.00		
Cake plate, 12", footed	26.00	65.00		
Candy jar and cover, 11½"	65.00	175.00		
***Celery dish, 10½", oblong	16.00	42.00		
Coaster, 5¾"	16.00	35.00		
Comport, 5"	17.50	30.00		
Creamer, footed	11.00	25.00		225.00
Cup	9.00	28.00	15.00	295.00
Goblet, 3¾", 3 oz., wine	22.00	120.00		325.00

	Crystal	Pink	Green	Royal Ruby
Goblet, 4¾", 5 oz., juice	27.00	110.00		325.00
Goblet, 5½", 10 oz., water	20.00	55.00		295.00
Pitcher, 8", 65 ounce	50.00	165.00		
Pitcher, 8½", 65 ounce, w/ice lip	70.00	225.00		
**Plate, 5¾", sherbet	6.00	13.00	8.00	55.00
Plate, 6¾"			14.00	
Plate, 8½", salad	7.50	27.00		165.00
***Plate, 10¼", dinner	16.00	38.00		
Plate, 10¼", grill	10.00	28.00		
Platter, 12¼", oval	15.00	38.00		
Relish, 8¾", 4-part	10.00	25.00		
Relish, 11¾", round, divided	25.00	6,000.00		
Salt and pepper, pair	35.00	67.50		
Saucer	3.00	8.00		75.00
**Sherbet	7.00	18.00		150.00
Sugar	9.00	25.00		225.00
***Tumbler, 4", 5 oz., juice	17.00	60.00		235.00
Tumbler, 4½", 10 oz., water	16.00	37.50	22.00	
Tumbler, 5¾", 14 ounce, iced tea	30.00	110.00		

*Absolute mint price   **Also in Ice Blue $50.00   ***Also in Ice Blue $150.00

Colors: Amethyst, cobalt blue; some crystal, pink, and Platonite fired-on colors.

Moderntone is admired first for its rich coloring and then for its simplistic style. It is more economically priced than many of its counterpart patterns. The certificate below shows a 36-piece set of cobalt blue Moderntone could be bought for $1.69 plus freight costs for 24 pounds. You had to send two or four coupons from flour—no hardship since baking was an everyday thing then. However, $1.69 was more than a day's wages for laborers.

There is no Moderntone tumbler per se. Tumblers sold, today, as Moderntone were just advertised alongside this pattern, but they were never sold as a part of the set. There are two different style tumblers that have been adopted for this set. The water tumbler and the juice to the left of the whiskey on page 138 are paneled and have a rayed bottom. The juice to the right of the whiskey is not paneled and has a plain bottom that is marked H over top A which is the Hazel Atlas trademark. Either tumbler is acceptable, but most collectors choose the circled, paneled one. All sizes of these tumblers are hard to find except for the water. Green, pink, or crystal tumblers were made, but there is little market for these except for the tiny shot glass that is sought by a growing cadre of those collectors.

The butter bottom and sugar were apparently sold to some company who made the tops. Lids come with black, red, or blue knobs, but red appears most often. By adding a lid, mustards were made from the handle-less custard. Speaking of that custard, there is a punch set being sold as Moderntone which uses a Hazel Atlas mixing bowl and either the plain, cobalt, roly-poly cups found with the Royal Lace toddy set or Moderntone custard cups. This was not Hazel Atlas assembled; but some embrace it to go with Moderntone.

In past editions, I have shown a boxed set with crystal Moderntone shot glasses in a metal holder that came with a Colonial Block creamer. The box was marked "Little Deb" Lemonade Server Set. That crystal pitcher has turned up in cobalt and several have been found with Shirley Temple's picture. These boxed, children's sets sell in the $100.00 range. Crystal shots go for $16.00 each. There are a few collectors pursuing crystal Moderntone. It brings about half the price of amethyst. Flat soups are rare in any color except crystal. Today's collectors combine colors; so, crystal soups may become desirable.

Ruffled cream soups have outdistanced the sandwich plates in price. Sandwich plates can be located, but nearly all are heavily scuffed or worn causing collectors to shun them. When you pick up a blue plate that looks white in the center from years of use, that is not a good sign. A collector gleefully related that she bought nearly a dozen of these sandwich trays on a table in a used furniture store for $18 not so long ago.

The cheese dish remains the highest priced piece of Moderntone. This cheese dish is essentially a salad plate with a metal cover and wooden cutting board.

Green, crystal, and pink ashtrays are found, but there is limited demand for them. Blue ashtrays still command a hefty price for an ashtray. Finding any Moderntone bowls without inner rim roughness (irr) is a difficult task. Prices are for mint condition pieces. That is why bowls are so highly priced. Used, nicked, and bruised bowls are the norm and should be priced accordingly. Bowls, themselves, are not rare; mint condition bowls are. Platonite Moderntone has been moved into the *Collectible Glassware from the 40s, 50s, 60s...* since it better fits the era covered by that book.

MODERNTONE

	Cobalt	Amethyst
* Ashtray, 7¾", match holder in center	175.00	
Bowl, 4¾", cream soup	22.00	20.00
Bowl, 5", berry	28.00	25.00
Bowl, 5", cream soup, ruffled	65.00	33.00
Bowl, 6½", cereal	75.00	75.00
Bowl, 7½", soup	150.00	100.00
Bowl, 8¾", large berry	52.00	40.00
Butter dish with metal cover	110.00	
Cheese dish, 7", with metal lid	395.00	
Creamer	12.00	11.00
Cup	10.00	11.00
Cup (handle-less) or custard	22.00	15.00
Plate, 5⅞", sherbet	6.00	5.00
Plate, 6¾", salad	11.00	10.00

	Cobalt	Amethyst
Plate, 7¾", luncheon	12.00	9.00
Plate, 8⅞", dinner	18.00	13.00
Plate, 10½", sandwich	60.00	40.00
Platter, 11", oval	52.00	37.50
Platter, 12", oval	85.00	45.00
Salt and pepper, pair	42.50	35.00
Saucer	4.00	3.00
Sherbet	15.00	12.00
Sugar	13.00	12.00
Sugar lid in metal	37.50	
Tumbler, 5 ounce	70.00	40.00
Tumbler, 9 ounce	40.00	30.00
Tumbler, 12 ounce	125.00	90.00
** Whiskey, 1½ ounce	45.00	

* Pink $75.00; green $95.00
** Pink or green $17.50

138

MONTICELLO; Later WAFFLE #698 IMPERIAL GLASS COMPANY, c. 1920 – 1960s

Colors: Crystal, Rubigold, milk, clambroth, teal.

Monticello was presented in the early 1920s in items of crystal and Rubigold, Imperial's name for their marigold colored carnival glass. Judging by the number of pieces made and the length of years they were manufactured, Monticello was a successful addition to their line. Most crystal pieces I see out are priced very reasonably. Years later, Monticello was offered by Imperial under the Waffle name, which is what it was being called at markets in the late 1960s when I first encountered it.

As with their other lines, Imperial reissued various items from this line throughout their production years in whatever colors were being run at that moment. So, it's possible you will find other, later colors than those listed above. I'm pricing crystal only for now. Colors will add to the prices listed, with teal and clambroth bringing the most. Forgive the older, pattern glass footed mug pictured.

Item	Crystal	Item	Crystal	Item	Crystal	Item	Crystal
Basket, 10"	20.00	Bowl, 8½", belled	17.50	Compote, 5¾", belled		Punch cup	8.00
Bonbon, 5½", 1 handle	12.00	Bowl, 8", lily (cupped)	40.00	rim	15.00	Relish, 8¼", divided	18.00
Bowl, 4½", finger	10.00	Bowl, 8", round veg	25.00	Creamer	12.50	Salt & pepper w/glass	
Bowl, 4½", fruit, 2 styles	8.00	Bowl, 8", round	15.00	Cup	10.00	tops	20.00
Bowl, 5½", crème soup	12.50	Bowl, 8", shallow	15.00	Cuspidor	50.00	Saucer	4.00
Bowl, 5", lily	20.00	Bowl, 9", round	20.00	Mayo set, 3-piece	30.00	Sherbet	10.00
Bowl, 5", fruit	10.00	Bowl, 9", shallow	17.50	Pickle, 6", oval	15.00	Stem, cocktail	12.50
Bowl, 6½", belled	12.50	Bowl, 10", belled	25.00	Pitcher, 52 oz., ice lip	55.00	Stem, water	15.00
Bowl, 6", lily	22.50	Bowl, 10", shallow	22.00	Plate, 6", bread	5.00	Sugar, open	12.50
Bowl, 6", round	10.00	Bowl, 12", deep	30.00	Plate, 8", salad	9.00	Tidbit, 2-tier	
Bowl, 7½", square	17.50	Buffet set, 3-pc. (mayo,		Plate, 9", dinner	20.00	(7½" & 10½")	45.00
Bowl, 7½", belled	15.00	spoon, 16½" rnd. plate)	75.00	Plate, 10½", square	25.00	Tumbler, 9 oz., water	12.00
Bowl, 7", flower		Butter tub, 5½"	35.00	Plate, 12", round	35.00	Tumbler, 12 oz., tea	15.00
(w/flower grid)	40.00	Celery, 9", oval	20.00	Plate, 16", cupped	50.00	Vase, 6"	22.50
Bowl, 7", lily	30.00	Cheese dish and cover	75.00	Plate, 16½", round	50.00	Vase, 10½", flat	35.00
Bowl, 7", nappy	12.50	Coaster, 3¼"	8.00	Plate, 17", flat	55.00		
Bowl, 7", round	12.50	Compote, 5¼"	12.50	Punch bowl, belled rim	65.00		

MOONDROPS NEW MARTINSVILLE GLASS COMPANY, 1932 – 1940

Colors: Amber, pink, green, cobalt, ice blue, red, amethyst, crystal, dark green, light green, Jadite, smoke, and black.

Red and cobalt blue are the colors most Moondrops collectors find irresistible; and these colors are selling briskly on the Internet auctions, though red is taking precedence. Every antique dealer knows that red and cobalt blue glass are expensive colors; therefore, prices are generally high even if they do not recognize Moondrops. Conversely, other colors escape unacknowledged; you might find a bargain if you know what to look for. A green cordial price recently surprised me on an Internet auction. So, other colors of Moondrops are being acknowledged in collecting circles. Amber was the least preferred color for a while, but even that is changing, not only in Moondrops, but in other patterns as well. Perfume bottles, powder jars, mugs, gravy boats, and triple candlesticks are symbols of more elegant glassware than most of its contemporaries. Bud vases, decanters, and coveted "rocket style" stems present a gallery of unusual pieces. Several colors of "rocket style" decanters are pictured in my *Very Rare Glassware* series.

Evidently New Martinsville or one of their glass distributors mismatched some of their Moondrops colors. I have found two powder jars with crystal bottoms and cobalt blue tops in antique malls in Ohio and Florida. I recently had a report of another one in Kansas; this may indicate how some of them were sold. I have seen a complete cobalt one. They can be found that way, too.

The butter has to have a matching glass top to obtain the prices listed below. The metal top with a bird finial found on some butter bottoms sells for about $35.00. However, a metal top with the fan finial sells for approximately $65.00. Those fan finials are not easily found. Collectors tend to want glass tops on their butter dishes.

	Blue, Red	Other Colors		Blue, Red	Other Colors
Ashtray	30.00	17.00	Goblet, 5¾" 8 ounce	40.00	20.00
Bowl, 4¼", cream soup	100.00	40.00	Goblet, 5⅛", 3 ounce, metal stem wine	16.00	11.00
Bowl, 5¼", berry	25.00	12.00	Goblet, 5½", 4 ounce, metal stem wine	20.00	11.00
Bowl, 5⅜", 3-footed, tab handle	75.00	40.00	Goblet, 6¼", 9 ounce, metal stem water	23.00	16.00
Bowl, 6¾", soup	90.00		Gravy boat	195.00	100.00
Bowl, 7½", pickle	35.00	20.00	Mayonnaise, 5¼"	65.00	40.00
Bowl, 8⅜", footed, concave top	45.00	25.00	Mug, 5⅛", 12 ounce	40.00	23.00
Bowl, 8½", 3-footed divided relish	40.00	20.00	Perfume bottle, "rocket"	250.00	195.00
Bowl, 9½", 3-legged, ruffled	70.00		Pitcher, 6⅞", 22 ounce, small	165.00	90.00
Bowl, 9¾", oval vegetable	75.00	45.00	Pitcher, 8⅛", 32 ounce, medium	185.00	115.00
Bowl, 9¾", covered casserole	225.00	125.00	Pitcher, 8", 50 ounce, large, with lip	195.00	115.00
Bowl, 9¾", handled, oval	52.50	36.00	Pitcher, 8⅛", 53 ounce, large, no lip	185.00	125.00
Bowl, 11", boat-shaped celery	32.00	23.00	Plate, 5⅞"	11.00	8.00
Bowl, 12", round, 3-footed console	85.00	32.00	Plate, 6⅛", sherbet	8.00	5.00
Bowl, 13", console with "wings"	120.00	42.00	Plate, 6", round, off-center sherbet indent	12.00	9.00
Butter dish and cover	500.00	275.00	Plate, 7⅛", salad	14.00	10.00
Butter dish bottom	75.00	50.00	Plate, 8½", luncheon	17.00	12.00
Butter dish top (glass)	425.00	225.00	Plate, 9½", dinner	30.00	20.00
Candles, 2", ruffled, pair	45.00	25.00	Plate, 14", round, sandwich	45.00	20.00
Candles, 4½", sherbet style, pair	30.00	20.00	Plate, 14", 2-handled, sandwich	60.00	25.00
Candlesticks, 5", ruffled, pair	40.00	25.00	Platter, 12", oval	45.00	25.00
Candlesticks, 5", "wings," pair	110.00	60.00	Powder jar, 3-footed	295.00	160.00
Candlesticks, 5¼", triple light, pair	150.00	95.00	Saucer	4.00	3.00
Candlesticks, 8½", metal stem, pair	45.00	33.00	Sherbet, 2⅝"	16.00	11.00
Candy dish, 8", ruffled	40.00	20.00	Sherbet, 4½"	30.00	16.00
Cocktail shaker with or without handle, metal top	60.00	35.00	Sugar, 2¾"	15.00	10.00
			Sugar, 3½"	16.00	11.00
Comport, 4"	27.50	18.00	Tumbler, 2¾", 2 ounce, shot	22.00	10.00
Comport, 11½"	95.00	55.00	Tumbler, 2¾", 2 ounce, handled shot	16.00	11.00
Creamer, 2¾", miniature	18.00	11.00	Tumbler, 3¼", 3 ounce, footed juice	20.00	11.00
Creamer, 3¾", regular	16.00	10.00	Tumbler, 3⅝", 5 ounce	18.00	10.00
Cup	16.00	8.00	Tumbler, 4⅜", 7 ounce	16.00	10.00
Decanter, 7¾", small	67.50	38.00	Tumbler, 4⅜", 8 ounce	20.00	11.00
Decanter, 8½", medium	70.00	42.00	Tumbler, 4⅞", 9 ounce, handled	30.00	16.00
Decanter, 11¼", large	100.00	50.00	Tumbler, 4⅞", 9 ounce	20.00	15.00
Decanter, 10¼", "rocket"	495.00	395.00	Tumbler, 5⅛", 12 ounce	30.00	14.00
Goblet, 2⅞", ¾ ounce, cordial	40.00	30.00	Tray, 7½", for mini sugar/creamer	37.50	19.00
Goblet, 4", 4 ounce, wine	20.00	13.00	Vase, 7¾" flat, ruffled top	60.00	57.00
Goblet, 4¾", "rocket", wine	60.00	30.00	Vase, 8½", "rocket" bud	275.00	185.00
Goblet, 4¾", 5 ounce	24.00	15.00	Vase, 9¼", "rocket" style	250.00	150.00

MT. PLEASANT, "DOUBLE SHIELD" L. E. SMITH GLASS COMPANY, 1920s – 1934

Colors: Black amethyst, amethyst, cobalt blue, crystal, pink, green, and white.

Many people are drawn to colored glassware for the color alone. Mt. Pleasant is often bought for its cobalt blue and black colors rather than for the fact that it is a Depression glass pattern. At shows I see pieces of Mt. Pleasant brought in to be identified and people are delighted to find it booked. You'd be surprised how many amateur glass lovers walk into a glass show for the first time not even knowing there are books on the subject.

I had to explain the "double shield" meaning to a novice collector recently, because you can't really see that moulded design element in the opaque pieces shown here, Sorry!

I received a letter from a lady telling me she had spotted her cobalt blue leaf dishes in a friend's book; she had unwrapped a set of one large and six smaller plates as a wedding gift in 1931. The larger leaf measures 11½" and is not easily found.

The picture below illustrates but a few of many decorations found on Mt. Pleasant. All are factory decorations except for the decaled flowers and chickens. A few undecorated pieces of white Mt. Pleasant are known, but the black stripes and handles dress up what is shown. Few pieces of color striped crystal are seen; I purchased these few for you to enjoy. I have had occasional reports of pink and green items, usually sugars and creamers. A few pink plates pop up once in a while suggesting a luncheon set.

Most cobalt blue Mt. Pleasant is found in the Midwest and in northern New York. We know that Mt. Pleasant was prominently displayed and used for premiums in hardware stores in those areas; black dominates in other areas of the country. Many pieces are found with a platinum (silver) band around them, a kind of trademark with Smith black ware. This decorated band faded with use. Price is generally less for worn decorations.

	Pink, Green	Amethyst, Black, Cobalt		Pink, Green	Amethyst, Black, Cobalt
Bonbon, 7", rolled-up, handle	16.00	23.00	Leaf, 11¼"		30.00
Bowl, 4" opening, rose	18.00	27.50	Mayonnaise, 5½", 3-footed	18.00	30.00
Bowl, 4⅞", square, footed, fruit	13.00	20.00	Mint, 6", center handle	16.00	25.00
Bowl, 6", 2-handle, square	13.00	18.00	Plate, 7", 2-handle, scalloped	9.00	16.00
Bowl, 7", 3-footed, rolled out edge	16.00	25.00	Plate, 8", scalloped or square	10.00	15.00
Bowl, 8", scalloped, 2-handle	19.00	35.00	Plate, 8", 2-handle	11.00	18.00
Bowl, 8", square, 2-handle	19.00	35.00	Plate 8¼", square w/indent for cup		16.00
Bowl, 9", scalloped, 1¾" deep, ftd.		32.00	Plate, 9", grill		20.00
Bowl, 9¼", square, footed, fruit	19.00	35.00	Plate, 10½", cake, 2-handle	16.00	37.00
Bowl, 10", scalloped fruit		45.00	Plate, 10½", 1¼" high, cake		40.00
Bowl, 10", 2-handle turned-up edge		35.00	Plate, 12", 2-handle	20.00	33.00
Cake plate, 10½", footed, 1¼" high		37.50	Salt and pepper, 2 styles	24.00	45.00
Candlestick, single, pair	20.00	30.00	Sandwich server, center-handle		45.00
Candlestick, double, pair	26.00	45.00	Saucer	2.50	4.00
Creamer	18.00	20.00	Sherbet, 2 styles	10.00	16.00
Cup (waffle-like crystal)	4.50		Sugar	18.00	20.00
Cup	9.50	14.00	Tumbler, footed		28.00
Leaf, 8"		17.50	Vase, 7¼"		35.00

MT. VERNON; Later WASHINGTON #699 IMPERIAL GLASS COMPANY, Late 1920s – 1970s

Colors: Crystal, red, green, yellow, milk, iridized, red flash.

A popular, prismatic design, Mt. Vernon appears mostly in crystal; limited pieces in color surfaced from time to time; cobalt and emerald items were made by another company entirely in a last ditch effort to raise money to "save Imperial glass." Available in markets, today, you should be able to gather a large set. The tall celery becomes a pickle by adding a lid; both sugar bowls, the 5¾" two-handled bowl, and the 69 ounce pitcher were sold with or without lids. Tiffin made a similar looking pattern called Williamsburg in the late 20s in crystal and in the 50s in colors. Williamsburg has a rayed star bottom design; Mt. Vernon's pattern shows a waffle type design in the bottom, square shapes, and tip handle protrusions.

	Crystal		Crystal
Bonbon, 5¾", one-handle	10.00	Pitcher, 69 ounce, straight edge	40.00
Bowl, 5", finger	12.00	Plate, 6", bread and butter	5.00
Bowl, 5¾", two-handle	10.00	Plate, 8", round	10.00
Bowl, 5¾", two-handle, w/cover	22.00	Plate, 8", square	10.00
Bowl, 6", lily	15.00	Plate, 11", cake	20.00
Bowl, 7", lily	18.00	Plate, 12½", sandwich	25.00
Bowl, 8", lily	20.00	Plate, 13¼", torte	27.00
Bowl, 10", console	25.00	Plate, 18", liner for punch	25.00
Bowl, 10", 3-footed	25.00	Saucer	2.00
Bowl, punch	30.00	Shaker, pair	22.00
Butter dish, 5"	30.00	Spooner	22.00
Butter dish, dome top	35.00	Stem, 2 ounce, wine	12.00
Butter tub, 5"	15.00	Stem, 3 ounce, cocktail	8.00
Candlestick, 9"	30.00	Stem, 5 ounce, sherbet	6.00
Celery, 10½"	22.00	Stem, 9 ounce, water goblet	10.00
Creamer, individual	8.00	Sugar lid, for individual	8.00
Creamer, large	12.00	Sugar lid, for large	12.00
Cup, coffee	8.00	Sugar, individual	8.00
Cup, custard or punch	8.00	Sugar, large	12.00
Decanter	35.00	Syrup, 8½ ounce, w/cover	45.00
Oil bottle, 6 ounce	30.00	Tidbit, two-tier	30.00
Pickle jar, w/cover	35.00	Tumbler, 7 ounce, old fashioned	10.00
Pickle, tall, two-handle	22.00	Tumbler, 9 ounce, water	8.00
Pickle, 6", two handle	15.00	Tumbler, 12 ounce, iced tea	12.50
Pitcher top, for 69 ounce	35.00	Vase, 10", orange bowl	50.00
Pitcher, 54 ounce	35.00		

Colors: Green; some crystal, pink, amethyst, and cobalt.

New Century, the official name for this Hazel Atlas pattern, was featured in a display at the Sanlando show as the new millennium rolled around. This classic "pillow optic" design, as it was advertised in a Butler Brothers catalog, has definitely withstood the test of time.

Green is the chosen color since sets can only be assembled in that color. A few pieces are found in crystal, but not enough to assemble a set according to some that tried to do so. Crystal prices are on par with green even with little demand. You can find crystal powder jars made from a sugar lid set atop a sherbet. The knob of the sherbet usually has decorative glass marbles or beads attached by a wire. One of these is pictured on the next page. I believe these were a legitimate product of the 30s. Unfortunately, a lady sent me a picture of a Cherry Blossom one she'd paid $250.00 as "rare unlisted," which doubtless was put together "last week." A $20.00 investment in a good book is my recommendation.

Thirty years into mass collecting Depression glass, New Century bowls are nearly impossible to find. I haven't had a 4½" berry bowl in years. That same company mentioned above sold them for 37 cents a dozen; and they were packed three dozen to a carton. Cream soups, casseroles, whiskeys, wines, grill plates, and cocktails are rarely seen. As with Adam, the casserole bottom is harder to find than the top. I saw a chipped casserole lid for $10.00. When I set it down, I was told any lid was worth that. Well, no, not yet; and particularly not damaged.

Pink, cobalt blue, and amethyst New Century have only been found in water sets and an occasional cup or saucer. Only flat tumblers have been encountered in these colors. By the way, in doing some other research, I found that most beverage sets in the 30s were priced $1.00 and were often used as a sales advertisement. If you visited the sales at thus and so stores, you could buy a seven-piece beverage set for a $1.00.

	Green, Crystal	Pink, Cobalt, Amethyst
Ashtray/coaster, 5⅜"	30.00	
Bowl, 4½", berry	30.00	
Bowl, 4¾", cream soup	22.00	
Bowl, 8", large berry	28.00	
Bowl, 9", covered casserole	95.00	
Butter dish and cover	65.00	
Cup	10.00	20.00
Creamer	15.00	
Decanter and stopper	75.00	

	Green, Crystal	Pink, Cobalt, Amethyst
Goblet, 2½ ounce, wine	33.00	
Goblet, 3¼ ounce, cocktail	33.00	
Pitcher, 7¾", 60 ounce, with or without ice lip	35.00	35.00
Pitcher, 8", 80 ounce, with or without ice lip	40.00	42.00
Plate, 6", sherbet	8.00	
Plate, 7⅛", breakfast	10.00	
Plate, 8½", salad	14.00	
Plate, 10", dinner	18.00	
Plate, 10", grill	20.00	
Platter, 11", oval	25.00	
Salt and pepper, pair	40.00	
Saucer	3.00	7.50
Sherbet, 3"	12.00	
Sugar	10.00	
Sugar cover	18.00	
Tumbler, 3½", 5 ounce	18.00	12.00
Tumbler, 3½", 8 ounce	28.00	
Tumbler, 4¼", 9 ounce	22.00	20.00
Tumbler, 5", 10 ounce	22.00	22.00
Tumbler, 5¼", 12 ounce	33.00	30.00
Tumbler, 4", 5 ounce, footed	22.00	
Tumbler, 4⅞", 9 ounce, footed	25.00	
Whiskey, 2½", 1½ ounce	22.00	

NEWPORT, "HAIRPIN" HAZEL ATLAS GLASS COMPANY, 1936 – 1940

Colors: Cobalt blue, amethyst; some pink, Platonite white, and fired-on colors.

In the last book I reported that some Newport collectors were slightly miffed with me for exposing the minute, 5⁄16" difference between a dinner and a luncheon plate. This time I had a dealer tell me that since I pointed out that 5⁄16" difference, his customers were buying luncheon plates and not paying for the higher priced dinners. Now, in talking to a mould worker, it's probable that the smaller plates were made in the later, reworked moulds which had to be cut down, resulting in slightly smaller sized items. At any rate, the larger dinner plate measures 8¹³⁄16" while the luncheon plate measures 8½"; and, frankly, after that initial flurry, few really seem to care. I only brought the matter up because of problems that mail-order dealers were having. ("The plates you sent me were smaller than the ones I have!") The only official listing I have states plates of 6", 8½", and 11½". However, after obtaining these plates, I found actual measurements quite different as you can see by the size listings in the price guide below. One of the problems with catalog measurements is that they are not always accurate and sometimes not even very close.

Cereal bowls, sandwich plates, large berry bowls, and tumblers have virtually vanished into collections in all colors. I finally bought a large amethyst berry bowl; but I am having trouble replacing the large cobalt berry bowl that was annihilated before a photography session. I have run across a few cobalt ones, but not at a reasonable enough price to suit me. Cathy did locate a damaged cobalt blue bowl at an antique show for $25.00. I thought that would fill the hole in the picture until I saw it was missing an entire scallop. There was even a 10% discount. The 2" missing piece didn't matter, because "it was old." It mattered to me! Author's can't afford to spend too much on photo items considering how many it takes to present an exceptional book in color!

Collectors favor cobalt blue Newport. Sets of pink Newport were given away as premiums for buying seeds from a catalog in the 1930s. (See ad below.) Very few of these pink sets are coming into the market because pink seems to be the rarest color in Newport. Newport and Moderntone are the only Depression ware sets you can assemble in amethyst. Moroccan Amethyst came much later. Price pink one third of amethyst due to less demand.

Platonite Newport from the 1950s can be found in my book *Collectible Glassware from the 40s, 50s, 60s....*

	Cobalt	Amethyst		Cobalt	Amethyst
Bowl, 4¾", berry	22.00	17.00	Plate, 8¹³⁄16", dinner	30.00	30.00
Bowl, 4¾", cream soup	25.00	24.00	Plate, 11¾", sandwich	45.00	40.00
Bowl, 5¼", cereal	40.00	35.00	Platter, 11¾", oval	50.00	43.00
Bowl, 8¼", large berry	45.00	45.00	Salt and pepper	50.00	40.00
Cup	14.00	12.00	Saucer	5.00	5.00
Creamer	16.00	14.00	Sherbet	16.00	15.00
Plate, 5⅞", sherbet	9.00	8.00	Sugar	16.00	16.00
Plate, 8½", luncheon	16.00	14.00	Tumbler, 4½", 9 ounce	45.00	40.00

No. 200. LADIES! Here's a gorgeous Dinner Set in that new shade Rose Crystal. It consists of 6 large plates, 6 small plates, 6 cups, 6 saucers, 6 cereal dishes, vegetable dish and large meat platter. This sparkling set, more beautiful than you can imagine, is given for one $4.00 order of Seeds. Weight 22 lbs. Sent Express collect.

32-Piece Rose Crystal Dinner Set

NORMANDIE, "BOUQUET AND LATTICE" FEDERAL GLASS COMPANY, 1933 – 1940

Colors: Iridescent, amber, pink, and crystal.

This very lovely old Depression pattern, appropriately dubbed "Bouquet and Lattice," is most desirable in pink; but it was also made in amber and iridescent colors, which these 30 years into collecting, you will have a better chance of finding. Buy any hard-to-find items first or whenever you find them. That guidance goes for collecting any pattern. Rarer, harder-to-find items have always increased in price faster than frequently found ones. Don't pass pieces of pink that cross your path; someone wants them.

Some iridescent Normandie is being displayed at Depression glass shows. There are people requesting it since rumors got around that it was getting hard to find. There were enough buyers to raise the prices. Iridescent is still reasonably priced in comparison to pink and amber.

Pink Normandie has been very elusive for several years; but amber tumblers, sugar lids, and dinner-sized plates have become scarce, also. Pink Normandie tumblers, should you discover any, rival prices of American Sweetheart; and Normandie collectors are vastly outnumbered by those buying American Sweetheart. Pink pitchers could be bought reasonably when compared to those in American Sweetheart were they available; but most are already tucked away in collections.

That console bowl and candlesticks (occasionally found with sets of iridized Normandie) are Madrid pattern. These were sold about the same time as Normandie. That does not make them Normandie; they are still Madrid. The design on the glass determines pattern, not the color. See Madrid for pricing of these console sets.

	Amber	Pink	Iridescent
Bowl, 5", berry	10.00	10.00	6.00
* Bowl, 6½", cereal	25.00	50.00	10.00
Bowl, 8½", large berry	27.50	40.00	15.00
Bowl, 10", oval vegetable	20.00	45.00	18.00
Creamer, footed	9.00	14.00	10.00
Cup	7.50	11.00	6.00
Pitcher, 8", 80 ounce	85.00	195.00	
Plate, 6", sherbet	4.50	7.00	3.00
Plate, 7¾", salad	10.00	14.00	
Plate, 9¼", luncheon	8.50	17.00	15.00
Plate, 11", dinner	33.00	125.00	11.50
Plate, 11", grill	15.00	25.00	9.00
Platter, 11¾"	22.00	45.00	12.00
Salt and pepper, pair	55.00	95.00	
Saucer	2.00	3.00	2.00
Sherbet	6.50	10.00	7.00
Sugar	9.00	12.00	6.00
Sugar lid	95.00	195.00	
Tumbler, 4", 5 ounce, juice	35.00	95.00	
Tumbler, 4¼", 9 ounce, water	25.00	60.00	
Tumbler, 5", 12 ounce, iced tea	45.00	120.00	

* Mistaken by many as butter bottom.

No. 610, "PYRAMID" INDIANA GLASS COMPANY, 1926 – 1932

Colors: Green, pink, yellow, white, crystal, blue, or black in 1974 – 1975 by Tiara.

"Pyramid" is the collectors' name for Indiana's pattern No. 610, which is being embraced by Art Deco enthusiasts as well as Depression glass collectors. Prices have advanced with increased demand from both sectors. Little is being found, and mint condition "Pyramid" is bringing premium prices. I did buy a beverage set recently simply because I asked how the two tumblers displayed were priced and was informed they belonged with a set. Better and better!

Crystal pitchers and tumblers in "Pyramid" are very scarce. Crystal pitchers are priced higher than all but yellow, even though yellow ones are encountered more often. There are so many collectors of yellow No. 610 that prices continue to increase. Ice buckets turn up fairly often, even in yellow. However, the yellow lid to the ice bucket is nearly impossible to find. No lids have yet been found for the other colors. I had a call from someone who wanted to sell me a yellow ice bucket lid with a chip on it. She couldn't comprehend why I would not buy it for book price. I hope she found a buyer at her price, but it wasn't going to be me. The prices below are for mint condition glassware; any with a "ding" or two should market for less.

Optimistically, I hope you read this paragraph about the crystal shaker pictured in previous books. This shaker was made by Indiana, and is often misrepresented as "Pyramid," but it is not. If you see one, look at it closely. The design is upside down from that of all No. 610 pieces and slightly different in make-up. It would serve as a great companion item since there are no shakers per se in this older Indiana pattern. I have only seen these shakers in crystal, but they could be found in other colors.

The bona fide sugar/creamer stand has squared indentations on each side to fit the bottoms of the sugar and creamer. These stands were common then in various patterns.

Oval bowls and pickle dishes are occasionally mixed up inasmuch as both measure 9½". The oval bowl has pointed edges, shown by bowls in white, green, and yellow. The pickle dish has rounded edges, instead of pointed and is handled.

Eight-ounce tumblers are found with two different sized bases. One has a 2¼" square foot while the other has a 2½" square foot, only noticeable when placed side by side.

No. 610 was, and still is, easily damaged. Be sure to examine all the ridged panels and all the corners on each piece. You will be amazed how often a chipped or cracked piece of "Pyramid" is offered as mint.

Indiana made blue and black pieces of "Pyramid" for Tiara during the 1970s. You will see two sizes of black tumblers, blue and black berry bowls, small and large, and the four-part center-handled relish in either color. It was advertised as their Art Deco collection. If you like these colors, it is fine to buy them as a reissue from the original company. Just realize that they are not Depression era. Do not pay antique glass prices for them. That handled, four-part relish is sometimes mistaken for Tea Room, but it is not.

	Crystal	Pink	Green	Yellow
Bowl, 4¾", berry	20.00	35.00	35.00	55.00
Bowl, 8½", master berry	30.00	55.00	55.00	75.00
Bowl, 9½", oval	30.00	40.00	45.00	65.00
Bowl, 9½", pickle, 5¾" wide, handle	30.00	35.00	35.00	55.00
Creamer	20.00	35.00	30.00	40.00
Ice tub	95.00	125.00	115.00	225.00
Ice tub lid				650.00
Pitcher	395.00	395.00	265.00	550.00
Relish tray, 4-part, handle	25.00	60.00	65.00	67.50
Sugar	17.50	35.00	30.00	40.00
Tray for creamer and sugar	25.00	30.00	30.00	55.00
Tumbler, 8 ounce, footed, 2 styles	55.00	55.00	55.00	75.00
Tumbler, 11 ounce, footed	75.00	65.00	85.00	95.00

No. 612, "HORSESHOE" INDIANA GLASS COMPANY, 1930 – 1933

Colors: Green, yellow, pink, and crystal.

The official name for this Indiana pattern is No. 612, but collectors have nicknamed it "Horseshoe." In reality, that design does not fit any form of horseshoe ever made, but I guess that would be considered nit picking. It's a whimsical horseshoe. Newcomers tend to shy away from this lovely pattern due to its prices; and that's a shame, really. If you genuinely like something, even a piece or two can give you pleasure. Life's too short to continually deny yourself the small pleasures.

A green "Horseshoe" butter dish is most often lacking from collections, although tumblers, both flat and footed tea, grill plates (which not all collectors want), and pitchers are scarce. The only "Horseshoe" butter I have seen at a show recently was priced about $500.00 above selling price. That same butter has made the show tour for several years now without anyone buying it. At least everyone gets to see one that way which is a service to the show-going public. The "Horseshoe" butter dish has always been highly priced. If you can find a first edition of my book, the butter dish was $90.00 in 1972. That was big money for a butter back then. Actually, putting rare pieces out for "show" is a time-honored tradition in the antique trade. It dresses a booth and speaks to the quality of your merchandise. Some items dealers really don't want to sell.

Yellow pitchers, grill plates, and footed iced teas also create problems for collectors of that color. I have never pictured a yellow grill plate, but I have found one to show. Amazingly, this yellow grill and a crystal one I found do not have the inner rim roughness (irr) that was on the six green grill plates I previously owned.

There are two types of plates and platters. Some are plain in the center, while others have a pattern.

Candy dishes only have the pattern on the top. The bottom is plain. A few pink candy dishes have been found, but that candy is the only piece to ever surface in pink.

	Green	Yellow
Bowl, 4½", berry	30.00	25.00
Bowl, 6½", cereal	30.00	40.00
Bowl, 7½", salad	25.00	25.00
Bowl, 8½", vegetable	40.00	35.00
Bowl, 9½", large berry	50.00	50.00
Bowl, 10½", oval vegetable	30.00	33.00
Butter dish and cover	800.00	
Butter dish bottom	200.00	
Butter dish top	600.00	
Candy in metal holder motif on lid	195.00	
also, pink	165.00	
Creamer, footed	18.00	20.00
Cup	12.00	13.00
Pitcher, 8½", 64 ounce	295.00	350.00

	Green	Yellow
Plate, 6", sherbet	8.00	9.00
Plate, 8⅜", salad	12.00	12.00
Plate, 9⅜", luncheon	14.00	16.00
Plate, 10⅜", grill	125.00	150.00
Plate, 11½", sandwich	25.00	28.00
Platter, 10¾", oval	32.00	35.00
Relish, 3-part, footed	30.00	45.00
Saucer	5.00	5.00
Sherbet	16.00	18.00
Sugar, open	18.00	20.00
Tumbler, 4¼", 9 ounce	175.00	
Tumbler, 4¾", 12 ounce	175.00	
Tumbler, 9 ounce, footed	32.00	32.00
Tumbler, 12 ounce, footed	165.00	185.00

No. 616, "VERNON" INDIANA GLASS COMPANY, 1930 – 1932

Colors: Green, crystal, yellow.

No. 616 attracts a few collectors. It is another numbered Indiana pattern that was christened "Vernon" in honor of another glass author's spouse. Little is being discovered today; and collectors looking for it quickly buy what is found. We once used crystal No. 616 as everyday dishes. It was attractive; but I warn you from experience that there are rough mould lines protruding from the seams of the tumblers. After a cut lip or two from using the tumblers, this set was retired to the sale box. Today, a glass grinder could quickly take care of those problems.

What "Vernon" is turning up today is usually crystal. Some pieces are found trimmed in platinum (silver). Decorated pieces seldom have worn platinum. Evidently, Indiana's process for applying this trim was superior to other companies.

The 11½" sandwich plate is great for dinner or barbecue plates when grilling out. They are certainly lighter than the Fiesta chop plates that are used for grilled steaks and pizza. If you do use this reasonably priced pattern, it is either sandwich plates or the little 8" luncheon. For healthy appetites, that is what is called a "no brainer."

Photographing this pattern is a major obstacle. No. 616 is very delicate and light passes through without picking up the design well. I think we have succeeded.

Sets of yellow and green "Vernon" are difficult to complete, but there is even less green than yellow available. I continue to have difficulty locating a green tumbler and creamer.

	Green	Crystal	Yellow			Green	Crystal	Yellow
Creamer, footed	30.00	12.00	30.00	Saucer		4.00	3.00	4.00
Cup	18.00	10.00	18.00	Sugar, footed		30.00	11.00	30.00
Plate, 8", luncheon	9.50	12.00	9.50	Tumbler, 5", footed		45.00	20.00	45.00
Plate, 11½", sandwich	27.50	12.00	27.50					

No. 618, "PINEAPPLE & FLORAL" INDIANA GLASS COMPANY, 1932 – 1937

Colors: Crystal, amber; some fired-on red, green, milk white; late 1960s, avocado; 1980s pink, cobalt blue, etc.

Indiana reissued diamond-shaped comports and 7" salad bowls in "Pineapple and Floral" in a multitude of colors including the original crystal. Most had sprayed-on colors, although the light pink was an excellent transparent color. ("Pineapple and Floral" was never made in pink originally.) Unfortunately, prices for these two older crystal pieces slumped as result. Amber and fired-on red are safe colors to collect to avoid reissued ware.

A crystal "Pineapple and Floral" set is not easily put together; but, it is not impossible. Tumblers, cream soups, and sherbets are the most bothersome pieces to find. As with most of Indiana's patterns, there is some mould roughness on the seams, an impediment for some collectors. This is distinctively true on both sizes of tumblers. Most times this roughness comes from extra and not missing glass. Search for the harder-to-find pieces. The set is extraordinarily attractive as a whole due to the design that reflects light vividly.

There are two different plates that have an indented center ring. One is pictured in the foreground of the bottom picture. No one has encountered a top or anything to fit that ring as yet. A cheese dish is the idea most often proposed for this; but no top has turned up. The usual one seen is 11½" in diameter. You may see these advertised as a servitor — defined in my dictionary as a human servant. Call it what you wish.

Amber No. 618 is not collected as often as the crystal because there is so little of it available. I have been unable to unearth an amber tumbler. A customer in Texas just talked with me about helping her find amber bowls. Only plates have been found in light green. These are old and will glow under ultraviolet light.

The two-tier tidbit with a metal handle is not priced in my listings although one is pictured. These sell in the $25.00 to $30.00 range. The glass companies seldom made tidbits. They can easily be made today if you can find the metal hardware. Many tidbits are a product of the early 1970s when a dealer in St. Louis would make up any pattern for $10.00 if you furnished the plates. He did a great job!

The fired-on red pitcher that has been found with fired red sets of "Pineapple and Floral" has also been located with sets of fired red Daisy. The color is dull, having no sheen, as is most of this fired-on red. There is a crosshatching design on the base of the pitcher similar to that of No. 618, but that is where the similarity to "Pineapple and Floral" ends. There is no resemblance to Daisy.

There are a few items to be found in milk glass that should please the burgeoning group of collectors for that.

	Crystal	Amber, Red		Crystal	Amber, Red
Ashtray, 4½"	17.50	20.00	Plate, 11½", w/indentation	25.00	
Bowl, 4¾", berry	25.00	20.00	Plate, 11½", sandwich	20.00	17.50
Bowl, 6", cereal	30.00	25.00	Platter, 11", closed handle	15.00	18.00
* Bowl, 7", salad	2.00	10.00	Platter, relish, 11½", divided	18.00	
Bowl, 10", oval vegetable	25.00	20.00	Saucer	4.00	4.00
* Comport, diamond-shaped	1.00	8.00	Sherbet, footed	18.00	20.00
Creamer, diamond-shaped	9.00	10.00	Sugar, diamond-shaped	9.00	10.00
Cream soup	22.00	22.00	Tumbler, 4¼", 8 ounce	32.00	25.00
Cup	10.00	10.00	Tumbler, 5", 12 ounce	50.00	
Plate, 6", sherbet	4.00	5.00	Vase, cone-shaped	60.00	
Plate, 8⅜", salad	8.50	8.50	Vase holder, metal 35.00		
** Plate, 9⅜", dinner	15.00	15.00			

* Reproduced in several colors   **Green $45.00

OLD CAFE HOCKING GLASS COMPANY, 1936 – 1940

Colors: Pink, crystal, and Royal Ruby.

Collectors adore this small pattern marketed over 60 years ago; and surprisingly, you seldom go to a market without finding a piece (alas, not plates), indicating it was in generous supply years ago. People evidently found it agreeable back then, also. Old Cafe lamps, pitchers, and dinner plates are very elusive and they are expensive compared to the rest of the pattern. Pitchers, pictured in earlier editions, have alternating large panels with two small panels that constitute the make-up of all Old Cafe pieces. The pitcher that is often mislabeled Old Cafe can be seen on pages 184 under Hocking's Pillar Optic. Some collectors are mistakenly buying Pillar Optic (evenly spaced panels) for Old Café because dealers are labeling them as such. I recommend some time spent in a good book to learn these differences. The juice pitcher is shaped like the Mayfair juice pitcher.

Lamps are found in pink and Royal Ruby colors. Lamps were sometimes made by drilling through a vase, but the pink one shown here has ball feet to raise it enough to allow the cord to pass under the edge. The 5" bowl has an open handle while the 4½" bowl has tab handles, as does the 3¾" berry. The footed sherbet (pictured in row 2) also measures 3¾".

Royal Ruby Old Cafe cups are found on crystal saucers (shown). No Old Cafe Royal Ruby saucers have ever surfaced. A 5½" crystal candy with a Royal Ruby lid is also pictured. No Royal Ruby bottom has been spotted.

The low candy (or footed tray) is 8⅜" including handles, and 6½" without. You can see a pink and crystal one on either side of the large pink plate.

Hocking made a cookie jar (a numbered line) which is an excellent "go-with" piece. It is ribbed up the sides similar to Old Cafe but has a crosshatched lid that does not conform to Old Cafe. There is also a similar looking Hocking-made candy box and lid that untutored people often mistake for Old Café.

	Crystal, Pink	Royal Ruby		Crystal, Pink	Royal Ruby
Bowl, 3¾", berry tab handles	14.00	9.00	Pitcher, 6", 36 oz.	125.00	
Bowl, 5½", cereal, no handles	35.00		Pitcher, 80 ounce	150.00	
Bowl, 6½", open handles	15.00		Plate, 6", sherbet	4.00	
Bowl, 9", closed handles	12.00	18.00	Plate, 10", dinner	65.00	
Candy dish, 8", low, tab handles	14.00	18.00	Saucer	5.00	
Candy jar, 5½", crystal with ruby cover		25.00	Sherbet, 3¾", low ftd.	16.00	12.00
Cup	12.00	12.00	Tumbler, 3", juice	18.00	20.00
Lamp	100.00	150.00	Tumbler, 4", water	22.00	30.00
Olive dish, 6", oblong	10.00		Vase, 7¼"	45.00	50.00

OLD COLONY "LACE EDGE," "OPEN LACE" HOCKING GLASS COMPANY, 1935 – 1938

Colors: Pink and some crystal and green.

In December 1990, I spent a day at Anchor Hocking going through old files and catalogs. I encountered some old store display photographs (page 160 and 161) promoting the name of this glass as Old Colony. I was thrilled to find an authentic name for the pattern which Hocking workers called "Lace." Don't you wish our ancestors had stocked up on those dime sherbets and underliners? No Old Colony sherbet plate has been seen. Regardless, one engineer wrote that he had tried to gauge the size of those plates with his instruments and his supposition was they were saucer size. Oh, to know for certain!

If you collect this popular Old Colony, always check the "lace" around the edge. It damages easily. Plates and bowls should be stored carefully. A paper plate between each piece is a must when stacking or packing glassware. Candlesticks, console bowls, and vases are hard to find in mint condition, but are available with chips and nicks.

Ribs on the footed tumbler extend approximately half way up the side as they do on the cup. This tumbler is often confused with the Coronation tumbler that has a similar shape and design. See the Coronation photograph and read there, also. Notice the fine ribbed effect from the middle up on the Coronation tumbler. This upper ribbing is omitted on Old Colony tumblers.

Satinized or frosted pieces presently sell for a fraction of the cost of their unfrosted counterparts in Old Colony. Lack of demand is one reason. Possibly vases and candlesticks are rare because so many of them were satinized. I have shown those items frosted this time. If satinized pieces still have the original painted floral decorations, they will fetch 25% more than the prices listed for them. So far, only a few collectors think frosted Old Colony is beautiful; but I have noticed lately that more are considering it because of price — or perhaps because "blending" has become more legitimate.

Notice the green bowl in the bottom photo. It was found in the basement of a former Anchor Hocking employee. He thought that they made other pieces, but was not sure. It is the only green piece I have ever verified as Hocking. I think it had a ground bottom.

The flower bowl with crystal frog becomes a candy jar with a cover added in place of the frog. It was marketed both ways. That cover is the same as fits the butter dish or bonbon as Hocking actually listed it. The 7" comport becomes a footed candy with a cookie lid added. This piece was listed as a covered comport; but today, many dealers call it a footed candy jar. Since both these lids fit two items, it doesn't take a genius to figure why there is a lid shortage today. There are two styles of 7¾" and 9½" bowls. Some are ribbed up the side and some are not. The smaller, non-ribbed salad bowl is also the butter bottom. Both sizes of ribbed bowls are harder to find than their non-ribbed counterparts. Moulds were expensive. It was common practice for as many pieces as possible to be obtained from as few moulds as possible.

The true 9" comport in Old Colony has a rayed base. There is a comparable comport that also measures 9". This "pretender" has a plain foot and was probably made by Standard or Lancaster Glass. It has been shown in earlier editions. Both Lancaster and Standard had very similar designs, but their glass generally was better quality and rings when gently tapped on the edge with your finger. Hocking's Old Colony makes a thud sound. If the piece is not shown in my listing, or is in any color other than pink or crystal, the likelihood of your having an Old Colony piece is meager at best.

	Pink		Pink
* Bowl, 6⅜", cereal	30.00	Flower bowl, crystal frog	30.00
Bowl, 7¾", ribbed, salad	60.00	Plate, 7¼", salad	30.00
Bowl, 8¼", crystal	12.00	Plate, 8¼", luncheon	25.00
Bowl, 9½", plain	32.00	Plate, 10½", dinner	37.50
Bowl, 9½", ribbed	35.00	Plate, 10½", grill	30.00
** Bowl, 10½", 3 legs, frosted $65.00	265.00	Plate, 10½", 3-part relish	30.00
Butter dish or bonbon with cover	70.00	Plate, 13", solid lace	65.00
Butter dish bottom, 7¾"	30.00	Plate, 13", 4-part, solid lace	70.00
Butter dish top	40.00	Platter, 12¾"	42.00
** Candlesticks, pair, frosted $95.00	350.00	Platter, 12¾", 5-part	40.00
Candy jar and cover, ribbed	50.00	Relish dish, 7½", 3-part, deep	75.00
Comport, 7"	30.00	Saucer	12.00
Comport, 7", and cover, footed	65.00	** Sherbet, footed	120.00
Comport, 9"	995.00	Sugar	30.00
Cookie jar and cover, frosted $60.00	75.00	Tumbler, 3½", 5 ounce, flat	150.00
Creamer	30.00	Tumbler, 4½", 9 ounce, flat	25.00
Cup	28.00	Tumbler, 5", 10½ ounce, footed	95.00
Fish bowl, 1 gallon, 8 ounce (crystal only)	30.00	Vase, 7", frosted $90.00	695.00

* Officially listed as cereal or cream soup, green $75.00   ** Price is for absolute mint condition

OLD ENGLISH, "THREADING" INDIANA GLASS COMPANY, Late 1920s

Colors: Green, amber, pink, crystal, crystal with flashed colors, and forest green.

Old English can be assembled in sets of green and possibly amber. All pieces are known in green. Some pieces have never surfaced in amber. That does not mean they were never produced. Amber Old English is a deep color more indicative of Cambridge or New Martinsville products which collectors find so enticing. Most of the amber pieces I've owned over the years have found willing buyers, but green is a bit easier to buy or sell.

Pink Old English is rarely seen with only the center-handled server, cheese and cracker, and sherbets found periodically. Additional pieces in pink exist, but seldom surface. I did find a pink pitcher and tumbler (below); it was only the second pink pitcher I had ever seen. Crystal Old English is found with artistic decorations; undecorated crystal is rarely seen.

Old English footed pieces are more readily available than flat items. I haven't seen a green center-handled server in almost 25 years. There are two styles of sherbets. One is pictured in green and the other in pink. Both large and small berry bowls and the flat candy dish are in meager supply. Sugar and candy jar lids have the same cloverleaf-type knob as the pitcher. The flat candy lid is comparable in size to the pitcher lid; but that pitcher lid is notched in the bottom rim to allow for pouring. You cannot co-mingle the two lids since the candy lid is not notched. That flat candy is often found in a metal holder.

Only crystal egg cups have turned up. A fan vase is the only piece I have ever seen in dark green. A flashed-lavender footed candy bottom is shown. Does anyone have a lid?

	Pink, Green, Amber
Bowl, 4", flat	22.00
Bowl, 9", footed fruit	40.00
Bowl, 9½", flat	35.00
Candlesticks, 4", pair	40.00
Candy dish and cover, flat	60.00
Candy jar with lid	60.00
Compote, 3½" tall, 6⅜" across, 2-handle	22.50
Compote, 3½" tall, 7" across	25.00
Compote, 3½", cheese for plate	20.00
Creamer	17.50
Egg cup (crystal only)	10.00
Fruit stand, 11", footed	45.00
Goblet, 5¾", 8 ounce	35.00
Pitcher	75.00
Pitcher and cover	135.00
Plate, indent for compote	20.00
Sandwich server, center handle	55.00
Sherbet, 2 styles	20.00
Sugar	17.50
Sugar cover	35.00
Tumbler, 4½", footed	28.00

	Pink, Green, Amber
Tumbler, 5½", footed	40.00
Vase, 5⅜", fan type, 7" wide	65.00
Vase, 8", footed, 4½" wide	55.00
Vase, 8¼", footed, 4¼" wide	55.00
Vase, 12", footed	75.00

OLIVE, LINE #134 IMPERIAL GLASS COMPANY, Late 1930s

Colors: Red, light blue, emerald, pink.

Imperial's Olive Line #134 is a smaller pattern whose major claim to fame is its confusion with Imperial's Old English, Line #166. Think round olives and that will help. Olive also has circles in its design near the bottom of the pieces and ribbed feet. Old English Line #166 has elongated designs reaching skyward from its base with olive type balls held between a dividing line ribbon above the elongation. The plates in Old English, however, do have a kind of ribbed flower center design raying from a ball circle. You will notice that the plates in Olive Line #134 have plain centers. Confusing? You bet! Actually, they are so compatible that should you care to collect both lines as one pattern, few will notice and you can get some tumblers from Old English that you will not have with Olive. Olive pattern has handled mugs instead.

	Emerald/Pink	Blue/Red		Emerald/Pink	Blue/Red
Bowl, 6½", flared, footed	15.00	20.00	Compote, 6½"	12.50	22.50
Bowl, 7", rose (cupped)	20.00	30.00	Creamer	10.00	15.00
Bowl, 7", shallow	15.00	25.00	Cup	8.00	10.00
Bowl, 9", fruit, pedestal foot	20.00	35.00	Mayonnaise	12.50	15.00
Bowl, 9", bun or fruit tray	20.00	35.00	Plate, 6"	4.00	5.50
Bowl, 9", shallow	25.00	35.00	Plate, 8"	8.00	10.00
Bowl, 10¼", salad	30.00	45.00	Plate, 12"	18.00	25.00
Candle, 2½"	15.00	20.00	Saucer	3.00	4.00
Candy jar w/lid	30.00	40.00	Sugar	10.00	15.00
Compote, 6"	10.00	20.00			

"ORCHID" PADEN CITY GLASS COMPANY, Early 1930s

Colors: Yellow, cobalt blue, crystal, green, amber, pink, red, and black.

"Orchid," as well as all other patterns manufactured by Paden City, are generating enormous price leaps. All Paden City patterns were more limited in production runs than those of some of the larger glass companies. Orchid growers and collectors may have sparked the interest for this one pattern, but the Internet has unveiled many pieces of these smaller patterns (like Orchid) that few previously had a chance to discover. Instead of dozens buying at shows, there are now thousands eyeing pieces. This "Orchid" pattern was not produced in hundreds of thousands of pieces as was Heisey's Orchid. Every piece of Paden's "Orchid" we have displayed at shows has sold not long after the show opened — if not before.

Many believed that "Orchid" etched pieces turned up only on #412 Line, the square, Crow's Foot blank made by Paden City. See the yellow sandwich server pictured below. However, "Orchid" has turned up on the #890 rounded blank as well (comport in center, bottom of page 166). Thus, "Orchid" may well turn up on any Paden City blank. A few pieces of "Orchid" are being found on black, but only a few. As a matter of fact, red and cobalt blue pieces seem to be the preferred colors and appear in proportional numbers. The pattern displays better on transparent colors, but they do not seem to be as popular with the buying public.

There are at least three distinct "Orchid" arrangements found on Paden City blanks. Collectors do not mind blending these varieties because so little of any one is found.

New reports of etched Paden City patterns are not unusual. Most pieces were shown in catalogs with no etchings; and until a piece shows up with a particular etching, there is no way to know if it exists in that pattern.

	All Other Colors	Red Black Cobalt Blue		All Other Colors	Red Black Cobalt Blue
Bowl, 4⅞", square	30.00	55.00	Comport, 6⅝" tall, 7" wide	65.00	135.00
Bowl, 8½", 2-handle	75.00	135.00	Creamer	55.00	100.00
Bowl, 8¾", square	75.00	125.00	Ice bucket, 6"	95.00	195.00
Bowl, 10", footed, square	95.00	195.00	Mayonnaise, 3-piece	85.00	165.00
Bowl, 11", square	85.00	195.00	Plate, 8½", square		125.00
Cake stand, square, 2" high	75.00	150.00	Sandwich server, center handle	75.00	125.00
Candlesticks, 5¾", pair	110.00	195.00	Sugar	50.00	100.00
Candy with lid, 6½", square, 3-part	110.00	195.00	Vase, 8"	95.00	275.00
Candy with lid, cloverleaf, 3-part	95.00	195.00	Vase, 10"	125.00	295.00
Comport, 3¼" tall, 6¼" wide	25.00	55.00			

OVIDE, "NEW CENTURY" HAZEL ATLAS GLASS COMPANY, 1930 – 1935

Colors: Green, black, white Platonite trimmed with fired-on colors in 1950s.

Varieties of decorated Ovide sets are available if you are wishing to find an economical one to use. Finding any specific decoration may prove to be a chore. Separating these decorations into time eras for my books has been a task. Call the decorated white one "Windmills" for categorizing purposes due to our dearth of actual names. This is priced below under the decorated white heading.

Hazel Atlas used a flock of different patterns on this popular Platonite, including one of flying geese. One of the more popular, judging from the amount being found today, was the black floral design with red and yellow edge trim. That set covered kitchenware items (stacking sets and mixing bowls) as well as a dinnerware line. You can see later made patterns in *Collectible Glassware from the 40s, 50s, 60s....* For some of these patterns I have found documentation and they are correctly named.

The "Flying Ducks" (actually geese) set is priced under decorated white and not as Art Deco. Only the Art Deco pieces are priced under that column and were shown in earlier editions. I have been unable to find a single piece of it in these last years. You will never be able to sell any other decorated Ovide for those Art Deco prices. The egg cup in the "Flying Ducks" pattern is selling in the $12.00 to $15.00 range. It is peculiar that no other patterns have had egg cups reported except for crystal ones in English Hobnail and Old English.

Very little black, transparent green, or yellow Ovide are ever seen, but there are a few collectors asking for it. A luncheon set should be possible; but it would be simpler to put together the type set in black or yellow Cloverleaf which would be admittedly be more costly but, also, more easily found. Depression glass dealers are prone to bring the Cloverleaf pattern to shows, but leave the Ovide home.

	Black	Green	Decorated White	Art Deco		Black	Green	Decorated White	Art Deco
Bowl, 4¾", berry			8.00		Plate, 8", luncheon		3.00	14.00	60.00
Bowl, 5½", cereal			13.00		Plate, 9", dinner			20.00	
Bowl, 8", large berry			22.50		Platter, 11"			22.50	
Candy dish and cover	45.00	22.00	35.00		Salt and pepper, pair	27.50	27.50	24.00	
Cocktail, footed, fruit	5.00	4.00			Saucer	3.50	2.50	6.00	20.00
Creamer	6.50	4.50	17.50	110.00	Sherbet	6.50	3.00	14.00	75.00
Cup	7.50	3.50	12.50	85.00	Sugar, open	6.50	6.00	17.50	110.00
Plate, 6", sherbet		2.50	6.00		Tumbler			17.50	110.00

OYSTER AND PEARL ANCHOR HOCKING GLASS CORPORATION, 1938 – 1940

Colors: Pink, crystal, Royal Ruby, Vitrock, and Vitrock with fired-on pink, blue, and green.

Royal Ruby Oyster and Pearl can be found under the Royal Ruby pattern shown on page 207, but prices are also found here. Pink Oyster and Pearl has often been used as complementary pieces for other Depression glass patterns. That pink relish dish and candlesticks sell rapidly since they are reasonably priced in comparison to other patterns. That is not as true as it once was, but Oyster and Pearl prices are cheaper than most patterns in this book. This pattern sells well and makes wonderful gifts. We habitually try to start newlyweds off with a gift of Depression glass, including a note telling the history. We have found this custom to be well received. Unfortunately, some of those marriages haven't lasted as long as the glass.

That Oyster and Pearl relish dish measures 11½" including the handles. I mention that because of letters I receive wondering what piece is 11½" when I list a 10½" relish. All measurements in this book are taken without handles unless otherwise mentioned. Glass companies rarely measured the handles. I have made a point to talk about measurements with handles in my commentary since I have been getting so many letters about measurements on pieces that I have already listed. There is no divided bowl in Oyster and Pearl; it was (and is) listed as a relish and pictured in the foreground on the bottom of page 169 in pink and crystal.

I had a report of a lamp made from candleholders; it was two candles glued together at their bases to make a ball. Obviously, someone had more time on his or her hands to play around than I do. Many patterns had lamps made out of candleholders or vases. Sometimes these were factory made; more often, some other company who bought the parts from the factory, fabricated these. When available, lamps do add appeal to your collection or décor.

I have seen a few crystal pieces decorated, and most of them were trimmed in red. They sell faster than undecorated crystal. The 10½" fruit bowl is a great salad bowl and the 13½" plate makes a wonderful server; several collectors have used these for a small punch bowl and liner. You will have to decide what punch cups to use.

Pink fired over Vitrock was called Dusty Rose; the fired green was called Springtime Green by Hocking. Most collectors love these shades; but I've met a few who loathe them. The undecorated Vitrock is infrequently seen, and not as fascinating. A few pieces have been found with fired blue, but this must have been very limited.

The pink, 6½", deep bowl is often found with metal attached to the handles for holding a spoon. This was another of the marketing gimmicks of that time. With tongs it could serve as a small ice bowl or serving dish. It was another way to retail this bowl.

The spouted, 5½" bowl is often referred to as heart shaped. It might serve as a gravy or sauce boat although most people use them for candy dishes. The same bowl is found without the spout in Royal Ruby, although I mistakenly listed it in the past. I investigated this a bit further after several collectors called it to my attention. This bowl always has a spout in Dusty Rose and Springtime Green.

	Crystal, Pink	Royal Ruby	White and Fired-On Green Or Pink
Bowl, 5¼", heart-shaped, 1-handled	15.00		12.00
Bowl, 5½", 1-handled		20.00	
Bowl, 6½", deep-handled	20.00	27.50	
Bowl, 10½", deep fruit	25.00	60.00	25.00
Candle holder, 3½", pair	40.00	65.00	30.00
Plate, 13½", sandwich	20.00	55.00	
Relish dish, 10½", oblong, divided	18.00		

"PARROT," SYLVAN FEDERAL GLASS COMPANY, 1931 – 1932

Colors: Green, amber; some crystal and blue.

"Parrot" is one of those Depression glass patterns having several rare pieces, which has a noticeable history of price surges. Prices will level off to a steady keel and then, suddenly, several collectors want "Parrot" at the same time, causing prices to increase very rapidly. I've watched these cycles repeat themselves for 30 years.

Parrot pitchers seem to have left the market at any price. Prices for the few made available reached a ballpark figure of $3,000. A few buyers willing to pay that price did. Very few pitchers are found. Originally, a cache of 37 was found in the basement of an old hardware store in central Ohio. Today, there are over 30 still in existence. I know at least a couple of those have been broken. One cracked from a dealer dusting it out and bumping a ring in a thin spot. The whole pitcher is thin, but where the pattern is moulded it gets even thinner.

There are two types of "Parrot" hot plates. One, shown in the pattern shot, is shaped like the pointed edged Madrid and the other, round, is more like the one in Georgian; it was photographed previously. One of these round ones has now appeared in amber.

The amber butter dish, creamer, and sugar lid are all harder to find than green; and even fewer mint butter dish tops or sugar lids surface. The less than mint ones are available. (Damaged glassware should not bring mint prices.) Frequently found butter bottoms have an indented ledge for the top. The jam dish is the same size as the butter bottom, but without the ledge. The jam dish has never been located in green, but is fairly common in amber. There are fewer collectors of amber "Parrot"; so, prices are not as volatile and affected by demand, as are those for green.

Notice that "Parrot" tumblers are found on Madrid-like moulds except for the heavy-footed tumbler, whose pointy edges sometimes chip. The supply of heavy, footed tumblers (in both colors), green water tumblers, and thin, flat iced teas in amber has met demand. Apparently, the thin, moulded, footed tumbler did not accept the "Parrot" design favorably and the heavier version was made. The thin, 10 ounce footed tumbler has only been found in amber. Prices for both those last two tumblers have remained steady during other "Parrot" price increases.

A cracked shaker is on the bottom row. It's my way to give otherwise useless old glass a function. You still get to see size, shape, and color, and a collector gets to enjoy a good piece. It seems better than having them thrown away or having desirable glass stored in photography boxes for years with no one able to enjoy it. It's a win-win situation. Actually, many dealers now offer me their damaged, hard-to-find pieces, at reasonable prices so I can photograph them for my books. At least one artist I met does her conserving part, too. She uses damaged pieces of Depression glass in her art, glass windows and such.

Blue "Parrot" sherbets turn up occasionally; one was pictured earlier.

Now, one last comment in the "for what it's worth" department. I was talking to another dealer about the stuff I see sitting in shops that was there five years ago and remarking that there is *no way* there was any profit left in that piece after paying rent, help, supplies, utilities, inventory tax, et al. He chimed in with this example. About a year before a dealer put out a large set of green and amber glassware. A week after he put it out, a buyer came in and offered him "book" price for all of it. He declined (!) since he had priced some of the harder to find pieces for 20% to 30% more than book. All the rest was commonly found flatware. Today, a year later, most of the harder to find pieces are gone; but stacks of flatware remain. Now, perhaps he's gotten all his money out of the good pieces and all that other stuff is "free." More likely, he's still got money tied up (for over a year) in what is left that isn't selling. It's our belief you can well *afford* to make a lesser profit *fast* and turn that profit into four or five more profits in a year's time and come out better in the long run. We think it's better to take that fast-offered smaller profit in hand and buy something else to resell than to take six months or longer to get a little more out of something which you're now *paying* to have the remainders sit idle.

	Green	Amber		Green	Amber
Bowl, 5", berry	30.00	23.00	Plate, 9", dinner	58.00	47.50
Bowl, 7", soup	55.00	38.00	Plate, 10½", round, grill	33.00	
Bowl, 8", large berry	100.00	90.00	Plate, 10½", square, grill		32.00
Bowl, 10", oval vegetable	70.00	75.00	Plate, 10¼", square (crystal only)	26.00	
Butter dish and cover	425.00	1,350.00	Platter, 11¼", oblong	65.00	75.00
Butter dish bottom	65.00	200.00	Salt and pepper, pair	295.00	
Butter dish top	360.00	1,150.00	Saucer	15.00	17.50
Creamer, footed	60.00	85.00	* Sherbet, footed cone	25.00	22.50
Cup	42.00	42.00	Sherbet, 4¼" high	1,450.00	
Hot plate, 5", pointed	895.00	995.00	Sugar	40.00	50.00
Hot plate, 5", round	995.00		Sugar cover	175.00	550.00
Jam dish, 7"		38.00	Tumbler, 4¼", 10 ounce	195.00	135.00
Pitcher, 8½", 80 ounce	2,995.00		Tumbler, 5½", 12 ounce	225.00	165.00
Plate, 5¾", sherbet	35.00	23.00	Tumbler, 5¾", footed, heavy	195.00	135.00
Plate, 7½", salad	40.00		Tumbler, 5½", 10 oz., ftd (Madrid mould)		175.00

*Blue $225.00

"PARTY LINE," "SODA FOUNTAIN" LINE #191, 191½, #192 PADEN CITY GLASS COMPANY, LATE 1920s – 1951; CANTON GLASS COMPANY, 1950s

Colors: Amber, crystal, green, pink (Cheriglo), red, some turquoise green.

People have asked me off and on for years why I didn't put this line in my books. I'm really not certain, perhaps because of a bit of personal bias and knowing it was continually made through the fifties; perhaps because it didn't exactly fit the time parameters I had set for this book and it didn't have a lot of dinnerware pieces. (Jerry Barnett reported in his Paden City book that factory workers called this "Soda Fountain," certainly an apt name judging by the pieces made.) Now, with so many traditional Depression wares disappearing from the collecting market, I still see this pattern languishing on shelves and know it has just as much right to be in the book as any other pattern; and, to be frank, Cathy took the bull by the horns and started buying it to be included and then went down and loaded it in the van for the photography session when I was complaining there was no way there would be enough room in the book for all the new patterns and this, too. We are running out of space in this book for adding listings. If we have to add more pages, the book is going to have to increase in price, something we've tried really hard not to do these many years of *color* production. (Have you noticed all the new books rolling off the presses with only a *few* pages of color clustered in the center of the book, and then miles of black and white history filling page after page?) They all cost more, too!

If you've been collecting this for years and have valuable knowledge of which of the multitude of tumblers are hard to find, we'd appreciate hearing from you.

	*All colors		*All colors		*All colors
Banana split, 8½", oval	25.00	Custard, 6 ounce	8.00	Shaker, sugar	155.00
Bottle, 22 ounce, wine w/stopper	45.00	Ice tub & pail	55.00	Sherbet, 3½ or 4½ ounce, footed	10.00
Bottle, 48 ounce, water, no stopper	40.00	Ice tub, 6½", w/tab handle	45.00	Shaker, sugar	155.00
Bowl, 4½", nappy	8.00	Jar w/lid, high, crushed fruit	65.00	Sherbet, 3½ or 4½ ounce, footed	10.00
Bowl, 6½", berry	10.00	Marmalade, w/cover, 12 ounce	35.00	Sherbet, 6 ounce, high foot	12.50
Bowl, 7", mixing	20.00	Mayo, 6", footed	25.00	Stem, 9 ounce	15.00
Bowl, 8", mixing	25.00	Parfait, 5 ounce (2 styles)	12.50	Sugar, 7 ounce	10.00
Bowl, 9", berry	25.00	Pitcher, 30 ounce, jug, w/cover	65.00	Sugar w/id, 10 ounce hotel	22.50
Bowl, 9", low foot comport, flare	27.50	Pitcher, 32 ounce, grape juice w/lid	95.00	Sundae, 4 or 6 ounce tulip	15.00
Bowl, 9", mixing	30.00	Pitcher, 36 ounce, measure w/5½"		Sundae, 9 ounce crimped	20.00
Bowl, 10½", high foot, flare	35.00	reamer	125.00	Syrup, 8 ounce	45.00
Bowl, 11", low foot comport	35.00	Pitcher, 70 ounce, jug w or w/optic,		Syrup w/glass cover, 12 ounce	75.00
Bowl, 11", vegetable, flare	35.00	w/lid	135.00	Tumbler, 1½ oz., footed, cordial	15.00
Butter box, w/cover, round flat lid	55.00	Plate 6"	6.00	Tumbler, 2½ or 3½ oz., ftd, cocktail	12.50
Candy, footed w/cover	35.00	Plate, 8"	10.00	Tumbler, 3 ounce, wine	12.00
Cigarette holder w/cover. footed	45.00	Plate, 10½" cracker, w/covered		Tumbler, 4½ ounce, juice	8.00
Cocktail shaker, 18 ounce, w/lid	65.00	cheese	65.00	Tumbler, 5 ounce, coke	12.00
Cologne, 1½ ounce	55.00	Saucer, 5¾"	3.00	Tumbler, 6 ounce, 3 styles	12.00
Creamer, 7 ounce	10.00	Server, 10", center handle	40.00	Tumbler, 7 ounce, 2 styles	12.00
Cup, 6 ounce	8.00	Shaker, pair	35.00	Tumbler, 8 ounce, 3 styles	14.00

	*All colors
Tumbler, 9 ounce, barrel	12.00
Tumbler, 10 ounce, 3 styles	12.00
Tumbler, 12 ounce, blown	15.00
Tumbler, 12 ounce, 4 styles	14.00
Tumbler, 14 ounce, 3 styles	14.00
Vase, 6", fan	40.00
Vase, 7", fan	45.00
Vase, 7", crimped	45.00

*Double the price for red and 50% for crystal.

PATRICIAN, "SPOKE" FEDERAL GLASS COMPANY, 1933 – 1937

Colors: Pink, green, crystal, and amber ("Golden Glo").

Patrician amber was extensively marketed, perhaps more than any other Federal pattern except Madrid. Amber is available to anyone wishing to start a set and it has never been reproduced like Madrid. Sets of green or pink Patrician can probably still be assembled with determination, but at greater cost. The plentiful, amber, 10½" dinner plates we've now discovered were given away with 20-pound sacks of flour as cake plates. Displays of these plates sat on the counter and when you paid for your flour, you were handed one of these as a bonus. Since I started buying Depression glass over 30 years ago, that plate has been called a dinner plate. I discovered my mom had stacks of these received with the purchase of flour when they first married and had been giving them away with meals sent home with her day care help. My dad had received a set as a gift for delivering newspapers as a boy. Two marketing ploys for this pattern were represented in my family.

As in Federal's "Parrot" and Sharon patterns, the jam dish is a butter bottom without the indented ledge for the top and measures 6¾" wide and stands 1¼" deep. This is the same measurement as the butter bottom; still, Patrician cereal bowls are often confused with jam dishes. Cereals are 6" in diameter and 1¾" deep. Prices differ; be aware of which is which.

There is more green Patrician available than either pink or crystal. Nevertheless, green dinner plates are infrequently found. Completing a set of pink is difficult, but it might be impossible in crystal since not all pieces have turned up.

Amber pitchers were supposedly made in two styles. The one pictured has a moulded handle. If anyone owns an applied handle amber pitcher, let me know as I am beginning to doubt it exists. In crystal and green, the applied handled pitcher is easier to find.

In Patrician, mint condition sugar lids, jam dishes, footed tumblers, cookie or butter bottoms, and footed tumblers are harder to find than other pieces. Check sugar lids for signs of repair. Many a glass grinder has cut his teeth on those. That cookie bottom is rare in green. There are several lids found for each bottom. This is another pattern where saucers are also harder to find than cups.

	Amber, Crystal	Pink	Green		Amber, Crystal	Pink	Green
Bowl, 4¾", cream soup	15.00	22.00	22.00	Plate, 6", sherbet	10.00	8.00	10.00
Bowl, 5", berry	14.00	12.00	16.00	Plate, 7½", salad	15.00	15.00	20.00
Bowl, 6", cereal	28.00	25.00	32.00	Plate, 9", luncheon	13.00	16.00	16.00
Bowl, 8½", large berry	45.00	35.00	40.00	Plate, 10½", dinner	8.00	40.00	45.00
Bowl, 10", oval vegetable	35.00	30.00	35.00	Plate, 10½", grill	14.00	15.00	20.00
Butter dish and cover	95.00	225.00	140.00	Platter, 11½", oval	32.00	25.00	30.00
Butter dish bottom	60.00	175.00	80.00	Salt and pepper, pair	60.00	110.00	75.00
Butter dish top	30.00	50.00	60.00	Saucer	9.50	10.00	9.50
Cookie jar and cover	95.00		650.00	Sherbet	13.00	17.00	14.00
Creamer, footed	11.00	12.00	15.00	Sugar	9.00	9.00	15.00
Cup	9.00	15.00	14.00	Sugar cover	60.00	65.00	80.00
Jam dish	30.00	30.00	40.00	Tumbler, 4", 5 ounce	33.00	33.00	33.00
Pitcher, 8", 75 ounce, moulded				Tumbler, 4¼", 9 ounce	30.00	26.00	30.00
handle	135.00	125.00	165.00	Tumbler, 5½", 14 ounce	48.00	45.00	55.00
Pitcher, 8¼", 75 ounce, applied				Tumbler, 5¼", 8 ounce, footed	57.50		70.00
handle	*110.00	150.00	175.00	*Crystal only			

"PATRICK" LANCASTER GLASS COMPANY, Early 1930s

Colors: Yellow and pink.

Yellow "Patrick" luncheon sets are being found, but other pieces are not. I had reports of some crystal being seen, but was unable to confirm this sighting. Look for a piece for me. A few pink "Patrick" luncheon sets have been discovered, but the price has scared away all but enthusiastic collectors, though prices have softened a bit for pink. Little has come up for sale, recently, which could account for that. This was a very limited production before anyone ever came up with the idea of limiting productions in order to sell you something for more money. Jubilee was distributed heavily in the Northwest and Florida, but "Patrick" seems infrequently found anywhere. It was very likely made as a small promotion item, a lure for some company's product.

Pink "Patrick" sugar or creamers had been selling for $75.00 each, but that has been slipping some, as new collectors seem to get sticker shock when asked that price. I only record market prices; I do not make them. The "Patrick" three-footed candy is shaped just as the Jubilee one shown in the twelfth edition.

"Patrick" serving pieces are rare. The pattern is bold on the 11" console bowl. I bought one not long ago from a dealer who "knows everything" about Depression glass (except what "Patrick" looks like). I've learned never to skip a booth just because there will probably not be any bargains to be had. There are similar serving pieces to be found in other patterns on the same blanks used for "Patrick" and Jubilee. However, these similar pieces should sell more reasonably than those with "Patrick" and Jubilee designs.

	Pink	Yellow		Pink	Yellow
Bowl, 9", handled fruit	185.00	145.00	Mayonnaise, 3-piece	195.00	150.00
Bowl, 11", console	165.00	145.00	Plate, 7", sherbet	20.00	12.00
Candlesticks, pair	195.00	150.00	Plate, 7½", salad	25.00	20.00
Candy dish, 3-footed	195.00	195.00	Plate, 8", luncheon	40.00	25.00
Cheese & cracker set	150.00	125.00	Saucer	20.00	12.00
Creamer	65.00	37.50	Sherbet, 4¾"	75.00	60.00
Cup	65.00	35.00	Sugar	65.00	37.50
Goblet, 4", cocktail	80.00	80.00	Tray, 11", 2-handled	75.00	60.00
Goblet, 4¾", 6 ounce, juice	80.00	75.00	Tray, 11", center-handled	155.00	110.00
Goblet, 6", 10 ounce, water	80.00	70.00			

"PEACOCK REVERSE" LINE #411, #412 & #991 PADEN CITY GLASS COMPANY, 1930s

Colors: Cobalt blue, red, amber, yellow, green, pink, black, and crystal.

Paden City's Line #412 ("Crow's Foot"), Line #991 ("Penny Line"), and Line #411 (square shapes with the corners cut off) comprise the standard blanks on which "Peacock Reverse" has been found. Add to those the octagonal plate pictured in the back and no telling which blank will turn up with "Peacock Reverse" etching. Paden City lines have various etched patterns. Often you will spot a piece from a distance which turns out to be the wrong etch when you get close enough for identification. (Those designs, which show white in the photograph, have been accentuated with chalk so you can see them better.)

That pink, eight-sided plate is the only plate or piece of pink I have seen in "Peacock Reverse." There are bound to be others. Adored red seems to be the most obtainable color. That blue sugar is the only blue luncheon item I have found with "Peacock Reverse" etch. We turned up two colored sugars, but have yet to spot a creamer in 16 years of searching. Few collectors of cups and saucers have "Peacock Reverse" represented. A lipped, footed comport which measures 4¼" tall and 7⅜" wide is pictured in the back on the right. You see this comport rather frequently without an etching.

There are two styles of candy dishes. Notice that both have patterns only on the lids. The plain bases can be discovered with lids sporting other etches or even without an etch. That should make bases easier to find, but that hasn't been the case. Prices for "Peacock Reverse" are not established by color as much as other patterns. Collectors welcome any piece in any color whatsoever.

"Peacock Reverse" could conceivably be etched on almost any piece listed under "Crow's Foot" (squared) or "Orchid." Let me know what unlisted pieces or colors you encounter. I was told by a granddaughter of a Paden City worker that he said to tell me the workers at the plants called all these bird patterns "pheasants."

	All Colors		**All Colors**
Bowl, 4⅞", square	45.00	Plate, 5¾", sherbet	25.00
Bowl, 8¾", square	125.00	Plate, 8½", luncheon	60.00
Bowl, 8¾", square with handles	125.00	Plate 10⅜", 2-handled	95.00
Bowl, 11¾", console	145.00	Saucer	35.00
Candlesticks, 5¾", square base, pair	165.00	Sherbet, 4⅝" tall, 3⅜" diameter	65.00
Candy dish, 6½", square	195.00	Sherbet, 4⅞" tall, 3⅝" diameter	65.00
Comport, 3¼" high, 6¼" wide	75.00	Server, center-handled	75.00
Comport, 4¼" high, 7⅜" wide	85.00	Sugar, 2¾", flat	100.00
Creamer, 2¾", flat	100.00	Tumbler, 4", 10 ounce, flat	95.00
Cup	145.00	Vase, 10"	250.00

"PEACOCK & WILD ROSE," "NORA BIRD" LINE #300 PADEN CITY GLASS COMPANY, 1929 – 1930s

Colors: Pink, green, amber, cobalt blue, black, light blue, crystal, and red.

I am repeating what was written in the last book about why we combined the "Nora Bird" pattern with "Peacock and Wild Rose." At a photography session where Cathy was outlining a pattern with chalk to make it show in the photograph, she made a fascinating discovery about Paden City's "Peacock and Wild Rose" and "Nora Bird." They are the same pattern with "Nora Bird" being a condensed (or sectioned off) version of the larger "Peacock and Wild Rose." Examine a tall vase, you will see the small bird at the bottom of the design that appears on the pieces formerly known as "Nora Bird." The bird on each piece can be found in flight or getting ready to take flight. Obviously, the larger pattern would not fit on the smaller pieces; so, a condensed version was used. That is why creamers, sugars, and luncheon pieces have never been discovered in "Peacock and Wild Rose." These pieces, both from Line #300, have formerly been attributed to a separate pattern and given the name "Nora Bird." Thus, the "Nora Bird" pattern has now been incorporated into "Peacock and Wild Rose" where it truly belongs. Copious amounts of accessory pieces in "Peacock and Wild Rose" can now be combined with cups, saucers, creamers, sugars, and luncheon plates of "Nora Bird" to give a fairly extensive pattern.

Pheasant patterns were popular during this era and a reader wrote to tell me that old time plant workers referred to any of the bird etches as "pheasant line." This agrees with the granddaughter's message received regarding "Peacock Reverse" which I related.

Note the green, #300 line, flat, three-part candy dish on the right. The lid to this candy also fits the footed 5¼" candy dish. There is also an octagonal flat candy pictured in the last book. Finding a candy in "Peacock and Wild Rose" should be easier now with three known. The green tray in the top photo was listed as a #210 Line refreshment tray. A few pieces of light blue have been found including a rolled edge bowl. Are there candles?

There are two styles of creamers and sugars. Both types are also found with "Cupid" etch. Recently, I borrowed an individual (smaller) sugar and creamer in green to photograph. I had not seen these in any Paden City pattern before. They have rounded handles. Additionally, a collector in Texas has found two green tumblers that are different from those previously listed. They are 2¼", 3 ounces; and 5¼", 10 ounces.

Be sure to check out the 8½", 64 ounce pitcher in *Very Rare Glassware of the Depression Years, Sixth Series*. There are very possibly more pieces in this pattern than I have listed; please let me know if you find something else.

	All Colors		All Colors
Bowl, 8½", flat	135.00	Ice tub, 4¾"	195.00
Bowl, 8½", fruit, oval, footed	225.00	Ice tub, 6"	195.00
Bowl, 8¾", footed	175.00	Mayonnaise and liner	110.00
Bowl, 9½", center-handled	165.00	Pitcher, 5" high	295.00
Bowl, 9½", footed	185.00	Pitcher, 8½", 64 ounce	395.00
Bowl, 10½", center-handled	125.00	Plate, 8"	25.00
Bowl, 10½", footed	195.00	Plate, cake, low foot	150.00
Bowl, 10½", fruit	185.00	Relish, 3-part	110.00
Bowl, 11", console	185.00	Saucer	20.00
Bowl, 14", console	195.00	Sugar, 4½", round handle	55.00
Candlestick, 5" wide, pair	175.00	Sugar, 5", pointed handle	55.00
Candlesticks, octagonal tops, pair	215.00	Tray, rectangular, handled	195.00
Candy dish w/cover, 6½", 3-part	195.00	Tumbler, 2¼", 3 ounce	55.00
Candy dish w/cover, 7"	250.00	Tumbler, 3"	60.00
Candy with lid, footed, 5¼" high	195.00	Tumbler, 4"	75.00
Cheese and cracker set	185.00	Tumbler, 4¾", footed	85.00
Comport, 3¼" tall, 6¼" wide	135.00	Tumbler, 5¼", 10 ounce	85.00
Creamer, 4½", round handle	55.00	Vase, 8¼", elliptical	395.00
Creamer, 5", pointed handle	55.00	Vase, 10", two styles	250.00
Cup	80.00	Vase, 12"	295.00
Ice bucket, 6"	210.00		

"PEBBLED RIM" Line #707 L. E. SMITH GLASS COMPANY, 1930s

Colors: Amber, green, pink.

"Pebbled Rim" is a small L. E. Smith pattern that a few would-be collectors are beginning to ignore because, they complain, it is overpriced. I personally know of one pink set being displayed at an astronomical sum in an antique mall that I visit once a year. Each piece averages $10.00 and that eight-place setting includes cups, saucers, and two sizes of small plates. I guess the owner believes that since its pink Depression glass, it must be worth a mint. Perhaps because of age it *should* be; but, right now, there are only a few collectors seeking it. Demand drives prices. If there's little demand, huge prices aren't going to fly.

The large, ruffled edge bowl and the platter appear to be the hardest pieces to locate, although any green is more difficult than pink. This simple pattern blends well with other patterns. In fact, I'm fairly certain that accounts for the scarcity of the above two pieces. People are using them with other sets.

	All colors
Bowl, 9½", oval	28.00
Bowl, berry	8.00
Bowl, ruffled edge vegetable, deep	30.00
Bowl, ruffled edge vegetable, shallow	28.00
Candleholder	20.00
Cream	13.00
Cup	7.50

	All colors
Plate, 6", bread/butter	5.00
Plate, 7", salad	6.00
Plate, 9", dinner	10.00
Plate, 9", two-handle	22.00
Platter, oval	25.00
Saucer	2.00
Sugar	13.00

"PENNY LINE" Line #991 PADEN CITY GLASS COMPANY, c. 1930

Colors: Red, green, pink (Cheriglo), amber, primrose (light yellow), black, white, amethyst, royal blue.

This pattern is featured here courtesy of a dealer friend who found it, called to ask if I needed a photo for use in a book sometime and then packaged it and shipped it to the Paducah studio to get it photographed. You can't get service any better than that — or friends; and humbly and gratefully, I've made several in this business who will go above and beyond to that degree. All collectors owe these generous people much for their time and efforts to assist the spread of knowledge any way they can. Believe me, my energy supplies can use all the help they can get. Where did that youthful, dynamo of energy go?

The Deco age in which this pattern has its beginning was all about form, lines, and shapes. This circular, stacked rings look was a definite product of its cultural surroundings and should be much appreciated by devotees of Depression wares. One of the articles from that era remarked that this ware was a standout among the many ringed lines appearing in the markets. That was probably true, particularly since it was being made in Paden City's rich colorings, so treasured by collectors, today.

Low foot apparently meant goblets with only one wafer and high foot pieces had two. If you have a pitcher, I need ounce sizes. The mayo was cataloged with a liner plate, which I assume was the 6" dessert plate also used as a sherbet liner. Notice the unusual handles on the cup. If you find other pieces, I would appreciate the information.

	*All colors
Bowl, finger	15.00
Candle	20.00
Creamer	12.50
Cup	10.00
Decanter, 22 ounce w/stopper	40.00
Goblet, low foot, grapefruit	15.00
Goblet, low foot, 9 ounce	15.00
Goblet, high foot	17.50
Pitcher	55.00
Plate, 6"	5.00
Plate, 8", salad	12.50
Saucer	3.00
Server, 10½", center handle	35.00

	*All colors
Shaker, pair	35.00
Sherbet, low foot	10.00
Stem, 1¼ ounce, cordial	32.50
Stem, 3½ ounce, cocktail	12.50
Stem, 3 ounce, wine	15.00
Stem, 6 ounce, cocktail	12.50
Sugar	12.50
Tray, rectangular, 2 handled, sugar/cream	20.00
Tumbler, 2½ ounce, wine	12.00
Tumbler, 5 ounce, juice.	10.00
Tumbler, 9 ounce, table	12.00
Tumbler, 12 ounce, tea	14.00

*Add 50% for royal blue or red

PETALWARE MacBETH-EVANS GLASS COMPANY, 1930 – 1950

Colors: Monax, Cremax, pink, crystal, cobalt and fired-on red, blue, green, and yellow.

Notice the original boxed set below. Straight sided tumblers with matching pastel bands were packed with these sets. Although these tumblers are not Petalware pattern, they were decorated to go with it. Unfortunately, there is no name in the box to settle that issue. Red-trimmed Petalware Mountain Flowers decoration has matching tumblers; now we know "Pastel Bands" did, too. Original boxed sets of sherbets unveiled the Mountain Flowers name, which also came with three sizes of decorated tumblers and a pitcher to match. I have listed the two sizes of tumblers I own. You can find these either frosted or unfrosted. The Mountain Flowers decorated pitcher was a frosted Federal Star juice pitcher. Mountain Flowers design is shown on page 51, Cremax.

Monax and Ivrene are names given these Petalware colors by MacBeth-Evans. Ivrene refers to the opaque, beige colored Petalware shown below and on page181; Monax is the white shown in all the other pictures. Pastel decorated Ivrene shown below and in the middle row on page 181 is the design now being pursued. I am continually asked for it at shows. Considering little of it is found, prices are rising. Notice the crystal tumblers with matching pastel bands in that photo. These are found in several sizes, all presently selling in the $7.00 to $10.00 range. I can guarantee the boxed ones below are right, but as long as the colored bands match the dinnerware, that is sufficient. No pitchers were originally made, but banded, decorated tumblers to match were advertised with the set in 1939. However, those 1939 tumblers were all straight sided and probably nearly impossible to locate now.

Collectors are also enamored with various Petalware decorations. We find that out when we photograph for a book and put those items in stock to sell at a show. Those Petalware items leave the booth before the show is over. Finding enough different types for the next book's display becomes one of my challenges.

Florette is the second most collected design. It is the pointed petal, red flower decoration without the red edge trim. It is pictured on the second and third shelves on page 182. Notice the flat soup on the third row. Soups are seldom seen in Petalware. Therefore, decorated Florette ones are a serious find. One group of these was located in a garage in Pennsylvania. Since I now own a 1949 company magazine showing a lady painting this Florette design on stacks of plates, it should move to the 50s book.

I have tried to show a sample of decorated Petalware focusing on fruits and some florals. We had additional pictures, but I had to limit my choice to three in order to add new patterns to the book. Look back over the last few editions for additional designs. There are series of fruits, birds, and flowers. Fruit-decorated Petalware (with printed names of fruits) is found in sets of eight. One such set consists of plates showing cherry, apple, orange, plum, strawberry, blueberry, pear, and grape. You may find other sets with different fruits. Some plates have labels, which read "Rainbow Hand Painted." Others have colored bands or 22K gold trim. All series of fruit and bird decorated Petalware sell well.

Pink Petalware (top 182) has captivated some collectors. This delicate pink is still less costly than most other pink patterns in Depression glass and can be found at markets.

	Crystal	Pink	Cremax Monax Plain	Cremax, Monax Florette, Fired-On Decorations	Red Trim Floral
Bowl, 4½", cream soup	4.50	18.00	12.00	15.00	
Bowl, 5¾", cereal	4.00	14.00	8.00	14.00	42.00
Bowl, 7", soup			65.00	100.00	
*Bowl, 9", large berry	8.50	25.00	20.00	35.00	135.00
Cup	3.00	8.00	5.00	11.00	27.50
**Creamer, footed	3.00	8.00	8.00	12.50	35.00
Lamp shade (many sizes) $8.00 to $15.00					
Mustard with metal cover in cobalt blue only, $10.00					
Pitcher, 80 ounce (crystal decorated bands)	35.00				
Plate, 6", sherbet	2.00	2.50	3.00	6.00	22.00
Plate, 8", salad	2.00	7.00	6.00	10.00	25.00
Plate, 9", dinner	4.00	14.00	14.00	16.00	37.50
Plate, 11", salver	4.50	15.00	12.00	27.50	
Plate, 12", salver		15.00	18.00		40.00
Platter, 13", oval	8.50	22.50	15.00	25.00	
Saucer	1.50	2.00	2.00	3.50	10.00
Saucer, cream soup liner			15.00		
Sherbet, 4", low footed			30.00		
**Sherbet, 4½", low footed	3.50	10.00	8.00	18.00	38.00
**Sugar, footed	3.00	9.00	8.00	10.00	35.00
Tidbit servers or Lazy Susans, several styles 12.00 to 17.50					
Tumbler, 3⅝", 6 ounce					35.00
Tumbler, 4⅝", 12 ounce					37.50
***Tumblers (crystal decorated pastel bands) 7.50 to 10.00					

*Also in cobalt at $65.00   **Also in cobalt at $35.00   ***Several sizes

PILLAR OPTIC, "LOGS," "LOG CABIN" ANCHOR HOCKING GLASS COMPANY, 1937 – 1942

Colors: Crystal, green, pink, Royal Ruby; amber and iridescent, possible Federal Glass Co.

After adding Pillar Optic to the book two years ago, I received letters with two divergent views from readers. One was from a collector thanking me for pointing out that this pattern's pitcher was not Old Café. She had a written guarantee that the pink pitcher she had purchased was Old Café and the dealer from whom she bought it had refunded her money. About a month later I had another letter saying I had cost two sales of "Old Café" pitchers with my new book, Unfortunately, not everyone who bought Pillar Optic pitchers as Old Café were able to recover their funds. Pillar Optic pitchers are collectible; just Old Café collectors don't want them presented as Old Café. This brings up one of the questions that I really can't answer as author. Someone will say, "I paid $xxx for this. Did I get a good deal or pay too much?" If you have already bought something and were happy enough with the price to pay that amount for it, then be happy, as they say. I continue to say only you and the seller determine a price — whether good for you or for the dealer isn't relative at this juncture of the deal.

I found Pillar Optic's name while researching old catalog files for the Fire-King book. Up until then, I'd heard it called "Log Cabin." The 60 ounce pitcher came in three colors. The two 80 ounce ones are shown below. The panels of the Pillar Optic are evenly spaced (note pretzel jars) and not like Old Cafe's alternating large panel with two small ones. Notice that there were two styles of Pillar Optic pitchers manufactured. It is the ice lip style that is similar to Old Café.

Most of you who have been collecting for some time will recognize Pillar Optic pattern from my Kitchenware book. Hocking promoted a beer and pretzel set with mugs and the pretzel jar. Most collectors call the 130 ounce jar a cookie, but it was not offered as such. The top is hard to find mint and, as you can see, it is totally missing in pink in my picture. These jars are sometimes found satinized and hand painted with flowers.

Royal Ruby, amber, and iridescent items are hard to find. Flat tumblers come in amber and the iridescent water shown here. However, Federal Glass Company is known to have manufactured like patterned tumblers and it's likely amber and iridescent wares came from them rather than Anchor Hocking.

I have seen Royal Ruby Pillar Optic in four items, the three footed tumblers like those found in Colonial and the 9" two-handled bowl. A picture of a creamer and sugar were e-mailed to me recently. Thanks! So, now there are six.

Two styles of cups appear, the rounded cup pictured in green and the flatter pink one, more reminiscent of Colonial styled cups. I finally found a green saucer, but no pink one as yet. I have not seen flat green cups or rounded pink ones. The pink sugar and creamer came out of the attic of a former Hocking employee. Crystal Pillar Optic tumblers have been a staple in Anchor Hocking's restaurant line for years. In fact, in one or their later catalogs, it's shown under the heading "Old Reliable." Many restaurants still use them today.

	Crystal	Amber Green Pink	Royal Ruby
Bowl, 9", two-handle		65.00	125.00
Creamer, footed		50.00	65.00
Cup	10.00	15.00	
Mug, 12 ounce	10.00	32.50	
Pitcher, w/o lip, 60 ounce	25.00	45.00	
Pitcher, w/lip, 80 ounce	30.00	55.00	
Pitcher, 80 ounce, tilt	35.00	65.00	
Plate, 8", luncheon	8.00	12.00	
Pretzel jar, 130 ounce	60.00	135.00	
Saucer	2.00	4.00	
Sugar, footed		50.00	65.00
Tumbler, 1½ ounce, whiskey	10.00	17.50	
Tumbler, 7 ounce, old fashioned	10.00	15.00	
Tumbler, 9 ounce, water	2.50	20.00	
Tumbler, 11 ounce, ftd., cone	12.00	20.00	
Tumbler, 13 ounce, tea	4.00	25.00	
Tumbler, 3¼", 3 ounce, footed	8.00	15.00	25.00
Tumbler, 4", 5 oz. juice, ftd.	10.00	17.50	30.00
Tumbler, 5¼", 10 ounce, ftd.	12.00	25.00	35.00

PRIMO, "PANELED ASTER" U.S. GLASS COMPANY, Early 1930s

Colors: Green and yellow.

New discoveries in Primo continue to be the rule rather than the exception. This time, a grill pate with an indent for a cup is the newest find. In 1932, Primo could be bought as a 14-piece bridge set (with plates, cups, saucers, and sugar and creamer), a 16-piece luncheonette (with grill plates, tumblers, cups, and saucers), an 18-piece occasional set (with plates, tumblers, sugar, creamer, cup, and saucer), a 19-piece hostess set (add a tray), and a 7-piece berry set.

A two-handled tray surfaced. The 11" three-footed console bowl (large berry in old ads) created a furor among Primo collectors when I listed it. No one seemed overly excited about the 6¼" sherbet plate not previously listed. Oh, I got thrilled enough for everybody when I first spied them in that antique mall. I bought the sherbet plates, but had to take the sherbets to get them. Finding new pieces for patterns is my fun. The large berry (console) bowl is beat up, but I had to pay the $20.00 asked because "it had to be rare since it wasn't in Gene Florence's book."

A friend, who was determined to collect yellow Primo, asked me to watch for this pattern, and I have for over seven years. Any bowls, dinner, grill, or cake plates will take some searching. Though I have discovered several new pieces, I have not yet found a green berry bowl to photograph.

An irritation in buying Primo comes from extreme mould roughness and inner rim damage on pieces that have rims. There appears to be more Primo along the Gulf Coast than any place I have searched. I have seen several sets in antique malls between Florida and Texas, but a majority of the pieces were very rough or chipped. Prices marked are for mint pieces.

The tumbler exactly fits the coaster/ashtray. These coasters have been found in boxed sets with Primo tumblers that were advertised as "Bridge Service Sets." The coasters are also found in pink and black, but no Primo design is found on the coasters.

	Yellow, Green		Yellow, Green
Bowl, 4½"	25.00	Plate, 7½"	14.00
Bowl, 7¾"	40.00	Plate, 10", dinner	30.00
Bowl, 11", 3-footed	60.00	Plate, 10", grill	18.00
Cake plate, 10", 3-footed	45.00	Saucer	3.00
Coaster/ashtray	8.00	Sherbet	14.00
Creamer	12.00	Sugar	12.00
Cup	13.00	Tray, 2-handle hostess	45.00
Plate, 6¼"	12.00	Tumbler, 5¾", 9 ounce	20.00

186

PRINCESS HOCKING GLASS COMPANY, 1931 – 1935

Colors: Green, Topaz yellow, apricot yellow, pink, and light blue.

While shopping near Lancaster last year I visited someone who has helped me find glass for my books over the years. That visit brought a new discovery. Pictured to the right is another style cup than previously known. It looks bigger, but is not. It is the one on the left in the picture, shaped differently from the regular cup.

Blue Princess pieces are encountered on rare occasions. The cookie jar, cup, saucer, and dinner plate are finding a ready market. I pictured a three-part relish in my *Very Rare Glassware of the Depression Years, Sixth Edition* and recently heard about a candy jar bottom. Blue Princess suffers the curse of many infrequently found patterns or colors of Depression glass. It seems too rare to collect a set. Keep looking, though, because you never know these 70 years later what is still waiting to be unearthed. There is some evidence that blue Princess was shipped to Mexico, which could explain its dearth here in the States.

Footed iced tea tumblers and all bowls are hard to locate in any color of Princess. Green Princess collectors have to search long and hard for the undivided relish and the elusive, square foot pitcher with tumblers to match. Some dealers promote the undivided Princess relish as a soup bowl. To me, it does not seem deep enough for a soup bowl, but in any case, it is rarely found. Collectors of pink Princess have problems finding coasters, ashtrays, and squared foot pitchers with matching tumblers. The hardest to find yellow pieces include the butter dish, juice pitcher, undivided relish, 10½" handled sandwich plate, coasters, and ashtrays. I bought two of the yellow handled plates in Kentucky. This plate is just like the handled grill plate without the dividers. You can see one in the background of the photograph at the bottom of this page. Bowls in Princess present a problem due to inner rim roughness, "irr" in ads. Some new collectors are always writing about that. Stacking the bowls together over the years caused some of this "irr" damage; but the very sharply defined inner rims were themselves ripe for trouble from the moulds. Mint condition bowls are seldom found, so buy them when you can.

There is some color variation in yellow Princess. Topaz is the official color name listed by Hocking, and it is a bright, attractive shade of yellow. However, some yellow turned out looking amber and has been christened apricot by collectors. Most prefer the Topaz, which makes the darker, amber shade hard to sell. The colors are so mismatched that it is almost as if Hocking meant to have two distinct colors. For some reason (probably distribution) yellow Princess bowls and sherbets prevail in the Detroit area. I pointed that out to a dealer who had a table full of yellow and he said he had never realized that yellow was commonly found there. All but one of the known yellow Princess juice pitchers have been found in northern and central Kentucky. Regional patterns are noticeable for Depression era wares.

The grill plate without handles and dinner plate have been corrected to read 9½" in the listing instead of the 9" listed in Hocking catalogs. Measure perpendicularly and not diagonally.

Reproduction cobalt blue, green, pink, and amber (candy dishes) have been reported. The colors are not close to those original ones. Cobalt or amber was never made originally. The green will not glow under ultraviolet (black) light and the pink has an orange hue.

PRINCESS

	Green	Pink	Topaz, Apricot		Green	Pink	Topaz, Apricot
Ashtray, 4½"	75.00	95.00	110.00	**Plate, 9½", grill	20.00	20.00	8.00
Bowl, 4½", berry	30.00	32.00	55.00	Plate, 10¼", handled sandwich	16.00	28.00	180.00
Bowl, 5", cereal or oatmeal	40.00	40.00	40.00	Plate, 10½", grill, closed			
Bowl, 9", octagonal, salad	45.00	55.00	150.00	handles	10.00	12.00	5.50
Bowl, 9½", hat-shaped	50.00	50.00	140.00	Platter, 12", closed handles	30.00	30.00	67.50
Bowl, 10", oval vegetable	32.00	28.00	65.00	Relish, 7½", divided, 4 pint	26.00	28.00	100.00
Butter dish and cover	100.00	115.00	750.00	Relish, 7½", plain	195.00	195.00	250.00
Butter dish bottom	35.00	40.00	250.00	Salt and pepper, 4½" pair	60.00	55.00	85.00
Butter dish top	65.00	75.00	500.00	Spice shakers, 5½", pair	40.00		
Cake stand, 10"	35.00	35.00		***Saucer (same as sherbet			
*Candy dish and cover	65.00	95.00		plate)	10.00	10.00	3.00
Coaster	42.00	85.00	115.00	Sherbet, footed	25.00	27.00	35.00
**Cookie jar and cover	60.00	70.00		Sugar	10.00	15.00	8.50
Creamer, oval	20.00	20.00	20.00	Sugar cover	25.00	25.00	17.50
***Cup	12.00	13.00	9.00	Tumbler, 3", 5 ounce, juice	33.00	33.00	33.00
Pitcher 6", 37 ounce	60.00	75.00	795.00	Tumbler, 4", 9 ounce, water	30.00	30.00	25.00
Pitcher, 7⅜", 24 ounce, ftd.	525.00	475.00		Tumbler, 5¼", 13 oz., iced tea	50.00	40.00	32.00
Pitcher, 8", 60 ounce	60.00	65.00	100.00	Tumbler, 4¾", 9 oz., sq. ftd	65.00	60.00	
****Plate, 5½" sherbet	11.00	12.00	4.00	Tumbler, 5¼", 10 ounce, ftd.	33.00	30.00	22.00
Plate, 8" salad	18.00	18.00	15.00	Tumbler, 6½", 12½ oz., ftd.	110.00	90.00	175.00
*****Plate, 9½", dinner	30.00	26.00	16.00	Vase, 8"	45.00	65.00	

*   Beware reproductions in cobalt blue and amber
**   Blue $895.00
*** Blue $125.00
**** Blue $60.00
***** Blue $200.00

QUEEN MARY (PRISMATIC LINE), "VERTICAL RIBBED"
ANCHOR HOCKING GLASS COMPANY, 1936 – 1949

Colors: Pink, crystal, and some Royal Ruby.

Price is making crystal Queen Mary more enticing to new collectors than pink. Availability and its slightly Deco look are others. Nothing is as annoying as trying to stumble onto pink Queen Mary dinner plates and footed tumblers; and prices for those same items in crystal are producing upward trends due to new demand. A few pink Queen Mary prices have softened, as new collectors are not latching onto it, as they are the crystal. A crystal set can still be completed at tolerable prices.

A crosshatched vase (shaped like Old Cafe with a 400-line number) is pictured along with Queen Mary items in Hocking catalogs.

The 6" cereal bowl has the same form as the butter bottom but is smaller in diameter. Butter dishes were labeled preserve dishes in Hocking's catalogs. There are two sizes of cups. The smaller sits on the saucer with cup ring. The larger cup rests on the combination saucer/sherbet plate. Lately, the pink smaller cup and saucer have outdistanced the larger in price. Some dealers are identifying the 5½" tab-handled bowl as a cream soup. The price on that bowl has gone up rather dramatically.

The frosted crystal butter dish with metal band looks somewhat like a crown. These were made about the time of the English Coronation in the mid-1930s. I have seen these priced as high as $150.00 in an Art Deco shop, but I had to think before paying $25.00 for the one pictured in a previous book. A pair of lampshades was found made from frosted candy lids (with metal-banded decorations similar to that butter).

I am now confident the little colored shakers pictured are Hazel Atlas; keep that in mind if they are offered to you as Queen Mary. They, alas, are not.

	Pink	Crystal
Ashtray, 2" x 3¾", oval	5.00	3.00
*Ashtray, 3¼", round		3.00
Ashtray, 4¼", square (#422)		4.00
Bowl, 4", one-handle or none	8.00	3.50
Bowl, 4½", berry	8.00	4.00
Bowl, 5", berry, flared	12.00	6.00
Bowl, 5½", two handle, lug soup	30.00	6.50
Bowl, 6", cereal	28.00	6.00
Bowl, deep, 7½" (#477)	30.00	14.00
Bowl, 8¾", large berry (#478)	20.00	15.00
Butter dish or preserve and cover (#498)	150.00	30.00
Butter dish bottom (#498)	40.00	7.00
Butter dish top (#498)	110.00	23.00
Candy dish and cover, 7¼" (#490)	40.00	22.00
**Candlesticks, 4½", double branch, pair		22.00
Celery or pickle dish, 5" x 10" (#467)	25.00	11.00
Cigarette jar, 2" x 3", oval	7.50	5.50
Coaster, 3½"	6.00	3.00
Coaster/ashtray, 3¼", round (#419)	6.00	5.00
Comport, 5¾"	25.00	15.00

	Pink	Crystal
Creamer, footed	50.00	25.00
Creamer, 5½", oval (#471)	14.00	5.50
Cup, large	9.00	5.50
Cup, small	7.00	8.00
Mayonnaise, 5" x 2¾" h, 6" plate	30.00	15.00
Plate, 6⅝"	6.00	4.00
Plate, 8¾", salad (#438)		5.50
Plate, 9¾", dinner (#426)	60.00	22.00
Plate, 12", sandwich (#450)	25.00	18.00
Plate, 14", serving tray	22.00	12.00
Relish tray, 12", 3-part	18.00	9.00
Relish tray, 14", 4-part	20.00	12.00
Salt and pepper, 2½", pair (#486)		19.00
Saucer/cup ring	5.00	2.50
Sherbet, footed	10.00	5.00
Sugar, footed	50.00	25.00
Sugar, 6", oval (#470)	14.00	4.50
Tumbler, 3½", 5 ounce, juice	14.00	4.00
Tumbler, 4", 9 ounce, water	18.00	6.00
Tumbler, 5", 10 ounce, footed	70.00	35.00
Vase, 6½" (#441)		10.00

*Royal Ruby $5.00; Forest Green $3.00   ** Royal Ruby $75.00

189

RADIANCE NEW MARTINSVILLE GLASS COMPANY, 1936 – 1939

Colors: Red, cobalt and ice blue, amber, crystal, pink, and emerald green.

Radiance punch, decanter, and condiment sets continue to be on collectors' want lists. A cake stand, 11½" x 4" tall has been reported in red and crystal. If you are a collector of Radiance and do not have my *Very Rare Glassware of the Depression Years, Sixth Series,* you need to find a copy. Radiance pictures include an 8" red candlestick with matching bobeches and several odd colored vases. While shopping recently, we saw a pair of vases with decorations of gold, blue, and flowers. I regretted leaving them, but they were so worn, I would have had trouble recouping my $70.00 had I purchased them. I would like to be able to resell photograph items for as much as I pay for them once they're captured for the books.

The punch set is difficult to find, but the punch ladle is nigh impossible. The ladle was formed by adding a long handle to a punch cup. If not broken through use, collectors and dealers have added to their demise by traveling with them. I have been told several times that the handle detaches from the cup very easily. One dealer has had that misfortune twice. He, personally, has helped elevate the price of punch ladles.

Crystal punch bowls being found on emerald green and black were made by Viking after they bought out New Martinsville. One such emerald green set was pictured previously. These are found rather frequently — unlike their older counterparts. The bowls flare outward rather than inward, like the older "bowling ball" style. Viking's ladle is plain. I have several collectors lobbying for me to move Radiance to my Elegant book as it is too fine a glassware to be included in this book. They are probably right. However, Radiance was collected as Depression glass long before my term "Elegant" was ever suggested.

Red and ice blue are the most coveted Radiance colors. The most troublesome pieces to find in those colors include the butter dish, pitcher, handled decanter, and the five-piece condiment set. Vases have been encountered made into lamps. I question this being a factory project, but it could have been.

Cobalt blue is striking, but few pieces were produced in that color.

Pink Radiance pieces including creamer, sugar, tray, cup, saucer, vase, and shakers are turning up occasionally. These are selling in the same range as the red since they are scarce at this time. The pieces suggest they were made as luncheon sets, save for the vase which could have been picked up in a florist grouping.

Price crystal about 50% of amber. Only crystal pieces that item collectors seek sell very well. These include pitchers, butter dishes, shakers, sugars, creamers, and cordials.

	Ice Blue, Red	Amber		Ice Blue, Red	Amber
Bowl, 5", nut, 2-handle	20.00	10.00	Condiment set, 4-piece w/tray	325.00	175.00
Bowl, 6", bonbon	33.00	17.50	Creamer	25.00	15.00
Bowl, 6", bonbon, footed	35.00	20.00	Cruet, individual	80.00	40.00
Bowl, 6", bonbon w/cover	110.00	55.00	Cup, footed	18.00	12.00
Bowl, 7", relish, 2-part	35.00	20.00	Cup, punch	15.00	7.00
Bowl, 7", pickle	35.00	20.00	** Decanter w/stopper, handle	225.00	125.00
Bowl, 8", relish, 3-part	50.00	35.00	Goblet, 1 ounce cordial	35.00	25.00
* Bowl, 9", punch	225.00	100.00	Honey jar, w/lid	125.00	75.00
Bowl, 10", celery	45.00	22.00	Ladle for punch bowl	150.00	100.00
Bowl, 10", crimped	55.00	30.00	Lamp, 12"	125.00	65.00
Bowl, 10", flared	50.00	25.00	Mayonnaise, 3-piece, set	115.00	65.00
Bowl, 12", crimped	60.00	35.00	*** Pitcher, 64 ounce	325.00	175.00
Bowl, 12", flared	65.00	32.00	Plate, 8", luncheon	16.00	10.00
Butter dish	465.00	210.00	**** Plate, 14", punch bowl liner	85.00	45.00
Candlestick, 6", ruffled, pair	175.00	80.00	Salt & pepper, pair	95.00	50.00
Candlestick, 8", pair	225.00	95.00	Saucer	8.50	5.50
Candlestick, 2-lite, pair	175.00	95.00	Sugar	25.00	15.00
Candy, flat, w/lid	100.00	50.00	Tray, oval	45.00	25.00
Cheese/cracker (11" plate) set	110.00	30.00	***** Tumbler, 9 ounce	30.00	20.00
Comport, 5"	30.00	18.00	****** Vase, 10", flared or crimped	125.00	75.00
Comport, 6"	35.00	22.00	Vase, 12", flared or crimped	175.00	

* Emerald green $125.00   ****Emerald green $25.00
** Cobalt blue $185.00   *****Cobalt blue $28.00
*** Cobalt blue $350.00   ******Cobalt blue $75.00

RAINDROPS, "OPTIC DESIGN" FEDERAL GLASS COMPANY, 1929–1933

Colors: Green and crystal.

As I write this, most of my area in Central Florida would love to hear some raindrops falling outside. We have had only two years of rain in the last three. A year's deficit will not easily be made up unless we get those dreaded hurricanes.

For novice collectors please heed that Raindrops has rounded bumps and not elongated ones. Elongated bumps belong to another pattern usually referred to as "Thumbprint." Almost all Raindrops pieces are embossed on the bottom with Federal's trademark of an F inside a shield.

There are two styles of cups. One is flat bottomed and the other has a slight foot. The flat-bottomed is 2⁵⁄₁₆" high and the footed is 2¹¹⁄₁₆" (reported by an enthusiastic Raindrops collector). I have not measured them myself. Prices for crystal tumblers run from 50% to 60% less than for green.

Raindrops makes a great little luncheon or bridge set. It even has a few accessory pieces that other smaller sets do not. You can find three sizes of bowls in Raindrops. The 7½" bowl will be the one you will probably find last. Raindrops will blend well with many other green sets; so, give that a try if you want additional pieces.

That 7½" berry bowl price continues an upward climb and is now the second most expensive piece in Raindrops. It has overtaken the price of the sugar bowl lid. However, both of these pieces have to take a back seat to the shakers. In actuality, Raindrops sugar lids have turned out to be common in comparison to shakers. Consequently, the price of shakers has skyrocketed over the last few years. A couple of shaker collectors have told me that these are harder to find than yellow and green Mayfair. Both collectors had at least one of those elusive shakers, but neither one had the Raindrops. One of them told me to name my price for the one shown. If I did, you might never be able to see one pictured again. I have never seen a Raindrops shaker for sale at any show I have attended in 29 years if that makes any kind of impression on you as to how rare it is. I have owned the one-footed Mayfair shaker and have held both genuine pairs of pink Cherry Blossom shakers known. One Raindrops shaker is all I have seen; though I have heard of others.

	Green			Green
Bowl, 4½", fruit	6.00		Sugar	7.50
Bowl, 6", cereal	12.00		Sugar cover	40.00
Bowl, 7½", berry	55.00		Tumbler, 3", 4 ounce	5.00
Cup	5.50		Tumbler, 2⅛", 2 ounce	5.00
Creamer	7.50		Tumbler, 3⅞", 5 ounce	6.50
Plate, 6", sherbet	2.50		Tumbler, 4⅛", 9½ ounce	9.00
Plate, 8", luncheon	6.00		Tumbler, 5", 10 ounce	9.00
Salt and pepper, pair	350.00		Tumbler, 5⅜", 14 ounce	14.00
Saucer	2.00		Whiskey, 1⅞", 1 ounce	7.00
Sherbet	7.00			

REEDED, WHIRLSPOOL, "SPUN," LINE #701 IMPERIAL GLASS COMPANY, c. 1936 – 60s

Colors: Crystal, cobalt, dark green, amber, tangerine, Midas gold, turquoise, pink, milk, mustard.

This line was first marketed as beverage sets. Through the years, various other pieces were added to the line, indicating it enjoyed a certain popularity with buyers. I was prompted to put it in the book because the factory closed, which makes their wares more collectible, and interest has been building in the pattern for some time at shows.

Interesting items in the pattern include what they called a console set, usually a rolled edge bowl with candles. In this pattern, the bowl is a bowling ball shaped rose bowl (see pink one in photo) with small ivy ball vases that have had glass candle inserts added to make these candles. Don't pass by any of these. The second is the smoker set, consisting of the cigarette ivy ball with a flat rim, three-groove ashtray on top.

	*All Colors
Ashtray, 2¼", cupped	10.00
Bottle, 3 ounce, bitters	35.00
Bowl, 4½", fruit	20.00
Bowl, 7", nappy, straight side	30.00
Bowl, 8" ,nappy	30.00
Bowl, 10", deep salad	45.00
Candle, 2½", ball w/crystal glass insert	35.00
Candy box, footed w/cone lid	50.00
Cigarette holder, wider mouth, 2½" ball	20.00
Cocktail shaker, 36 ounce, w/or w/o handles	75.00
Creamer, footed	25.00
Cup	20.00
Ice tub	55.00
Jar, Whirlspool, 4", tall, w/lid or w/metal knob	55.00
Jar, Whirlspool, 5", tall, w/lid or w/metal knob	65.00
Jar, Whirlspool, 6", tall, w/lid or w/metal knob	75.00
Jar, Whirlspool, 7", tall, w/lid or w/metal knob	85.00
Muddler, 4½"	10.00
Perfume w/triangle stop	45.00
Pitcher, 80 ounce, ice lip	60.00
Plate, 8", salad, belled rim	20.00

	*All Colors
Plate, 13½", cupped edge	30.00
Plate, 14", server, flat	32.50
Powder jar w/lid	45.00
Saucer	8.00
Sherbet	17.50
Sugar, footed	25.00
Syrup, ball w/chrome spout & handle	60.00
Tumbler, 2 ounce, shot	20.00
Tumbler, 3½ ounce, cocktail	12.50
Tumbler, 5 ounce, juice, straight	12.00
Tumbler, 7 ounce, old fashioned	14.00
Tumbler, 9 ounce	14.00
Tumbler, 12 oz., tea, straight side	15.00
Tumbler, 12 ounce, tea, bulb top	16.00
Vase, 2½", ball	15.00
Vase, 3½", ivy ball, footed	35.00

	*All Colors
Vase, ivy ball, 6½", footed	55.00
Vase, 4", ball	17.50
Vase, 5", bud	35.00
Vase, 5", bulbous, tall neck rose	45.00
Vase, 5", rose	40.00
Vase, 6", ball, rose	45.00
Vase, 6", bud	40.00
Vase, 6", slender	40.00
Vase, 8½"	40.00
Vase, 9"	50.00

*Add 50% for red or blue; deduct 25% for crystal

"RIBBON" HAZEL ATLAS GLASS COMPANY, Early 1930s

Colors: Green; some black, crystal, and pink.

"Ribbon" is one of those multitudes of 1930s wares that echo the Deco age in which they began, filled with simplistic lines and clean shapes, which manage to have grace and movement all at the same time.

"Ribbon" bowls are among the most difficult to find in all of Depression glass. They are even scarcer than those of its sister pattern, Cloverleaf. The mould shapes are the same. Were there more collectors for "Ribbon," it would be interesting to see where the price of bowls would level off considering the prices brought by Cloverleaf bowls with tons of collectors. Several "Ribbon" seekers informed me that they lusted over the display of both the berry and the cereal in my previous book. In fact, I had a letter from a long-time collector explaining that I was wrong in listing the cereal because it didn't exist. He had an older book. I suggested he order the current book to see one. He did and then called to ask how much for that bowl? The cereal and berry are sitting flat in this photo since they looked ovoid when sitting on their sides in the last book. I found four berry bowls and kept one for photography. A dealer bought the other three for her sister's collection. Sorry, that's all the berry bowls I have ever owned; and you are looking at the only cereal I have seen.

I rarely see "Ribbon" for sale at shows any more. "Ribbon" is another of the patterns not found in the West according to dealers who travel those areas. Tumblers, sugars, and creamers are not yet as hard to find as bowls, but even they are beginning to disappear. The candy dish prevails as the repeatedly seen piece of "Ribbon."

The panel design on pieces flaring at the top will expand, as seen on the sugar and creamer in the picture. The normally found "Ribbon" design has evenly spaced small panels. This flared expansion is especially noticeable on a belled rim vegetable bowl you sometimes find in both black and green coloring. I had a letter questioning that the flared bowl was even the "Ribbon" pattern because it looked so different. This flared version has been accepted as "Ribbon" for the 30 years I've been in this business. There is an 8" bowl with straight sides like the berry and cereal pictured below. This bowl is analogous to a Cloverleaf bowl.

I have never been convinced that the shakers exist in green. All those represented as "Ribbon" have always made me wonder if they are. Notice I do not have one pictured.

	Green	Black		Green	Black
Bowl, 4", berry	35.00		Plate, 6¼", sherbet	3.00	
Bowl, 5", cereal	45.00		Plate, 8", luncheon	8.00	14.00
Bowl, 8", large berry, flared	35.00	40.00	*Salt and pepper, pair	30.00	45.00
Bowl, 8", straight side	75.00		Saucer	2.50	
Candy dish and cover	45.00		Sherbet, footed	10.00	
Creamer, footed	15.00		Sugar, footed	15.00	
Cup	5.00		Tumbler, 6", 10 ounce	35.00	

*Pink — $35.00

194

RING, "BANDED RINGS" LINE #300 HOCKING GLASS COMPANY, 1927 – 1933

Colors: Crystal, crystal w/bands of pink, red, blue, orange, yellow, black, silver, etc.; green, pink, "Mayfair" blue, and Royal Ruby.

Crystal Ring with colored bands fascinates more collectors than the ever abundant, ordinary crystal. Crystal with platinum (silver) bands is the second most collected form of crystal Ring. Worn trims aggravate collectors. Colored rings do not seem to suffer from that problem. It may be because the paint did not decorate the rims, as did platinum; but I speculate that fired-on trims proved more impervious to wear than metal ones.

There is a predominant colored Ring arrangement involving black, yellow, red, and orange in that order. Other assortments drive the punctilious crazy. The foot of the crystal cocktail is plain and does not have the normal block/grid design of other footed pieces.

A reader enlightened me that obtaining a subscription to *Country Gentleman* in the 1930s got you a green Ring berry bowl set consisting of an 8" berry and six 5" berry bowls. That must not have been too enticing since I have seen few green bowls over the years. You could put a set of green together over time. You will notice that my green accumulation is not building fast, though, thanks to a reader, I now have two berry bowls to show in the future.

Pink pitcher and tumbler sets are the only pieces I see in that color. A Wisconsin collector reported that the pink pitchers were given away as a dairy premium. The tumblers were packed with cottage cheese and she could not remember what you had to do to receive the pitcher. Pink sets are plentiful only in that part of the country.

A few pieces of Ring are discovered occasionally in Royal Ruby and "Mayfair" blue. The luncheon plate and 10-ounce tumbler are fairly common in Royal Ruby, but flat juice tumblers and cups have turned up in inadequate quantities. I have had no reports of saucers to go with those cups. Let me know if you spot any Royal Ruby or blue Ring saucer/sherbet plates.

You may see items decorated with Ring-like colors, only to find that these pieces have no actual rings moulded into the design. A reader sent me an ad from the mid-30s that described these as Fiesta. Hocking had a number of different striped patterns in ads of this period. I assume the Fiesta was one version of those.

	Crystal	Green/Dec.		Crystal	Green/Dec.
Bowl, 5", berry	4.00	8.00	Plate, 11¼", sandwich	7.00	14.00
Bowl, 7", soup	10.00	14.00	****Salt and pepper, pair, 3"	20.00	45.00
Bowl, 5¼", divided	12.00	40.00	Sandwich server, center handle	16.00	27.50
Bowl, 8", large berry	7.00	12.00	Saucer	1.50	2.00
Butter tub or ice tub	25.00	38.00	Sherbet, low (for 6½" plate)	8.00	15.00
Cocktail shaker	20.00	27.50	Sherbet, 4¾", footed	6.00	11.00
** Cup	6.00	6.00	Sugar, footed	4.50	5.50
Creamer, footed	4.50	6.00	Tumbler, 3", 4 ounce	4.00	12.00
Decanter and stopper	28.00	45.00	Tumbler, 3½", 5 ounce	5.00	12.00
Goblet, 7¼", 9 ounce	12.00	15.00	Tumbler, 4", 8 ounce, old fashioned	15.00	17.50
Goblet, 3¾", 3½ ounce, cocktail	11.00	18.00	Tumbler, 4¼", 9 ounce	4.50	14.00
Goblet, 4½", 3½ ounce, wine	13.00	20.00	Tumbler, 4¾", 10 ounce	7.50	13.00
Ice bucket	20.00	35.00	^ Tumbler, 5⅛", 12 ounce	8.00	10.00
Pitcher, 8", 60 ounce	17.50	25.00	Tumbler, 3½" footed, juice	6.00	10.00
* Pitcher, 8½", 80 ounce	22.00	35.00	Tumbler, 5½" footed, water	6.00	12.00
Plate, 6¼", sherbet	2.00	2.50	Tumbler, 6½" footed, iced tea	8.00	15.00
Plate, 6½", off-center ring	5.00	7.00	Vase, 8"	17.50	35.00
***Plate, 8", luncheon	4.00	5.00	Whiskey, 2", 1½ ounce	7.00	15.00

* Also found in pink. Priced as green.   ** Red $65.00. Blue $45.00   *** Red $17.50   **** Green $55.00

ROCK CRYSTAL, "EARLY AMERICAN ROCK CRYSTAL" McKEE GLASS COMPANY, 1920s and 1930s in colors

Colors: Four shades of green, aquamarine, Canary yellow, amber, pink and frosted pink, red slag, dark red, red, amberina red, crystal, frosted crystal, crystal with goofus decoration, crystal with gold decoration, amethyst, milk glass, blue frosted or "Jap" blue, and cobalt blue.

Rock Crystal is a very attractive, graceful pattern with its design firmly rooted in the past. It may interest you to know that hand-cut wares made for a king's table centuries ago reportedly inspired the design itself. Now you know why you like it!

Crystal production started about 1915 and lasted into the 1940s. Hence the volume of pieces available. Unfortunately, catalogs illustrating *all* the pieces do not exist. Colored glassware production years are fairly well authenticated, but unexpected pieces are still showing up. A red syrup pitcher turned up a few years ago, which is a piece from a time period when red was presumably not made. Thus, an older syrup pitcher mould was resurrected and used during the red production. That gives hope for red shakers, cruets, and other pieces not yet seen in red. You can view this syrup in *Very Rare Glassware of the Depression Years, Fourth Series*. We bought a large collection of red Rock Crystal from a former McKee employee in the late 1970s. He had eight or nine flat candy bottoms, which he explained, were soup bowls. I gather that may have been a method to get rid of excess stock.

Red, crystal, and amber sets can be completed with tenacity. There are diverse pieces available; you need to determine what items you want. Instead of buying every tumbler and stem made, you can pick a couple of each, choosing a style you prefer. Even collectors with limited budgets can start a small crystal or amber set. Red will take a deeper pocket. Red coloration varies. It runs from very light to a very deep red that almost looks black. We collected it for about 20 years and many times we passed on a piece we needed because it was too dark or too light a color, something I would not do, today, because it's so scarce.

Rock Crystal pieces are often bought by collectors of other patterns to use as accessory items. Vases, cruets, candlesticks, and an abundance of serving pieces are some of the items obtained. Serving pieces abound; enjoy using them.

There are two different sizes of punch bowls. The recent purchase of a smaller-based bowl absolutely confirms this. The base for the larger bowl has an opening 5" across, and stands 6⅟16" tall. This base fits a punch bowl that is 4³⁄₁₆" across the bottom. The other style base has only a 4³⁄₁₆" opening, but is also 6⅟16" tall. The bowl to fit this base is only 3¼" across the bottom.

The egg plate is shown standing up in the rear of the photo on page 198. Often these are found with gold trim; they were probably a promotional item. In this part of Florida, I find Lazy Susans quite often. They consist of a revolving metal stand with a Rock Crystal relish for a top. I have only found these here; so, they may have been a give-away or premium in this region.

In the 20s and 30s, Tiffin also made a Rock Crystal similar to McKee's. Their wares had one 8-to-11-petaled daisy flower with ruffled rim lines above it, round pedestal feet, and ribbed type handles. Too, McKee, itself, made a similar pattern to their Rock Crystal, which was called Puritan and was part of their Prescut series as was Rock Crystal. Some of the earliest made Rock Crystal pieces are marked Prescut. Puritan had two 11-petaled daisy flowers, honeycombed effect stems, and ribbed handles, but no long, "S" type scrolls surrounding the (five-petal) flower that enhances the Rock Crystal design. I'm beginning to get letters about these "almost" Rock Crystal finds.

	Crystal	All Other Colors	Red
* Bonbon, 7½", s.e.	22.00	35.00	60.00
Bowl, 4", s.e.	12.00	22.00	32.00
Bowl, 4½", s.e.	20.00	22.00	32.00
Bowl, 5", s.e.	22.00	24.00	45.00
** Bowl, 5", finger bowl with 7" plate, p.e.	35.00	45.00	95.00
Bowl, 7", pickle or spoon tray	30.00	40.00	75.00
Bowl, 7", salad, s.e.	24.00	37.50	75.00
Bowl, 8", salad, s.e.	27.50	37.50	85.00
Bowl, 8½", center handle			250.00
Bowl, 9", salad, s.e.	45.00	50.00	125.00
Bowl, 10½", salad, s.e.	25.00	50.00	100.00
Bowl, 11½", 2-part relish	38.00	50.00	85.00
Bowl, 12", oblong celery	27.50	45.00	95.00
*** Bowl, 12½", footed center bowl	85.00	125.00	295.00
Bowl, 12½", 5-part relish	45.00		
Bowl, 13", roll tray	45.00	60.00	125.00
Bowl, 14", 6-part relish	50.00	65.00	
Butter dish and cover	335.00		
Butter dish bottom	200.00		
Butter dish top	135.00		
**** Candelabra, 2-lite, pair	50.00	105.00	295.00
Candelabra, 3-lite, pair	65.00	195.00	395.00
Candlestick, flat, stemmed, pair	40.00	65.00	150.00
Candlestick, 5½", low, pair	40.00	65.00	195.00
Candlestick, 8", tall, pair	100.00	165.00	475.00
Candy and cover, footed, 9¼"	75.00	90.00	295.00
Candy and cover, round	75.00	85.00	195.00
Cake stand, 11", 2¾" high, footed	35.00	52.50	125.00
Cheese stand, 2¾"	22.00	30.00	50.00
Comport, 7"	50.00	50.00	95.00
Creamer, flat, s.e.	37.50		
Creamer, 9 ounce, footed	20.00	32.00	67.50
Cruet and stopper, 6 ounce, oil	115.00		
Cup, 7 ounce	15.00	27.50	70.00
Egg plate	35.00		
Goblet, 7½ ounce, 8 ounce, low footed	20.00	27.50	57.50
Goblet, 11 ounce, low footed, iced tea	20.00	30.00	67.50
Ice dish (3 styles)	40.00		
Jelly, 5", footed, s.e.	30.00	27.50	52.50
Lamp, electric	250.00	395.00	695.00
Parfait, 3½ ounce, low footed	25.00	37.50	85.00
Pitcher, quart, s.e.	165.00	225.00	
Pitcher, ½ gallon, 7½" high	135.00	195.00	
Pitcher, 9", large covered	175.00	250.00	850.00
Pitcher, fancy tankard	195.00	695.00	995.00
Plate, 6", bread and butter, s.e.	9.00	9.50	22.00
Plate, 7½", p.e. & s.e.	10.00	12.00	25.00
Plate, 8½", p.e. & s.e.	15.00	12.50	35.00
Plate, 9", s.e.	18.00	22.00	55.00
Plate, 10½", s.e.	25.00	30.00	65.00
Plate, 10½", dinner, s.e. (large center design)	47.50	70.00	195.00
Plate, 11½", s.e.	18.00	25.00	57.50
Punch bowl and stand, 14" (2 styles)	695.00		
Punch bowl stand only (2 styles)	250.00		
Salt and pepper (2 styles), pair	90.00	125.00	
Salt dip	60.00		
Sandwich server, center-handle	30.00	40.00	145.00

* s.e. McKee designation for scalloped edge **p.e. McKee designation for plain edge
*** Red Slag $350.00; Cobalt $325.00 **** Cobalt $325.00

ROCK CRYSTAL (Cont.)

	Crystal	All Other Colors	Red
Saucer	7.50	8.50	22.00
Sherbet or egg, 3½ ounce, footed	20.00	25.00	60.00
Spooner	45.00		
Stemware, 1 ounce footed, cordial	20.00	40.00	60.00
Stemware, 2 ounce, wine	25.00	28.00	50.00
Stemware, 3 ounce, wine	22.00	33.00	55.00
Stemware, 3½ ounce, footed, cocktail	16.00	21.00	45.00
Stemware, 6 ounce, footed, champagne	16.00	23.00	35.00
Stemware, 7 ounce	16.00	25.00	52.50
Stemware, 8 ounce, large footed goblet	22.00	26.00	57.50
Sundae, 6 ounce, low footed	12.00	18.00	38.00
Sugar, 10 ounce, open	15.00	22.00	45.00
Sugar, lid	35.00	50.00	135.00
Syrup with lid	195.00		895.00
Tray, 5⅜" x 7⅜", ⅞" high	65.00		
Tumbler, 2½ ounce, whiskey	20.00	30.00	50.00
Tumbler, 5 ounce, juice	16.00	25.00	57.50
Tumbler, 5 ounce, old fashioned	20.00	27.50	60.00
Tumbler, 9 ounce, concave or straight	22.00	26.00	52.50
Tumbler, 12 ounce, concave or straight	30.00	35.00	75.00
Vase, 6", cupped	90.00		
Vase, cornucopia	125.00	150.00	275.00
Vase, 11", footed	85.00	125.00	225.00

"ROMANESQUE" L. E. SMITH GLASS COMPANY, Early 1930s

Colors: Black, amber, crystal, pink, yellow, and green.

This jeweled arches "Romanesque" pattern is drawing in more and more collectors with its magnetic charm.

See the black 10½" console bowl that is not footed, but comes in two parts. The bowl rests on that plain, detached base. I imagine these may have been a tad precarious; but a number of companies made bowls during this era, which resided on matched or different colored stands. You may find the bowl separate from the base these days, making it appear something like a turned edge plate. These were originally designed as console sets, having a pair of candles at each side, to be used as centerpieces on the rectangular "sideboards" and buffets of that era. The stands made the bowls taller than the candles.

Pink is hard to find, so notice the footed console in that color. At a recent show, an attendee offered me another one for $500.00, and when I said I wasn't interested, he wanted an offer. I had bought the one pictured for $40.00 less a discount, so I didn't want to insult him with an offer. I did wonder where he came up with his price though.

Green and amber seem to be the prevailing colors; we have, so far, spotted plates, candles, ruffled sherbets, and the bowl part of the console in amber. Notice the newly listed two-handled plate in the photo. The yellow is a bright, canary yellow that is often called vaseline by collectors. Those tri-cornered candles stand 2½" high.

The snack trays were sold with a sherbet to hold fruit or dessert. An original ad called these a luncheon set.

Black pieces have the design on the bottoms; thus, the console bowl was turned over so you could see the pattern. I have only seen bowls and cake stands in black. If you have other information or unlisted pieces in this pattern, please let me know.

	* All Colors		* All Colors
Bowl, 10", footed, 4¼" high	75.00	Plate, 8", round	9.00
Bowl, 10½"	45.00	Plate, 10", octagonal	22.00
Cake plate, 11½" x 2¾"	40.00	Plate, 10", octagonal, 2-handled	30.00
Candlestick, 2½", pair	25.00	Tray, snack	15.00
Plate, 5½", octagonal	5.00	Sherbet, plain top	8.00
Plate, 7", octagonal	7.00	Sherbet, scalloped top	10.00
Plate, 8", octagonal	10.00	Vase, 7½", fan	55.00

*Black or canary add 30%

ROSE CAMEO BELMONT TUMBLER COMPANY, 1931

Color: Green.

Belmont Tumbler Company patented Rose Cameo in 1931. It only has seven pieces and it is possible that the actual production was done at Hazel Atlas. After all, Belmont was basically a tumbler-making company. Glass shards have been found in excavations at a Hazel Atlas factory site in West Virginia. Contrarily, a yellow Cloverleaf shaker was dug up at the site of Akro Agate's factory in Clarksburg, West Virginia; and we believe Akro had nothing to do with making Cloverleaf. (Did you know some glass collectors apparently engage in archaeological pursuits of glass?) Actually, the more we learn about how the companies farmed out their moulds and/or, contract glass runs, anything is possible. Rather than lose a contract, a company could make some arrangement with another company producing the requested color rather than change over vats to run it themselves. A bonded person transferred the valuable moulds between the plants.

All three Rose Cameo bowls are difficult to find; but the smaller berry is the easiest. Most collectors are not finding the straight-sided 6" bowl. That is the bowl sitting on its edge on the right that makes it look like a plate.

Rose Cameo is not puzzling new collectors as it once did. Cameo, with its dancing girl, and this cameo-encircled rose were often confused in bygone days. An informed collecting public rarely makes those mistakes today.

There are two styles of tumblers; one flares and one does not. Some day I'll find the other style and show them together.

Bowl, 4½", berry	15.00	Plate, 7", salad	15.00
Bowl, 5", cereal	22.00	Sherbet	15.00
Bowl, 6", straight sides	30.00	Tumbler, 5", footed (2 styles)	25.00

ROSEMARY, "DUTCH ROSE" FEDERAL GLASS COMPANY, 1935 – 1937

Colors: Amber, green, pink; some iridized.

The Rosemary pattern came about because of Hocking's earlier patent to the Mayfair name. The story of Rosemary's being redesigned from Federal's Mayfair pattern can be read on page 128. Rosemary is an engaging pattern. I've never heard anybody say they were sorry they chose it to collect — even those still searching for pieces.

Pink is found in minute amounts. Tumblers and grill plates have vanished into collections. It is frustrating to try to collect a color or pattern that is not being found at any price. An amber set can be assembled; there are only a few pieces being found irregularly, particularly the cereal. I cannot remember when I have seen green cream soups.

The transitional green cream soups (see Federal Mayfair) could be substituted for Rosemary in a pinch. An entire set of green Rosemary will probably take quite some time to gather.

Cereal bowls, cream soups, grill plates, and tumblers are few and far between. I noticed a want list for green Rosemary cream soups on the Internet. I wish I had one for photography. New collectors should know that grill plates are the divided plates usually associated with diners or grills (restaurants) in that time. Food was kept from flowing together by those raised partitions (normally three).

The sugar has no handles and is often mislabeled as a sherbet. There is no sherbet.

	Amber	Green	Pink
Bowl, 5", berry	6.00	9.00	14.00
Bowl, 5", cream soup	18.00	30.00	45.00
Bowl, 6", cereal	30.00	38.00	50.00
Bowl, 10", oval vegetable	18.00	30.00	50.00
Creamer, footed	10.00	12.50	25.00
Cup	7.50	9.50	12.00
Plate, 6¾", salad	6.00	8.50	13.00
Plate, dinner	10.00	15.00	25.00
Plate, grill	10.00	20.00	30.00
Platter, 12", oval	16.00	25.00	38.00
Saucer	5.00	5.00	6.00
Sugar, footed	10.00	12.50	25.00
Tumbler, 4¼", 9 ounce	32.00	40.00	75.00

ROULETTE, "MANY WINDOWS" HOCKING GLASS COMPANY, 1935 – 1938

Colors: Green, pink, and crystal.

This "winning" pattern, as Hocking once advertised it, has six different tumblers.

I now know why. These were promotional sets, usually meaning beverage sets with various configurations of tumblers which were offered retailers as product "lures" to entice customers to their shops. Once there for the "special" (usually a pitcher and six tumblers for around $1.00), then they could expect impulse buying to take over. Since this appears to have been a widely accepted practice, it obviously worked. Sometimes an entire luncheon set of 14 or 19 pieces was the lure. This pattern was intended for these purposes.

Roulette is the bona fide name of the pattern which collectors formerly called "Many Windows."

Pink pitchers and tumblers are easier to find than green ones, but pink Roulette was only made in those pieces. Both colors are similarly priced. There are five sizes of pink flat tumblers; but I have never found a pink-footed tumbler. Have you?

Cups, saucers, sherbets, and luncheon plates can be found in green rather easily. The 12" sandwich plate and fruit bowls are seldom encountered. Juice tumblers and the old fashioned are most elusive. I still have not found a green juice; but thanks to a reader I was finally able to buy a green whiskey. The whiskeys sell very well to the shot glass collecting group that is making its presence increasingly known in our collecting world.

Crystal tumbler and pitcher sets are very seldom found; however, there is limited demand for the few that have surfaced. Some crystal sets are decorated with colored stripes. In fact, this striped effect gives them an Art Deco look that impresses me.

	Crystal	Pink, Green		Crystal	Pink, Green
Bowl, 9", fruit	9.50	25.00	Sherbet	3.50	6.00
Cup	4.00	8.00	Tumbler, 3¼", 5 ounce, juice	7.00	28.00
Pitcher, 8", 65 ounce	30.00	45.00	Tumbler, 3¼", 7½ oz., old fashioned	23.00	45.00
Plate, 6", sherbet	3.50	5.00	Tumbler, 4⅛", 9 ounce, water	13.00	28.00
Plate, 8½", luncheon	5.00	8.00	Tumbler, 5⅛", 12 ounce, iced tea	16.00	35.00
Plate, 12", sandwich	11.00	17.50	Tumbler, 5½", 10 ounce, footed	14.00	35.00
Saucer	1.50	3.50	Whiskey, 2½", 1½ ounce	14.00	18.00

"ROUND ROBIN" POSSIBLY ECONOMY GLASS CO., Probably early 1930s

Colors: Green, iridescent, and crystal.

The Domino tray is the fancier, unanticipated piece in this small pattern. Hocking's Cameo is another pattern in Depression glass which offers a sugar cube tray. This tray has, so far, only been found in green "Round Robin." It is shown standing up behind the creamer and sugar in the picture. For new readers, the Domino tray held the creamer in the center ring with sugar cubes surrounding it. Sugar cubes were made by a famous sugar company, and the tray became synonymous with this name. I have seen few of these over the years. A damaged one sold for $50.00 recently. Grab one if you can!

Sherbets and berry bowls are the most difficult green pieces to come across in "Round Robin" outside the Domino tray. I have not even found a green berry bowl myself. Sherbets and berry bowls are plentiful in iridescent. Saucers seem to be harder to find than the cups. Only a few patterns can claim that. The "Round Robin" cup is one of the few footed ones available in Depression glass. I have not found an iridescent cup and saucer. Do you have one?

Some crystal "Round Robin" is found today. Crystal was sprayed and baked to accomplish the iridized look. Obviously, not all the crystal was sprayed, since we find it occasionally. Too, Cathy just found a "Round Robin" creamer that is top half irridized and bottom half crystal. Their spraying hand, or technique, wasn't too precise, either!

A reader sent me word that author James Merrell has identified the manufacturer of this pattern as Economy Glass. Finally we know the pattern's origins.

	Green	Iridescent
Bowl, 4" berry	10.00	9.00
Cup, footed	7.00	7.00
Creamer, footed	12.50	9.00
Domino tray	110.00	
Plate, 6", sherbet	3.00	2.50
Plate, 8", luncheon	8.00	4.00
Plate, 12", sandwich	12.00	10.00
Saucer	2.00	2.00
Sherbet	9.00	10.00
Sugar	12.50	9.00

ROXANA HAZEL ATLAS GLASS COMPANY, 1932

Colors: "Golden Topaz," crystal, and some white.

I pictured a plate with its design highlighted in gold in hopes the Roxana pattern would show better in the photograph.

Thanks to a couple of Michigan collectors, we now know why Roxana seemed to be more prevalent there. An ad they supplied has been shown in previous editions. If you ate Star Brand Oats, you were able to receive one piece of "Golden Topaz" table glassware in every package. This "Golden Topaz" is what we now call yellow Roxana. That ad may show why the deep 4½" bowl and the 5½" plates are so hard to find. They were not packed as a premium in these oats. I am presuming that the plate shown in the ad is the 6" one for the sherbet although no descriptions are noted.

All seven known pieces are shown below. This small pattern was obviously created strictly as promotional ware for product; thus, its deficiency of pieces. Hazel Atlas only chronicled Roxana for one year.

Only the 4½" deep bowl has been found in Platonite.

	Yellow	White
Bowl, 4½" x 2⅜"	15.00	20.00
Bowl, 5", berry	16.00	
Bowl, 6", cereal	20.00	
Plate, 5½"	12.00	
Plate, 6", sherbet	10.00	
Sherbet, footed	12.00	
Tumbler, 4¼", 9 ounce	22.00	

ROYAL LACE HAZEL ATLAS GLASS COMPANY, 1934 – 1941

Colors: Cobalt blue, crystal, green, pink; some amethyst. (See Reproduction Section.)

Royal Lace in cobalt blue is ever dear to my heart because I took box loads of it to my first Depression glass show in Springfield, Missouri, in 1971 and very nicely supplemented my then $7,200.00 nine month pay teaching salary by selling it to dealers and authors alike. I also got a crash course in Depression glass and met the pioneer author, Weatherman. I had questions galore. She told me that the cobalt color for Royal Lace pattern was something of a fluke according to a factory employee she interviewed. It seems a cereal contractor rather suddenly didn't need any more Shirley Temple mugs and they had all this blue glass left in the vats and began looking around for something to do with it. Thus, the ever popular, cobalt blue Royal Lace pattern was born. (She also told me that Hocking didn't make either green cookie jars or yellow Mayfair indented butter dish bottoms and was bowled over when I pulled examples of each from my "sack of goodies.")

There are almost as many collectors for green Royal Lace as for blue. Green is found in quantity in England. A wealth of basic "tea" sets are there, i.e. cups, saucers, creamers, and sugars. I had a source for a couple of years that shipped me American Depression glass from there. The straight-sided pitcher must be prevalent in England as I bought six or seven of those in a couple of years. I never bought any other style pitcher and only water tumblers. Shakers with original Hazel Atlas labels proclaiming "Made in America" were on several sets I purchased. You have to wonder if Hazel Atlas named this pattern specifically for this "royal" market. It seems likely since this would have been made before the coronation that so enthralled everybody.

There were five different pitchers made in Royal Lace: a) 48 ounce, straight side; b) 64 ounce, 8", no ice lip; c) 68 ounce, 8", w/ice lip; d) 86 ounce, 8", no ice lip; e) 96 ounce, 8½", w/ice lip. The 10-ounce difference in the last two listed is caused by the spout on the pitcher without lip dipping below the top edge of the pitcher. This causes the liquid to run out before you get to the top. All spouted pitchers will vary in ounce capacity (up to eight ounces) depending upon how the spout tilts or dips. Always measure ounce capacities until no more liquid can be added without running out. The 68-ounce pitcher with ice lip is rare in green and cobalt blue.

The 4⅞", ten ounce tumblers have all been gobbled up into collections; but the number of Iced teas and juice tumblers is rapidly dwindling. Some collectors only purchase water tumblers and the straight-sided pitcher for their collections. This style of pitcher and water tumblers are more prolific and, therefore, more inexpensively priced; but demand continues to drive up the price.

Be aware that the cookie jar, juice, and water tumblers have been reproduced in a very dark cobalt blue which is quite dull looking in comparison to the real thing. These are also out now in pink and I think, green.

Both a rolled-edge console bowl and rolled-edge candlesticks have been found in amethyst. The only other amethyst pieces are the sherbets in metal holders and the cookie jar bottom used for toddy sets. There were reports of shakers.

Like many other patterns we longingly pursue, today, this was sold at Sears.

ROYAL LACE

	Crystal	Pink	Green	Blue
Bowl, 4¾", cream soup	17.50	32.00	38.00	48.00
Bowl, 5", berry	15.00	33.00	35.00	52.00
Bowl, 10", round berry	20.00	40.00	30.00	75.00
Bowl, 10", 3-legged, straight edge	35.00	65.00	75.00	95.00
* Bowl, 10", 3-legged, rolled edge	295.00	125.00	135.00	650.00
Bowl, 10", 3-legged, ruffled edge	55.00	115.00	135.00	750.00
Bowl, 11", oval vegetable	28.00	35.00	40.00	70.00
Butter dish and cover	80.00	195.00	275.00	695.00
Butter dish bottom	50.00	140.00	180.00	495.00
Butter dish top	30.00	55.00	95.00	200.00
Candlestick, straight edge, pair	40.00	75.00	95.00	165.00
** Candlestick, rolled edge, pair	60.00	155.00	175.00	550.00
Candlestick ruffled edge, pair	50.00	150.00	195.00	550.00
Cookie jar and cover	35.00	60.00	100.00	375.00
Cream, footed	16.00	22.00	28.00	60.00
Cup	9.00	22.00	20.00	45.00
Nut bowl	295.00	450.00	450.00	1,595.00
Pitcher, 48 ounce, straight sides	40.00	100.00	135.00	190.00

	Crystal	Pink	Green	Blue
Pitcher, 64 oz., 8", w/o lip	45.00	110.00	120.00	295.00
Pitcher, 8", 68 oz., w/lip	50.00	115.00		310.00
Pitcher, 8", 86 oz., w/o lip	50.00	135.00	175.00	395.00
Pitcher, 8½", 96 oz., w/lip	75.00	150.00	160.00	495.00
Plate, 6", sherbet	8.00	9.00	12.00	17.00
Plate, 8½", luncheon	8.00	15.00	16.00	43.00
Plate, 9⅞", dinner	18.00	30.00	35.00	45.00
Plate, 9⅞", grill	11.00	22.00	28.00	40.00
Platter, 13", oval	20.00	45.00	42.00	65.00
Salt and pepper, pair	42.00	65.00	140.00	325.00
Saucer	5.00	7.00	10.00	14.00
Sherbet, footed	17.00	19.00	25.00	55.00
*** Sherbet in metal holder	4.00			42.00
Sugar	11.00	20.00	22.00	40.00
Sugar lid	20.00	60.00	60.00	195.00
Tumbler, 3½", 5 ounce	20.00	33.00	35.00	60.00
Tumbler, 4⅛", 9 ounce	16.00	28.00	32.00	52.50
Tumbler, 4⅞", 10 ounce	40.00	85.00	95.00	140.00
Tumbler, 5⅜", 12 ounce	40.00	75.00	75.00	135.00
**** Toddy or cider set includes cookie jar metal lid, metal tray, 8 roly-poly cups, and ladle				295.00

* Amethyst $900.00   ** Amethyst $900.00   *** Amethyst $40.00   **** Amethyst $195.00

ROYAL RUBY ANCHOR HOCKING GLASS COMPANY, 1938 – 1940

Color: Ruby red.

The inauguration of Anchor Hocking's patented Royal Ruby color was in 1938 using their contemporary moulds. I am identifying and pricing only pieces of Royal Ruby introduced before 1940 in my listing here. Royal Ruby pieces made after 1940 are now in the *Collectible Glassware from the 40s, 50s, 60s....* Remember, only Anchor Hocking's red can rightfully be called Royal Ruby. Oyster and Pearl, Old Cafe, and Coronation were among the patterns used in the original Royal Ruby campaign. A smattering of pieces in Royal Ruby have been found in other Anchor Hocking lines including Colonial, Ring, Manhattan, Queen Mary, and Miss America. These Royal Ruby pieces are generally considered rare in these highly collected patterns and most are of exceptional quality for Anchor Hocking, having ground bottoms which are usually not found on the normal mass-produced glassware. There were other designs produced that were never given pattern names. None of those items are priced in the listing below.

I suspect that the name of the color was inspired by our country's enchantment with the English coronation of Edward VIII in 1936 and his ensuing relinquishing of that royal crown. Witness our fascination with celebrities in today's world and you have an inkling of the impact then.

Bonbon, 6½"	8.50	Cup (Old Cafe)	12.00
Bowl, 3¾", berry (Old Cafe)	9.00	Cup, round	6.00
Bowl, 4½", handled (Coronation)	7.00	Goblet, ball stem	12.00
Bowl, 4⅞", smooth (Sandwich)	12.50	Jewel box, 4¼", crystal w/Ruby cov.	12.50
Bowl, 5¼" heart-shaped, 1-handled (Oys & Prl)	20.00	Lamp (Old Cafe)	150.00
Bowl, 5¼", scalloped (Sandwich)	20.00	Marmalade, 5⅛", crystal w/Ruby cov.	7.50
Bowl, 5½", 1-handled (Oys & Prl)	20.00	Plate, 8½", luncheon (Coronation)	10.00
Bowl, 6½", deep-handled (Oys & Prl)	27.50	Plate, 9⅛", dinner, round	11.00
Bowl, 6½", handled (Coronation)	18.00	Plate, 13½", sandwich (Oys & Prl)	55.00
Bowl, 6½", scalloped (Sandwich)	27.50	Puff box, 4⅝", crystal w/Ruby cov.	9.00
Bowl, 8", handled (Coronation)	15.00	Relish tray insert (Manhattan)	4.00
Bowl, 8¼", scalloped (Sandwich)	50.00	Saucer, round	2.50
Bowl, 9", closed handles (Old Cafe)	18.00	Sherbet, low footed (Old Cafe)	12.00
Bowl, 10½", deep fruit (Oys & Prl)	60.00	Sugar, footed	7.50
Candle holder, 3½", pair (Oys & Prl)	65.00	Sugar, lid	11.00
Candle holder, 4½", pair (Queen Mary)	75.00	Tray, 6" x 4½"	12.50
Candy dish, 8" mint, low (Old Cafe)	18.00	Tumbler, 3" juice (Old Cafe)	20.00
Candy jar, 5½", crystal w/Ruby cov. (Old Cafe)	25.00	Tumbler, 4" water (Old Cafe)	30.00
Cigarette box/card holder, 6⅛" x 4", crystal w/Ruby top	65.00	Vase, 7¼" (Old Cafe)	50.00
Creamer, footed	9.00	Vase, 9", two styles	17.50
Cup (Coronation)	6.50		

"S" PATTERN, "STIPPLED ROSE BAND" MacBETH-EVANS GLASS COMPANY, 1930 – 1933

Colors: Crystal; crystal w/trims of silver, blue, green, amber; pink; some amber, green, fired-on red; ruby, Monax, and light yellow.

When collecting Depression glass first started in the early '70s, there was real excitement about "S" pattern. It came in various colors and trims, with a couple of styles of pitchers and a huge cake plate like the much ballyhooed Dogwood one; and when the first pieces were discovered in red, it was as exciting as a 100 point rise in the stock market! Now, I see this dear, delicate little pattern, which wasn't long in production, languishing at markets. Why?

"S" Pattern with platinum or pastel bands commands more respect than does plain crystal. Amber, blue, or green banded crystal was made. Crystal luncheon plates could be striking against a colored charger plate that would emphasize the romanticized fleur de lis pattern occurring as a scrolled rim design.

Amber "S" Pattern sometimes appears more yellow than amber. The color is almost the hue of Hocking's Princess. A dinner plate does occur in amber "S" Pattern and the amber pitcher in this pattern is considered rare. No crystal (nor crystal with trim) dinner plates have been spotted.

A pink or green pitcher and tumbler set appears occasionally. Years ago, there were a number of pitcher collectors per se; rare pitchers sold fast in the $200.00 – 500.00 range. Now, those same pitchers are commanding four figure prices.

Finding a pink tumbler that has a moulded blossom design will indicate a "Dogwood" moulded tumbler and not "S" Pattern. The only pink or green tumblers found in "S" Pattern have an applied, silk-screened "S" design on the glass. However, crystal tumblers come with moulded "S" designs. MacBeth-Evans made a generic beverage set having this mould blank shape with *no* pattern that was sold to go with various patterns, but which collectors consider to be *no* pattern beverage sets.

Fired-on red and true red "S" Pattern items are rare.

	Crystal	Yellow, Amber, Crystal W/ Trims			Crystal	Yellow, Amber, Crystal W/Trims
*Bowl, 5½", cereal	5.00	9.00		Plate, grill	6.50	8.00
Bowl, 8½", large berry	15.00	20.00		Plate, 11¾", heavy cake	40.00	60.00
*Creamer, thick or thin	5.00	7.00		***Plate, 13", heavy cake	65.00	85.00
*Cup, thick or thin	3.50	4.50		Saucer	2.00	2.50
Pitcher, 80 ounce (like "Dogwood"), green or pink 550.00	60.00	150.00		Sherbet, low footed	4.50	7.00
Pitcher, 80 ounce (like "American Sweetheart")	85.00			*Sugar, thick and thin	5.00	6.50
Plate, 6", sherbet, Monax 8.00	2.50	3.00		Tumbler, 3½", 5 ounce	5.00	8.00
**Plate, 8¼", luncheon	7.00	6.00		Tumbler, 4", 9 ounce, green or pink 50.00	10.00	12.00
Plate, 9¼", dinner		10.00		Tumbler, 4¾, 10 ounce	11.00	12.00
				Tumbler, 5", 12 ounce	12.00	15.00

* Fired-on red items will run approximately twice price of amber   **Red $40.00; Monax $10.00   ***Amber $77.50

SANDWICH INDIANA GLASS COMPANY, 1920s–1980s

Colors: Crystal late 1920s – today; teal blue 1950s – 1980s; milk white mid-1950s; amber late 1920s – 1980s; red 1933, 1970s; Smokey Blue 1976 – 1977; pink, green 1920s – early 1930s.

Since green Indiana Sandwich was chosen for the cover of my *Pocket Guide to Depression Glass, 12th Edition*, I have received numerous calls and letters from people who think they have old Sandwich, but who actually have Tiara's 1980s version called Chantilly. On the bottom of page 210, I have attempted to show an old Sandwich and a new Chantilly decanter with a black light below them. None of the Tiara green will glow under ultraviolet light. I hasten to add that this is not a general test for age of glass. There is glass made yesterday which will glow under black light. It is a test for this particular green Sandwich vs. Chantilly pattern. Any green piece that has no price listed is presumably new. Indiana also made a lighter pink in recent years.

Amber Sandwich is priced here with crystal. Realize that most all amber found today is from the Tiara issues and is not Depression era glass. There is no easy way to distinguish old crystal from new.

Only six items in red Sandwich date from 1933, i.e., cups, saucers, luncheon plates, water goblets, creamers, and sugars. In 1970s, Tiara Home Products marketed red Sandwich. Today, there is no difference in pricing red unless you have some marked 1933 Chicago World's Fair, which will fetch considerably more.

	Amber Crystal	Teal Blue	Red	Pink/ Green
Ashtrays (club, spade, heart, diamond shapes, each)	3.25			
Basket, 10" high	33.00			
Bowl, 4¼", berry	3.50			
Bowl, 6"	4.00			
Bowl, 6", hexagonal	5.00	14.00		
Bowl, 8½"	11.00			
Bowl, 9", console	16.00			40.00
Bowl, 11½", console	18.50			50.00
Butter dish and cover, domed	22.00	*155.00		
Butter dish bottom	6.00	42.50		
Butter dish top	16.00	112.50		
Candlesticks, 3½", pair	16.00			45.00
Candlesticks 7", pair	30.00			
Creamer	9.00		45.00	
Celery, 10½"	16.00			
Creamer and sugar on diamond shaped tray	16.00	32.00		
Cruet, 6½ ounce and stopper	26.00	135.00		175.00
Cup	3.50	8.50	27.50	
Decanter and stopper	22.00		80.00	150.00

	Amber Crystal	Teal Blue	Red	Pink/ Green
Goblet, 9 ounce	13.00		45.00	
Mayonnaise, footed	13.00			35.00
Pitcher, 68 ounce	22.00		130.00	
Plate, 6", sherbet	3.00	7.00		
Plate, 7", bread and butter	4.00			
Plate, 8", oval, indent for cup	5.50			15.00
Plate, 8⅜", luncheon	4.75		20.00	
Plate, 10½", dinner	8.00			20.00
Plate, 13", sandwich	12.75	24.00	35.00	25.00
Puff box	16.00			
Salt and pepper, pair	17.50			
Sandwich server, center	18.00		45.00	35.00
Saucer	2.50	4.50	7.50	
Sherbet, 3¼"	5.50	14.00		
Sugar, large	9.00		45.00	
Sugar lid for large size	13.00			
Tumbler, 3 ounce, footed, cocktail	7.50			
Tumbler, 8 ounce, footed, water	9.00			
Tumbler, 12 ounce, footed, iced tea	10.00			
Wine, 3", 4 ounce	6.00		12.50	25.00

*Beware recent vintage sell $22.00

SHARON, "CABBAGE ROSE" FEDERAL GLASS COMPANY, 1935 – 1939

Colors: Pink, green, amber; some crystal. (See Reproduction Section.)

Notice the old ad showing a coupon exchange for amber Sharon. We reproduced only parts of this advertisement. The numbers in the right column under Golden Glow (amber) tableware represent the number of coupons from large cans of Grand Union Tea product needed to order the item. Labels from small cans were worth only one half. In any case, most of the items shown were for amber Sharon and Patrician. This ad also listed pieces from Hocking (Manhattan), Jeannette (Jennyware), and McKee (Glasbake), although the major portion of the ad was for Federal wares. Those refrigerator containers are priced in my *Kitchen Glassware of the Depression Years*. The pitcher, without design, sells in the $35.00 range.

Prices have softened a bit for common pieces of amber Sharon, which are presently sitting at markets. Footed amber tumblers in Sharon are rare and pitchers with ice lips are twice as difficult to locate as pink. However, there are definitely fewer collectors for them right now which translates into fewer dollars commanded due to lack of demand.

Calls for pink Sharon have risen, causing some inflation in those prices. New collectors were timid about starting this extremely popular pink pattern a few years ago due to some reproductions flooding markets. However, once everyone learned how to recognize them (see the reproduction section), demand for this durable, 65-year-old pattern flourished once again. Cathy's grandmother told her she remembered the drummer who came around selling Sharon put the plate on the floor and stood on it to show how sturdy this was. The price for a pink Sharon cheese dish has crossed into four figures. The top for the cheese and butter dish is the same piece. The bottoms are different. The butter bottom is a 1½" deep bowl with a sloping, indented ledge while the cheese bottom is a salad plate with a raised band of glass on its surface within which the lid rests. The bottom piece is the rare part of this cheese. Amber cheese dishes were also made; but none have ever surfaced in green. A collector told me he'd found an old ad showing these were a special promotion item run for some cheese products. It would appear no one much wanted the product, else more of these dishes would have been produced and we wouldn't have such a scarcity of them, today. Other infrequently found pink Sharon items include flat, thick iced teas and jam dishes. The jam dish is like the butter bottom except it has no indentation for the top. It differs from the 1⅞" deep soup bowl by standing only 1½" tall. Once in a while, you can find a jam dish priced as a soup bowl; but that happens rarely.

Green Sharon pitchers and tumblers in all sizes are difficult to find. Surprisingly, the green pitcher without ice lip is

(Sharon continued on page 212)

211

SHARON

rarer than the one with an ice lip. You will find thick or thin flat iced teas and waters. The thick tumblers are easier to find in green; and the price reflects that. In amber and pink, the heavy iced teas are more rarely seen than the waters. There are no green soup bowls, only jam dishes.

The Sharon cereal was redesigned into a child's feeding dish. One is pictured below. I have only seen this bowl in amber and few of those.

	Amber	Pink	Green
Bowl, 5", berry	8.50	14.00	18.00
Bowl, 5", cream soup	28.00	50.00	55.00
Bowl, 6", cereal	22.00	30.00	30.00
Bowl, 7¾", flat soup, 1⅞" deep	55.00	60.00	
Bowl, 8½", large berry	5.00	35.00	38.00
Bowl, 9½", oval vegetable	18.00	38.00	35.00
Bowl, 10½", fruit	22.00	45.00	42.50
Butter dish and cover	50.00	60.00	90.00
Butter dish bottom	25.00	30.00	40.00
Butter dish top	25.00	30.00	50.00
* Cake plate, 11½", footed	27.50	42.00	65.00
Candy jar and cover	45.00	50.00	175.00
Cheese dish and cover	195.00	1,500.00	
Creamer, footed	14.00	20.00	22.50
Cup	10.00	14.00	20.00
Jam dish, 7½"	40.00	285.00	60.00

	Amber	Pink	Green
Pitcher, 80 ounce, w/ice lip	155.00	195.00	450.00
Pitcher, 80 ounce, w/o ice lip	140.00	185.00	475.00
Plate, 6", bread and butter	5.00	8.00	9.00
** Plate, 7½", salad	15.00	23.00	25.00
Plate, 9½", dinner	11.00	22.00	25.00
Platter, 12½", oval	16.00	33.00	35.00
Salt and pepper, pair	40.00	60.00	70.00
Saucer	6.00	12.00	12.00
Sherbet, footed	12.00	16.00	37.50
Sugar	9.00	14.00	16.00
Sugar lid	22.00	35.00	40.00
Tumbler, 4⅛", 9 ounce, thick	26.00	42.00	80.00
Tumbler, 4⅛", 9 ounce, thin	26.00	42.00	85.00
Tumbler, 5¼", 12 ounce, thin	55.00	55.00	110.00
Tumbler, 5¼", 12 ounce, thick	65.00	95.00	110.00
*** Tumbler, 6½", 15 ounce, footed	100.00	60.00	

*Crystal $10.00   **Crystal $50.00   ***Crystal $20.00

"SHIPS" or "SAILBOAT" also known as "SPORTSMAN SERIES"
HAZEL ATLAS GLASS COMPANY, Late 1930s

Colors: Cobalt blue w/white, yellow, and red decoration, crystal w/blue.

Unfortunately, cobalt Moderntone decorated with white "Ships" is now seldom seen. Sherbet plates are harder to find than dinner plates, but both have disappeared into collections. There is no ship on the Moderntone cup that fits the saucer having a "Ships" decoration. Prices below are for mint pieces. Discolored (beige) or worn items should sell for less. When the "Ships" pattern is partially missing, it would be easier to sell if the whole ship had sunk and you only had a cobalt blue piece to sell.

The confusing "Ships" shot glass is the smallest (2¼", two ounce) tumbler, not the heavy bottomed tumbler that holds four ounces and is 3¼" tall. I have letters from people who purchased this four ounce tumbler under the impression (or having been told) it was a shot glass. It was sold as a liquor tumbler beside the shaker, but never as the shot. You will notice there is a large price difference between the authentic, two-ounce shot and the four-ounce tumbler. The price for that four-ounce tumbler has increased, but not nearly to the level of the tiny shot glass. Do you suppose they made that tumbler heavy bottomed for unsteady hands?

At least one yellow "Ships" old-fashioned tumbler has surfaced in "raincoat" yellow. Pieces come with red and white "Ships" or crystal tumblers with a blue boat.

I am fond of the decorations that have the red boats with white sails. Only pitchers and tumblers seem to be found with this patriotic red-white-blue combination.

I might mention that no red glass pitcher has ever been found to go with the red glass (different design) ships tumblers ($9.00) often found in the markets.

	Blue/White
Cup (Plain) "Moderntone"	11.00
Cocktail mixer w/stirrer	30.00
Cocktail shaker	38.00
Ice bowl	40.00
Pitcher w/o lip, 82 ounce	65.00
Pitcher w/lip, 86 ounce	75.00
Plate, 5⅞", sherbet	30.00

	Blue/White
Plate, 8", salad	30.00
Plate, 9", dinner	40.00
Saucer	20.00
Tumbler, 2 oz., 2¼", shot glass	225.00
Tumbler, 3½", whiskey	27.50
Tumbler, 4 oz., heavy bottom	27.50
Tumbler, 4 oz., 3¼", heavy bottom	27.50

	Blue/White
Tumbler, 5 ounce, 3¾", juice	14.00
Tumbler, 6 ounce, roly poly	12.00
Tumbler, 8 oz., 3⅜", old fashioned	18.00
Tumbler, 9 oz., 3¾", straight, water	14.00
Tumbler, 9 oz., 4⅝", water	11.00
Tumbler, 10½ oz., 4⅞", iced tea	16.00
Tumbler, 12 ounce, iced tea	25.00

213

"SHIPS"

SIERRA, "PINWHEEL" JEANNETTE GLASS COMPANY, 1931 – 1933

Colors: Green, pink, and some Ultra Marine.

Sierra, with its Spanish derivation meaning saw or sawtooth, is an excellent name for this delightful 30s product which is becoming very hard to find in both colors. Pink and green pitchers, tumblers, and oval vegetable bowls have disappeared into collections and few are being marketed. I rushed to check out a vegetable bowl in a mall, recently, only to notice one of the points was missing. An unparalleled problem with Sierra is finding mint conditioned items. If they were used much, one of those points chipped.

Always, always, always examine any pink Sierra butter dishes to check for the Adam/Sierra combination lid. That is the way I found my first one. Be sure to read about this elusive and pricey butter under Adam. You can see one pictured in *Very Rare Glassware of the Depression Years, Fifth Series.*

Wrong cups are often found on Sierra saucers. *Any* pink cup of nondescript origin can be found atop the saucers. Original cups have the design on the cup, albeit without the serrated rim. You have to be vigilant when you are out shopping. Saucers are becoming harder to find than cups because of damaged points. The cups, pitchers, and tumblers all have smooth edges instead of the serrated edges of the other pieces.

Mint sugar bowls are harder to find than lids.

There have been four Sierra Ultra Marine cups found, but no saucer has been spotted. Why? Were these a sample run made at the time Jeannette was producing Ultra Marine Doric and Pansy or Swirl? You might even find some fired colors of Sierra. They have been reported, though I haven't seen them.

	Pink	Green		Pink	Green
Bowl, 5½", cereal	16.00	18.00	Platter, 11", oval	55.00	75.00
Bowl, 8½", large berry	35.00	40.00	Salt and pepper, pair	45.00	45.00
Bowl, 9¼", oval vegetable	75.00	150.00	Saucer	8.00	9.00
Butter dish and cover	70.00	75.00	Serving tray, 10¼", 2 handles	22.50	20.00
Creamer	20.00	22.50	Sugar	22.00	28.00
Cup	13.00	16.00	Sugar cover	16.00	16.00
Pitcher, 6½", 32 ounce	135.00	165.00	Tumbler, 4½", 9 ounce, footed	70.00	90.00
Plate, 9", dinner	20.00	24.00			

215

SPIRAL HOCKING GLASS COMPANY, 1928 – 1930

Colors: Green, crystal, and pink.

Hocking's Spiral is one of many serpentine patterns from the Depression era which have their roots in older, pattern glass lines. Availability of Spiral in pink is limited; but green can be collected with some effort. The real difficulty lies in recognizing Hocking's Spiral among the many others produced. Notice several pieces of Spiral, the ice tub, platter, creamer, and sugar, are shaped like Hocking's popular Cameo and Block Optic patterns. The seldom seen platter has closed or tab handles, as do many made by Hocking.

A luncheon set can be assembled rather inexpensively in Spiral. However, this is not a pattern often carried to glass shows. You will have to request it.

The Spiral center-handled server has a solid handle while its Imperial Glass Company look-alike, Twisted Optic (Line #313), has a center-handled server with an open handle. The pitcher shown has the rope top treatment like found in Cameo and Block Optic. There is also a 7⅝", 54 ounce bulbous based one (like shown in Block Optic) available in the Spiral pattern. Notice there are two styles of sugars and creamers found in Swirl, one a flat based, utilitarian style and one footed with a fancier handle. Generally speaking, Spiral swirls go to the left or clockwise while Twisted Optic spirals go to the right or counterclockwise. (Westmoreland's #1710 Spiral line and Duncan's Spiral Flutes have hand-polished bottoms on flat pieces, something not found on Hocking's machine-made Spiral; also the pattern lines have different shapes from the Hocking line; so, there should be no confusion between these and Hocking Spiral).

A few pieces of Hocking Spiral have turned up in crystal though few collectors care at the moment. Green is the Spiral color dear to collector's hearts.

	Green		Green
Bowl, 4¾", berry	7.00	Preserve and cover	35.00
Bowl, 7", mixing	15.00	Salt and pepper, pair	35.00
Bowl, 8", large berry	12.50	Sandwich server, center handle	25.00
Creamer, flat or footed	9.00	Saucer	2.00
Cup	5.00	Sherbet	5.00
Ice or butter tub	30.00	Sugar, flat or footed	9.00
Pitcher, 7⅝", 54 ounce, bulbous	40.00	Tumbler, 3", 5 ounce, juice	4.50
Pitcher, 7⅝", 58 ounce	35.00	Tumbler, 5", 9 ounce, water	10.00
Plate, 6", sherbet	2.50	Tumbler, 5⅞", footed	18.00
Plate, 8", luncheon	3.50	Vase, 5¾", footed	55.00
Platter, 12"	35.00		

SQUARE "HAZEN" Line #760 et al. IMPERIAL GLASS COMPANY, c. 1930s

Colors: Crystal, green, pink, ruby

This was a small line of Imperial's which was packaged as luncheon sets having 15, 21, or 27 pieces and it's included since I was able to find a large set in an antique mall close to our home. I was intrigued by the unusual style handles and the rich, ruby coloring.

Although the owner only knew it was red glass, she had a high opinion of its value. Often, it is difficult to buy red, cobalt blue, black, or older canary glass from sellers who do not know what they have for sale. Color is frequently highly overrated. As an example, about daylight yesterday morning, I was shopping an outside antique show and picked up a piece of Emerald green Cambridge to look for a price. The owner informed me that it was an old piece of "vaseline" and he only wanted $125.00 (for that $45.00 item). I causally mentioned that the company that made it called it Emerald green and he looked at me as if I had sprouted horns. You cannot deal with uniformed sellers since they already know more than you do. Just watch for their mistakes in pricing; they will make some.

	Crystal/Pink/Green	Ruby		Crystal/Pink/Green	Ruby
Bowl, 4½", nappy	12.50	17.50	Plate, 8", salad	12.50	17.50
Bowl, 7", square, soup/salad	15.00	22.50	Saucer	5.00	7.50
Creamer, footed	20.00	25.00	Server, 10½", center handled	35.00	45.00
Cup	15.00	20.00	Shaker, square, foot, pair	35.00	50.00
Plate, 6" dessert	7.50	10.00	Sugar, footed	20.00	25.00

STARLIGHT HAZEL ATLAS GLASS COMPANY, 1938 – 1940

Colors: Crystal, pink; some white, cobalt.

Starlight can be collected economically; the difficulty (nearly 30 years into Depression glass mania) lies in finding it to buy. This small pattern has never been gathered by large numbers of collectors, but the ones who do try for a set report shortages of plates, sherbets, cereals, and the large salad bowl and liner/serving plate. One collector told me they used that bowl as a punch bowl. Pink and blue bowls make nice accessory pieces with the crystal, but only bowls are available in those colors.

The 5½" cereal is handled and measures 6" including the handles. All measurements in this book do not include handles, unless directly noted.

Do notice the Starlight punch bowl set pictured which a number of collectors wish were theirs. This set is similar in make up to the Royal Lace toddy set, having a bowl in a metal holder with an extending flat rim to accommodate cups. A metal ladle with a red knob rests in the bowl. I owe this find to an eagle-eyed collector who bought it just for me to use in my book, a gesture mightily appreciated. She told me, "I knew the moment they put that up for auction that you would like that for your book."

I often pondered why Starlight shakers were found with a one hole shaker top. I now know. It was a specially designed top made to keep the salt "moisture proof." Airko shakers with these tops are often seen in southern areas where the humid air caused shaker holes to clog. One of these moisture-proof shakers is pictured here with an original label.

	Crystal, White	Pink
Bowl, 5½", cereal, closed handles	7.00	12.00
* Bowl, 8½", closed handles	10.00	20.00
Bowl, 11½", salad	28.00	
Bowl, 12", 2¾" deep	35.00	
Creamer, oval	8.00	
Cup	5.00	
Plate, 6", bread and butter	3.00	
Plate, 8½", luncheon	5.00	

	Crystal, White	Pink
Plate, 9", dinner	7.50	
Plate, 13", sandwich	15.00	18.00
Relish dish	15.00	
Salt and pepper, pair	22.50	
Saucer	2.00	
Sherbet	15.00	
Sugar, oval	8.00	

* Cobalt $32.50

218

STRAWBERRY U.S. GLASS COMPANY, Early 1930s

Colors: Pink, green, crystal; some iridized.

The shapes and to some extent, the Strawberry pattern itself, is a direct throwback to pattern lines of U.S. Glass and other pattern glassware companies of the late 1890s and early 1900s. Since both Strawberry and it's sister pattern, Cherryberry, are so popular with today's collectors, this bespeaks a certain ageless, seamless continuity of appreciation which is nice to behold in this age of throw-away-everything. Strawberry is requested at every show I attend.

The crystal and iridescent pitchers are in few collections. Crystal is priced along with iridescent because it is, categorically, rare. Iridescent Strawberry pitchers and tumblers are cherished by carnival collectors more highly than Depression glass collectors. By cherish, I mean they will pay more for them. The paramount carnival glass test is that it has to have full, vivid color that does not fade out toward the bottom, as many do. I'm wondering if this prejudice will hold with Depression glass collectors, however, since a strong movement for bi-colored wares is beginning to unfold.

Green Strawberry commands more attention than pink and matching color tones of green seems to be an insignificant issue. Green or pink Strawberry can be collected in a set; however, there are no cups, saucers, or dinner-sized plates. There is mould roughness on the seams. Even pieces that are considered mint may have extra glass roughness where it came out of the mould.

Strawberry sugar covers and the 6¼", 2" deep bowl are hard to find. Some mistakenly label the sugar with no lid and no handles as a spooner. Sometimes in older wares a topless, handled sugar was sold with breakfast sets as a spooner. However, most handless spooners in these same older wares were taller.

Strawberry has a plain butter dish bottom that is adaptable to other U.S. Glass patterns. This is the pattern for which other U.S. Glass butter bottoms were taken to use with Strawberry tops. Strawberry butter dishes have been desirable to collectors since day one.

	Crystal, Iridescent	Pink, Green		Crystal, Iridescent	Pink, Green
Bowl, 4", berry	6.50	12.00	Olive dish, 5", one-handle	9.00	20.00
Bowl, 6¼", 2" deep	60.00	150.00	Pickle dish, 8¼", oval	9.00	20.00
Bowl, 6½", deep salad	15.00	25.00	Pitcher, 7¾"	175.00	210.00
Bowl, 7½", deep berry	20.00	30.00	Plate, 6", sherbet	5.00	12.00
Butter dish and cover	135.00	195.00	Plate, 7½", salad	12.00	18.00
Butter dish bottom	77.50	100.00	Sherbet	8.00	10.00
Butter dish top	57.50	75.00	Sugar, small, open	12.00	22.00
Comport, 5¾"	18.00	35.00	Sugar, large	22.00	45.00
Creamer, small	12.00	22.00	Sugar cover	40.00	65.00
Creamer, 4⅝", large	22.50	40.00	Tumbler, 3⅝", 8 ounce	20.00	40.00

"SUNBURST," "HERRINGBONE" JEANNETTE GLASS COMPANY, Late 1930s

Colors: Crystal.

I have found no catalog or advertisement broadcasting any name for this pattern which I have heard called both "Sunburst" and "Herringbone." I do not know which, if either, is correct; but more people use "Sunburst."

"Sunburst" candlesticks are the most commonly found pieces, while sherbets, dinner plates, and tumblers are the hardest to find. The tumbler is similar in style to the flat Iris one, since it was made from the same shaped moulds as Iris. A divided relish and "Sunburst's" form of berry bowl would have made sensational pieces for Iris. Look this pattern over carefully, since inner rims are easily nicked and should be stacked with paper plates. Collectors would probably not have noticed "Sunburst" had it not been for the popular Iris.

I am listing only pieces I have found or pieces that have been in photographs sent me over the years. I will not be surprised by additional finds. Let me know what you have in your collections.

Item	Price		Item	Price
Bowl, 4¾", berry	8.00		Plate, 11¾", sandwich	25.00
Bowl, 8½", berry	18.00		Relish, 2-part	15.00
Bowl, 10¾"	27.50		Saucer	4.00
Candlesticks, double, pair	30.00		Sherbet	16.00
Creamer, footed	10.00		Sugar	10.00
Cup	10.00		Tray, small, oval	12.00
Plate, 5½"	9.00		Tumbler, 4", 9 ounce, flat	33.00
Plate, 9¼", dinner	22.00			

SUNFLOWER JEANNETTE GLASS COMPANY, 1930s

Colors: Pink, green, some Delphite; some opaque colors and Ultra Marine.

Sunflower is a well-recognized pattern of Depression glass. The ubiquitous cake plate may help explain that since they were packed in 20 pound bags of flour which sold in huge quantities in the 1930s because home baking was the norm then. A pink cake plate is shown in the center of the picture. If you look closely you can see a couple of the legs showing through. A quandary occurring with the green cake plate is that many are found in a deep, dark green that does not even approximate the coloration of other pieces of green Sunflower shown here. No other pieces of green are found in this hue. The heavy, round piece in the center is a paperweight found in a former Jeannette employee's home.

Judging by the inquiries I get, there is still some bafflement over the cake plate and the rarely found Sunflower trivet. The 7" trivet has an edge that is slightly upturned and it is three inches smaller than the omnipresent 10" cake plate. The 7" trivet remains the most elusive piece of Sunflower. Collector demand for the trivet keeps prices accelerating. Green Sunflower pieces are found less often than pink as evidenced by my photo; consequently, prices for green are greater than those of pink.

Today, Sunflower suffers a lack of saucers in both colors. The last few groups of Sunflower I have seen have had more cups than saucers. Two lots of green had no saucers at all. In total, there were 29 cups and only 13 saucers. Maybe the cups were a premium, which never offered saucers, or the cups were offered longer than the saucers. If you run into a stack of Sunflower saucers, remember that they could be a buy if the price is right.

The Ultra Marine ashtray pictured is the only piece I have found in that color. Opaque colors show up sporadically, usually creamers and sugars. Only a creamer, plate, 6" tab-handled bowl, cup, and saucer have been spotted in Delphite blue. You can see all but the creamer in *Very Rare Glassware of the Depression Years, Fifth Series.*

	Pink	Green		Pink	Green
* Ashtray, 5", center design only	9.00	12.00	Saucer	8.00	10.00
Cake plate, 10", 3 legs	15.00	15.00	Sugar, opaque $85.00	25.00	25.00
** Creamer, opaque $85.00	25.00	25.00	Tumbler, 4¾", 8 ounce, footed	35.00	35.00
Cup, opaque $75.00	16.00	18.00	Trivet, 7", 3 legs, turned up edge	350.00	350.00
Plate, 8", luncheon	35.00				
Plate, 9", dinner	22.00	24.00			

* Found in Ultra Marine $25.00   **Delphite $85.00

SUNSHINE LINES #731 – #737 LANCASTER GLASS COMPANY, c. 1932

Colors: Pink, green w/crystal.

This was another of those small lines sold as an assortment of pieces. There appear to have been sequences of hexagonal blanks used for the pattern, however; and you could buy up to a 36-piece assortment. I have never seen any dinner plates, though they may have been made judging from the other luncheon type pieces we do know were available. Let me know what else you turn up.

I will warn you, you will seldom find a piece of this line for a small price, not because the dealer has any notion what it is, just because it "looks like better glass." Most of the pieces shown here started at $40 up when we found them for sale.

	Pink/Green		Pink/Green
Bowl, 8", 2-handled, hex edge	55.00	Plate, 10½", 2-handled, hex edge	40.00
Bowl, 9", 2-handled, hex edge	65.00	Plate, 14", serving, hex edge	50.00
Bowl, 10", oval, 2 raised sides, hex edge	75.00	Server, 11", center handled sandwich, hex edge	50.00
Bowl, 12", flat rim, hex edge	65.00	Sugar, round, footed	22.50
Candle, single, hex foot	35.00	Tray, 10", roll edge, "bun" tray, hex edge	55.00
Creamer, round, footed	22.50		

SWANKY SWIGS 1930s – Early 1940s

"Why, I remember those. We used them when I was a child," is a comment I often hear when Swanky Swigs are spotted. Serious collectors seek all types and sizes; casual collectors like flowers, particularly daffodils, red tulips, violets, and bachelor buttons. See *Collectible Glassware from the 40s, 50s, 60s...* for later made Swanky Swigs and their metal lids.

Top Row:

Band No.1	Red & Black	3⅜"	2.00 – 3.00
	Red & Blue	3⅜"	3.00 – 4.00
	Blue	3⅜"	3.50 – 5.00
Band No. 2	Red & Black	4¾"	4.00 – 5.00
	Red & Black	3⅜"	3.00 – 4.00
Band No. 3	Blue & White	3⅜"	3.00 – 4.00
Circle & Dot:	Blue	4¾"	8.00 – 10.00
	Blue	3½"	5.00 – 6.00
	Red, Green	3½"	4.00 – 5.00
	Black	3½"	5.00 – 6.00
	Red	4¾"	8.00 – 10.00
Dot	Black	4¾"	7.00 – 9.00
	Blue	3½"	5.00 – 6.00

2nd Row:

Star	Blue	4¾"	7.00 – 8.00
	Blue, Red, Green, Black	3½"	3.00 – 4.00
	Cobalt w/White Stars	4¾"	18.00 – 20.00
Centennials	W.Va. Cobalt	4¾"	22.00 – 25.00
	Texas Cobalt	4¾"	35.00 – 40.00

	Texas Blue, Black, Green	3½"	35.00 – 40.00
Checkerboard	Blue, Red	3½"	30.00 – 35.00

3rd Row:

Checkerboard	Green	3½"	30.00 – 35.00
Sailboat	Blue	4½"	12.00 – 15.00
	Blue	3½"	10.00 – 12.00
	Red, Green	4½"	12.00 – 15.00
	Green, Light Green	3½"	10.00 – 15.00
Tulip No. 1	Blue, Red	4½"	15.00 – 20.00
	Blue, Red	3½"	3.00 – 4.00

4th Row:

Tulip No. 1	Green	4½"	15.00 – 20.00
	Green, Black	3½"	3.00 – 4.00
	Green w/Label	3½"	10.00 – 12.00
*Tulip No. 2	Red, Green, Black	3½"	30.00 – 35.00
Carnival	Blue, Red	3½"	5.00 – 7.00
	Green, Yellow	3½"	5.00 – 7.00
Tulip No. 3	Dark Blue, Light Blue	3¾"	2.50 – 3.50

*West Coast slightly lower price

223

SWIRL, "PETAL SWIRL" JEANNETTE GLASS COMPANY, 1937 – 1938

Colors: Ultra Marine, pink, Delphite; some amber and "ice" blue.

Almost all pieces of Swirl can be found with two different borders, ruffled and plain. Pink comes mostly with plain borders while Ultra Marine comes with both. This makes a big difference if you mail order or shop the Internet for your pattern. It is your responsibility to specify what style you want.

Ultra Marine Swirl pitchers (pictured in previous editions) are found once in a blue moon. Three have turned up. So far, none have been discovered in pink. Some collectors of Jeannette Swirl combine this pattern with Jeannette's "Jennyware" kitchenware line that does have a flat, 36-ounce pink pitcher in it. If you find mixing bowls, measuring cups, or reamers, then you have crossed into the kitchenware line and out of Swirl dinnerware. See *Kitchen Glassware of the Depression Years* for "Jennyware" listings.

Swirl candy and butter dish bottoms are more plentiful than are tops. Remember that before you buy only the bottom. That dearth of tops holds true for 90 percent of the butter and candy dishes in Depression glass. Unless you are good at remembering color hues, it might be sensible to take your half with you to match this Ultra Marine color. Swirl has some green-tinged pieces as well as the normally found color. This green tint is hard to match, and some collectors avoid this shade. Because of this, many times you can buy this green tint at a bargain price if you are willing to accumulate that shade. This problem occurs with all Jeannette patterns made in Ultra Marine. The smaller, flat tumbler and the 9" rimmed salad bowl beside it have this green tint. A boxed console set labeled "One 1500/3 Console Set, Ultra Marine from Jeannette Glass Co., Jeannette, Pa." was bought for my candlestick book. It had the footed console and candles in the green shade.

Pink candleholders are not considered rare even though they were omitted from some of my earlier editions. Omissions on my part do not make a piece rare. Sorry!

The pink coaster is usually found inside a small rubber tire and used for ashtrays. These tire advertisements have, themselves, become collectible. Those with a tire manufacturer's name on the glass insert are more in demand; but those with a non-advertising glass insert (such as this coaster) are collected if the miniature tire is embossed with the name of a tire company. Many of these tires dried up or decayed over the years leaving only the glass inserts as reminders. I certainly see few in Florida, but they are seen frequently in Ohio and Pennsylvania. Rubber in Florida's heat rapidly breaks down.

Swirl was produced in several scarce colors. A smaller set can be assembled in Delphite blue; it would only have basic pieces and a serving dish or two. Vegetable bowls (9") were made in several trial colors. A recent find was a small amethyst berry bowl pictured in *Very Rare Glassware of the Depression Years, Fifth Series*.

	Pink	Ultra Marine	Delphite
Bowl, 4⅞" & 5¼", berry	14.00	16.00	14.00
Bowl, 9", salad	26.00	32.00	30.00
Bowl, 9", salad, rimmed	30.00	32.00	
Bowl, 10", footed, closed handles	40.00	35.00	
Bowl, 10½", footed, console	20.00	30.00	
Butter dish	200.00	285.00	
Butter dish bottom	35.00	50.00	
Butter dish top	165.00	235.00	
Candle holders, double branch, pair	90.00	60.00	
Candle holders, single branch, pair			125.00
Candy dish, open, 3 legs	15.00	20.00	
Candy dish with cover	115.00	180.00	
Coaster, 1" x 3¼"	15.00	16.00	
Creamer, footed	10.00	16.00	12.00
Cup	11.00	16.00	10.00
Pitcher, 48 ounce, footed		1,950.00	

	Pink	Ultra Marine	Delphite
Plate, 6½", sherbet	7.00	8.00	6.00
Plate, 7¼"	12.00	15.00	
Plate, 8", salad	10.00	15.00	9.00
Plate, 9¼", dinner	17.00	22.00	12.00
Plate, 10½"			25.00
Plate, 12½", sandwich	22.00	30.00	
Platter, 12", oval			38.00
Salt and pepper, pair		45.00	
Saucer	3.00	4.00	5.00
Sherbet, low footed	18.00	22.50	
Soup, tab handle (lug)	45.00	50.00	
Sugar, footed	10.00	16.00	12.00
Tray, 10½", 2-handle			27.50
Tumbler, 4", 9 ounce	22.00	35.00	
Tumbler, 4⅝", 9 ounce	20.00		
Tumbler, 5⅛", 13 ounce	60.00	130.00	
Tumbler, 9 ounce, footed	25.00	47.50	
Vase, 6½" footed, ruffled	23.00		
Vase, 8½" footed, two styles		27.50	

TEA ROOM INDIANA GLASS COMPANY, 1926 – 1931

Colors: Pink, green, amber, and some crystal.

As the name suggests, the very Deco appearing Tea Room pattern was manufactured to be used in the tea rooms and ice cream parlors of the day. That's the reason you find so many soda fountain items.

Tea Room prices are not soaring as they once did due to a lack of available merchandise in the market to stimulate buying. This sometimes occurs when newer collectors cannot find enough to start a set. Rarely found pieces are not coming on the market unless a previously collected set is being dispersed. Thus, the dilemma in gathering Tea Room is finding it to buy.

The second problem is finding mint condition pieces. Check the underneath sides of flat pieces, which are inclined to chip and flake on all the unprotected points. I once witnessed the opening of a factory box of Tea Room that had 32 each cups, saucers, and luncheon plates. There were less than a dozen in mint condition as we define it today. These had never been used; so, there was doubtless a mould release problem with Tea Room initially. It's perfectly fine to buy and use flawed pieces; just don't pay mint prices for them.

Green Tea Room is sought more than pink; and some people are starting to request crystal. Crystal pieces are fetching about 75 to 80 percent of the pink prices listed except for the commonly found 9½" ruffled vase and the rarely found pitcher, priced separately below. That crystal pitcher is even harder to find than the amber one. I have bought and sold four amber pitchers, but only one crystal. I have only seen two. Amber pitchers and tumblers are often found in the Atlanta metro area. I was told they were Coca-Cola premiums. Creamers and sugars emerge occasionally in amber; and a 9½" ruffled top vase just appeared for the first time. I got an e-mail about it from a collector in New Zealand. Our glass does (or did) get around.

A couple of pink parfaits turned up in Houston. There are two styles of banana splits. Both the footed and flat are very desirable in any color. The green, flat one is the hardest to find. Many times you can find banana splits priced reasonably because they are not recognized as Tea Room.

The flat sugar and marmalade bottoms are the same. However, the marmalade has a notched lid; the sugar lid is not notched. Finding either is not an easy task. The mustard comes with a plain or notched lid.

Some interesting lamps are showing up which used frosted Tea Room tumblers in their makeup. We recently photographed a chandelier, which employed a ruffled top vase. The regular lamp is not as plentiful as it once was.

Prices are for mint items. These prices are high because mint condition items are difficult to obtain. I cannot emphasize that too much. Damaged pieces are often bought to supplement sets until mint items can be found. Not everyone can afford to buy only mint items, and they are willing to accept Tea Room pieces with some minor flaws at lesser prices. New collectors may have to accept some damage on items or do without.

	Green	Pink		Green	Pink
Bowl, finger	70.00	70.00	Salt and pepper, pair	75.00	65.00
Bowl, 7½", banana split, flat	200.00	200.00	* Saucer	30.00	30.00
Bowl, 7½", banana split, footed	95.00	90.00	Sherbet, low, footed	25.00	22.00
Bowl, 8¼", celery	35.00	27.50	Sherbet, low flared edge	30.00	26.00
Bowl, 8¾", deep salad	95.00	85.00	Sherbet, tall, footed	50.00	50.00
Bowl, 9½", oval vegetable	75.00	65.00	Sugar w/lid, 3"	110.00	100.00
Candlestick, low, pair	80.00	85.00	Sugar, 4½", footed, amber $100.00	20.00	20.00
Creamer, 3¼"	27.50	27.50	Sugar, rectangular	25.00	20.00
Creamer, 4½", footed, amber $100.00	20.00	20.00	Sugar, flat with cover	200.00	165.00
Creamer, rectangular	25.00	20.00	Sundae, footed, ruffled top	95.00	75.00
Creamer & sugar on tray, 4"	85.00	85.00	Tray, center-handle	200.00	145.00
* Cup	60.00	60.00	Tray, rectangular sugar & creamer	50.00	40.00
Goblet, 9 ounce	75.00	65.00	Tumbler, 8 ounce, 4³⁄₁₆", flat	110.00	120.00
Ice bucket	60.00	55.00	Tumbler, 6 ounce, footed	35.00	35.00
Lamp, 9", electric	150.00	135.00	Tumbler, 8 ounce, 5¼", high, footed,		
Marmalade, notched lid	225.00	175.00	amber $110.00	35.00	35.00
Mustard, covered	195.00	160.00	Tumbler, 11 ounce, footed	50.00	45.00
Parfait	100.00	100.00	Tumbler, 12 ounce, footed	75.00	70.00
** Pitcher, 64 ounce, amber $600.00	175.00	150.00	Vase, 6½", ruffled edge	110.00	110.00
Plate, 6½", sherbet	32.00	30.00	*** Vase, 9½", ruffled edge	150.00	150.00
Plate, 8¼", luncheon	35.00	30.00	Vase, 9½", straight	100.00	95.00
Plate, 10½", 2-handle	55.00	45.00	Vase, 11", ruffled edge	250.00	295.00
Relish, divided	25.00	20.00	Vase, 11", straight	160.00	165.00

* Prices for absolutely mint pieces   ** Crystal $400.00   *** Crystal $16.00

THISTLE MacBETH-EVANS, 1929 – 1930

Colors: Pink, green; some yellow and crystal.

Thistle pattern is definitely the nettle that every photographer whom I have worked with since 1972 hates to see placed before them. Photography lights cause Thistle to do a vanishing act, which is an act familiar to Thistle collectors. Our new photographer seems to have captured Thistle by placing the cake plate askew.

Green Thistle is even more sparse than pink except for the large fruit bowl that is practically a mirage in pink. I have owned the one pictured here for over 25 years, and I have only seen two others.

Thistle pieces have the same mould shapes as the thin Dogwood; there is no Thistle creamer or sugar known. The Thistle grill plate has the pattern on the edge only. Those plain centers scratched very easily; be aware of that problem should you locate a grill plate to scrutinize. Frankly, if you find one with a distinguishable pattern, buy it. Eventually, there'll be glass polishers available to the public to fix scratching.

If you find a thick butter dish, pitcher, tumbler, creamer, sugar, or other heavy moulded pieces with Thistle designs, they are new. Mosser Glass Company in Cambridge, Ohio, is making these pieces. They are not a part of this pattern, but copies of a much older pattern glass. If you have a piece of Thistle not in the photograph, then you probably do not have a piece of MacBeth-Evans Thistle pattern; all seven pieces known to have been made by them are shown. Many companies made thistle patterns during America's rural heyday.

	Pink	Green
Bowl, 5½", cereal	33.00	35.00
Bowl, 10¼", large fruit	495.00	295.00
Cup, thin	25.00	28.00
Plate, 8", luncheon	22.00	24.00
Plate, 10¼", grill	30.00	35.00
Plate, 13", heavy cake	195.00	225.00
Saucer	12.00	12.00

"TOP NOTCH," "SUNBURST" New Martinsville, c. 1930s

Colors: Red, green, cobalt, amber.

I have found several names in use for this pattern. In the north, the name "Top Notch" or "Top Prize" is used; but in the south, "Sunburst" is the label. I questioned one dealer where her name label came from and she said she "found it in some old magazine a couple of years ago" though she couldn't pin point which one. A northern dealer asked me at the last show if I had any of that "Top Notch" pattern, and it took a moment to realize he was speaking of this ware. No matter what it's being called, it is a wonderful design and comes in rich jewel colors.

We know these items from a luncheon set were made. I don't remember seeing other type pieces, though I would presume there could well be some. I have, however, run into a second set having these same green items here in Florida. Based on that, it might be safe to assume these were distributed here. We located the red cup and saucer in Kentucky and I've seen one in blue. A friend with whom I was discussing the pattern believes she's seen amber. That would fit with New Martinsville colors from this time frame; so, I feel fairly confident in listing that color. Let me hear from you about what you have or find.

	All colors
Cup	20.00
Creamer	25.00
Plate, luncheon	18.00
Plate, serving tray	35.00
Saucer	8.00
Sugar	25.00

TULIP DELL GLASS COMPANY, Late 1930s – Late 1940s

Color: Amethyst, turquoise (blue), crystal, green.

Tulip has found an enthusiastic following among collectors since its inclusion here. Please notice that we now have a photo of that elusive decanter found with the tulip stoppers that have been pictured in several colors. The decanter bottom is not tulip design, though it does have an optic in the glass itself, rather than being totally plain glass. Now, you know what to look for at markets. Happy hunting!

The blue candy shown is the result of a marriage between my candy base and the top from a collector in the Midwest. You get to see the entire candy that way. I offered to sell him my candy top or buy his base. He chose to buy my top; so, I am looking again. You would not believe the gyrations made to get this glass photographed for you.

One style of candleholder is made from an ivy bowl (not a sherbet as the piece was previously thought to be). That ivy bowl (sherbet) is shown in the 1946 Montgomery Ward catalog with ivy growing in it. Though dropped this time to make room for new pattern listings, we pictured that ad in past books and I had a letter the other day from someone who had found the violin vase pictured with the pattern. That vase wouldn't be considered to be part of the pattern, merely an interesting accompaniment.

The juice tumbler (cigarette holder in ad in previous books) is 2¾" tall and holds three ounces while the whiskey is only 1¾" and holds one ounce. The ad for Tulip shows no stippling on the pieces. Early in buying this pattern, I ignored some pieces without stippling; both styles are acceptable to collectors. I am finding about half with and half without. Personally, I prefer the stippled look.

I started buying Tulip about 11 years ago, when I found nine green sugar bowls for $10.00. I could not turn them down at that price though I did not know whether there were collectors for it or not. I soon found out! Those sugars are often found in sets of four or more, making me believe they may also have been marketed as cream soups. I see about a dozen sugars for every creamer.

In buying Tulip, I have found that the scalloped rims have a tendency to have some damage. Most of the damage occurs under the rim edge; be sure to turn the piece over and check each of the pointed scallops. Many times a scallop or two will be absent and not show from the top side.

I have priced the crystal with the green since you will not see much of it. Crystal may be the rarest "color."

	Amethyst, Blue	Crystal, Green		Amethyst, Blue	Crystal, Green
Bowl, oval, oblong, 13¼"	110.00	90.00	Plate, 6"	11.00	10.00
Candleholder, 3¾" (ivy bowl)	38.00	30.00	Plate, 7¼"	16.00	13.00
Candleholder, 5¼" base, 3" tall	65.00	45.00	Plate, 10"	40.00	34.00
Candy w/lid, footed (6" w/o lid)	195.00	165.00	Saucer	7.00	6.00
Creamer	24.00	20.00	Sherbet, 3¾", flat (ivy bowl)	22.00	20.00
Cup	20.00	16.00	Sugar	22.00	20.00
Decanter w/stopper	495.00		Tumbler, 2¾", juice	33.00	22.00
Ice tub, 4⅞" wide, 3" deep	95.00	75.00	Tumbler, whiskey	35.00	25.00

Colors: Pink, green, amber; some blue and Canary yellow.

First, you should realize that many glass companies made twisting patterns besides Imperial and Hocking. Second, I need to own up to the round, green candy pictured below being Hocking's Spiral pattern and not Imperial's Twisted Optic, something I had exactly backwards in last book. Sorry. The true, rounded style Twisted Optic candy is shown in the Canary photo on the following page. Maybe we can fix this better in everyone's mind by having the two here to compare.

Page 233 shows a photograph of Imperial's striking Canary color. This color is often mislabeled vaseline. I was able to buy enough pieces from a dealer selling a set to illustrate the color. Seeing all the items he had accumulated in one display was absolutely breathtaking and I was tempted to buy it all. However, I couldn't justify to myself so large an expenditure on one photograph for the relatively few collectors there are at present.

	Blue, Canary Yellow	All Other Colors		Blue, Canary Yellow	All Other Colors
Basket, 10", tall	95.00	60.00	Plate, 6", sherbet	6.00	3.00
Bowl, console, scroll tab hdld., oval, ftd.			Plate, 7", salad	8.00	4.00
Bowl, 4¾", cream soup	25.00	15.00	Plate, 7½" x 9", oval with indent	12.00	5.00
Bowl, 5", cereal	16.00	9.00	Plate, 8", luncheon	8.00	6.00
Bowl, 7", crimped	30.00	20.00	Plate, 9½", cracker	30.00	18.00
Bowl, 7", salad	25.00	15.00	Plate, 10", sandwich	20.00	9.00
Bowl, 9"	35.00	15.00	Plate, 12"	20.00	15.00
Bowl, 9¼", salad	40.00	25.00	Plate, 14", buffet	35.00	25.00
Bowl 10", salad	45.00	30.00	Platter, oval	35.00	25.00
Bowl, 10½", console	45.00	25.00	Powder jar w/lid	65.00	40.00
Bowl, 11½", 4¼" tall	55.00	30.00	Preserve (same as candy w/slotted lid)		30.00
Candlesticks, 3", pair (2 styles)	45.00	50.00	Sandwich server, open center handle	35.00	20.00
Candlesticks, 8", pair	75.00	55.00	Sandwich server, two-handle	18.00	12.00
Candy jar w/cover, flat	85.00	50.00	Saucer	4.00	2.00
Candy jar w/cover, flat, flange edge	90.00	55.00	Server, center handle, bowl shape	35.00	20.00
Candy jar w/cover, ftd., flange edge	90.00	55.00	Sherbet	10.00	6.00
Candy jar w/cover, ftd., short, fat	100.00	60.00	Sugar	12.50	7.00
Candy jar w/cover, footed, tall	125.00	60.00	Tumbler, 4½", 9 ounce		6.00
Compote, cheese	20.00	12.00	Tumbler, 5¼", 12 ounce		8.00
Creamer	15.00	8.00	Vase, 7¼", 2-handle, rolled edge	75.00	45.00
Cup	12.00	5.00	Vase, 7¼", flat rim	65.00	40.00
Mayonnaise	50.00	30.00	Vase, 8", 2-handle, fan	95.00	50.00
Pitcher, 64 ounce		45.00	Vase, 8", 2-handle, straight edge	95.00	45.00

"U.S. SWIRL" U.S. GLASS COMPANY, Late 1920s

Colors: Green, some pink, iridescent, and crystal.

"U.S. Swirl" pattern has shapes and pieces very like those of the popular Aunt Polly also made by them. Pink, iridescent, and crystal items are located very infrequently in "U.S. Swirl." I have only found one pink shaker and a butter dish in the 14 years I have been searching. Probably very little pink was manufactured, or perhaps not a complete line, just some occasional items. In the listings, I separated the colors based on demand for green outweighing that of pink. Occasionally, I see crystal sherbets. The 5⅜" tall, rarely found comport is pictured behind the sherbet for size comparison. I know some collectors prefer I call it a martini glass, the modern use for compotes. (That's why Manhattan comports are so scarce. Collectors are buying six or more for drinks instead of one for candy.)

Several "U.S. Swirl" iridescent butter dishes have been discovered, but those and sherbets are the only pieces surfacing in that color. The tumbler listing 3⅝" conforms with the only known size of Aunt Polly and Cherryberry/Strawberry tumblers; but the 12 ounce tumbler has only been found in "U.S. Swirl." The footed piece in the back on the left is officially a vase, although it has been incorrectly labeled a tumbler at times.

"U.S. Swirl" has the plain butter bottom that is compatible with other patterns made by U.S. Glass. The butter dish in this pattern is the one that many Strawberry collectors have purchased over the years to borrow the base for their Strawberry lids. This plundering has stressed butters in "U.S. Swirl" pattern, particularly in scarce pink.

The shallow, 1¾" deep, 8⅜" oval bowl in front of the 2¾" deep, oval bowl is seldom found; it may be rare.

	Green	Pink		Green	Pink
Bowl, 4⅜", berry	5.50	6.50	Creamer	20.00	20.00
Bowl, 5½", 1-handle	9.50	10.50	Pitcher, 8", 48 ounce	85.00	85.00
Bowl, 7⅞", large berry	15.00	16.00	Plate, 6⅛", sherbet	2.50	2.50
Bowl, 8¼", oval (2¾" deep)	45.00	45.00	Plate, 7⅞", salad	5.50	6.50
Bowl, 8⅜", oval (1¾" deep)	55.00	55.00	Salt and pepper, pair	65.00	65.00
Butter and cover	120.00	120.00	Sherbet, 3¼"	4.50	5.00
Butter bottom	100.00	100.00	Sugar w/lid	40.00	40.00
Butter top	20.00	20.00	Tumbler, 3⅝", 8 ounce	10.00	10.00
Candy w/cover, 2-handle	27.50	32.00	Tumbler, 4¾", 12 ounce	14.00	15.00
Comport	35.00	30.00	Vase, 6½"	30.00	25.00

"VICTORY" DIAMOND GLASS-WARE COMPANY, 1929 – 1932

Colors: Amber, pink, green; some cobalt blue and black.

Amber and black "Victory" are pictured below. That color combination is appealing and started one new collector looking for "Victory." Combining colors is catching on amongst collectors. The black with gold trim shows up better in the photo than the gold-trimmed amber. As with most black glass of this time, the pattern is on the back; you have to turn it over to see that the piece is "Victory" unless you can distinguish it from the indented edges. Collectors of black glass are more likely to own black "Victory" than Depression glass people, though they often appear with it at shows having no clue its an actual pattern with a name. Diamond used several techniques of ornamentation besides the 22K gold trim. Floral decorations and even a Deco looking black design on pink and green is found. I have spied more floral decorated console sets (bowl and candlesticks) than anything. I presume that complete sets of gold decorated pink and green can be found while black pieces decorated with gold appear to be available only in luncheon or console sets.

Sets of "Victory" can be completed in pink and green with a great deal of searching. Amber, cobalt blue, and black will take more hunting and some good fortune. It can be done even in today's market, but it will be expensive, at best. After I mentioned that cobalt blue "Victory" was being spotted in the northeast, especially in Maine, I have heard of other sets there, the latest of which were in antique malls. Elsewhere, I see little blue.

Gravy boats and platters are the most desirable pieces to own in any color. I have only seen one amber and one green set, but five cobalt blue ones. A green gravy and platter can be seen at the bottom of page 236. The "Victory" goblet, candlestick, cereal, soup, and oval vegetable bowls will keep you looking long and hard in all colors.

"VICTORY"

	Black, Amber, Pink, Green	Blue
Bonbon, 7"	11.00	20.00
Bowl, 6½", cereal	14.00	45.00
Bowl, 8½", flat soup	20.00	70.00
Bowl, 9", oval vegetable	32.00	115.00
Bowl, 11", rolled edge	28.00	50.00
Bowl, 12", console	33.00	65.00
Bowl, 12½", flat edge	30.00	70.00
Candlesticks, 3", pair	35.00	125.00
Cheese & cracker set, 12" indented plate & compote	40.00	
Comport, 6" tall, 6¾" diameter	15.00	
Creamer	15.00	50.00
Cup	12.00	30.00
Goblet, 5", 7 ounce	25.00	95.00
Gravy boat and platter	250.00	350.00
Mayonnaise set: 3½" tall, 5½" across, 8½" indented plate, w/ladle	42.00	100.00
Plate, 6", bread and butter	6.00	16.00
Plate, 7", salad	7.00	20.00
Plate, 8", luncheon	7.00	30.00
Plate, 9", dinner	20.00	55.00
Platter, 12"	30.00	95.00
Sandwich server, center handle	29.00	75.00
Saucer	4.00	8.00
Sherbet, footed	13.00	26.00
Sugar	15.00	50.00

VITROCK, "FLOWER RIM" HOCKING GLASS COMPANY, 1934 – 1937

Colors: White and white w/fired-on colors, usually red or green.

Vitrock was not a pattern per se, but a mid-1930s stark white color of Hocking's similar to Hazel Atlas' Platonite. There are many different patterns found on this very durable line, but collectors have adopted the decorated Lake Como and the "Flower Rim" dinnerware sets as patterns to collect.

Vitrock was Hocking's headlong leap into the milk glass market. Today, platters, soup plates, and cream soups are pieces that are nearly impossible to find. If you locate a flat soup, you are usually wishing it had the Lake Como decoration. I have been unable to obtain a regular Vitrock flat soup. These are rarer than I previously thought.

Vitrock's claim to fame with collectors is for its kitchenware line of reamers, measuring cups, and mixing bowls. It was advertised as ware that "will not craze or check," a major flaw for many pottery wares of the times. Those large Vitrock mixing bowls are probably so hard to find today because they cost a quarter which may have accounted for a half day's wage for a working man. At the time, Vitrock competed with Hazel Atlas's Platonite; and by all indications now, Platonite won the battle.

You can see more Vitrock in my book *Kitchen Glassware of the Depression Years*. Some collectors are assembling patterns that cross other fields. This is a prime example of a pattern that fits into both collecting areas. Hazel Atlas did the same with their Platonite. It made perfect business sense to sell auxiliary items that matched your everyday dishes.

	White		White
Bowl, 4", berry	5.00	Plate, 7¼", salad	4.00
Bowl, 5½", cream soup	16.00	Plate, 8¾", luncheon	5.00
Bowl, 6", fruit	5.50	Plate, 9", soup	33.00
Bowl, 7½", cereal	8.00	Plate, 10", dinner	10.00
Bowl, 9½", vegetable	15.00	Platter, 11½"	35.00
Creamer, oval	6.00	Saucer	2.50
Cup	6.00	Sugar	6.00

WATERFORD, "WAFFLE" HOCKING GLASS COMPANY, 1938 – 1944

Colors: Crystal, pink; some yellow, Vitrock; forest green 1950s.

Waterford conjures images of exclusive, costly cut lead crystal when mentioned to most. Well, this pattern was Hocking's answer to that, a sort of poor man's Waterford. This Waterford sells very well because it is available and priced reasonably. It also looks impressive. Unfortunately, pink is rarely seen anymore. Most collectors would adore pink cereal bowls, a pitcher, or a butter dish residing at their table. Of these three pieces, the cereal is the most elusive. It has always been annoying to find, and worse, difficult to find mint. The inside rim is predictably damaged from stacking or use. A little roughness is typical; do not let that keep you from owning a hard-to-find piece. Because of the scalloped rim design, Waterford has been known to chip or flake.

There are some scarce crystal pieces. Cereal bowls, pitchers, and even water goblets are declining in number. Those shakers on the right in the top photograph were used by many restaurants through the 1960s, which is why they are frequently seen today. There are two styles of sherbets. One has a scalloped top and base. It is not as commonly found and is not as accepted as the regular plain edged one.

There is a Waterford "pretender" footed cup that is occasionally sold as a Waterford punch cup. These cups, and the larger lamps that are often displayed as Waterford, are only similar to Waterford. Waterford has a flattened (not rounded) diamond shape on each section of the design. There is also a large pink pitcher with an indented, circular design in each diamond, which is not Waterford. This pitcher was made by Hocking, but has more of a bull's-eye look. These pink pitchers with circular designs only sell for $35.00 and crystal for $20.00; do not pay Waterford prices for one.

A few pieces of Vitrock Waterford and some Dusty Rose and Springtime Green ashtrays turn up occasionally; these sell near crystal prices. Examples of those rose and green colors can be seen in Oyster and Pearl pattern. Forest green Waterford 13¾" plates were made in the 1950s promotion of Forest Green; these are usually found in the $30.00 range. Many of these have white sections sitting around them similar to those found in Manhattan. Some crystal has also been found trimmed in red. There is not enough of the red trim to collect a set piece by piece.

Advertising ashtrays, such as the "Post Cereals" shown below, are selling for $20.00 to $25.00 depending upon the significance of the advertising on the piece. An advertisement for Anchor Hocking itself will bring $35.00 to $40.00.

Items listed below with Miss America shape noted in parentheses are Waterford patterned pieces with the same mould shapes as Miss America. Some of these are shown in the seventh edition of this book or the first *Very Rare Glassware of the Depression Years.*

Those yellow and amber goblets shown below are compliments of Anchor Hocking's photographer from items stored in their morgue. I have not seen yellow ones for sale, but amber ones sell for around $25.00.

	Crystal	Pink
* Ashtray, 4"	7.50	
Bowl, 4¾", berry	7.00	20.00
Bowl, 5½", cereal	19.00	38.00
Bowl, 8¼", large berry	15.00	28.00
Butter dish and cover	30.00	235.00
Butter dish bottom	8.00	30.00
Butter dish top	22.00	205.00
Coaster, 4"	4.00	
Creamer, oval	6.00	12.00
Creamer (Miss America shape)		40.00
Cup	6.50	15.00
Cup (Miss America shape)		45.00
Goblets, 5¼", 5⅝"	16.00	
Goblet, 5½" (Miss America shape)	40.00	125.00
Lamp, 4", spherical base	26.00	
Pitcher, 42 ounce, tilted, juice	24.00	
Pitcher, 80 ounce, tilted, ice lip	40.00	165.00
Plate, 6", sherbet	4.00	7.00
Plate, 7⅛", salad	7.00	15.00

	Crystal	Pink
Plate, 9⅝", dinner	12.00	25.00
Plate, 10¼", handled cake	12.00	20.00
Plate, 13¾", sandwich	13.00	34.00
Relish, 13¾", 5-part	18.00	
Salt and pepper, 2 types	9.00	
Saucer	3.00	6.00
Sherbet, footed	5.00	20.00
Sherbet, footed, scalloped base	6.00	
Sugar	6.00	12.50
Sugar cover, oval	12.00	30.00
Sugar (Miss America shape)		40.00
Tumbler, 3½", 5 oz. juice (Miss America shape)		125.00
Tumbler, 4⅞", 10 ounce, footed	15.00	27.00

* With ads $15.00 – 40.00 depending on item popularity

WINDSOR, "WINDSOR DIAMOND" JEANNETTE GLASS COMPANY, 1936 – 1946

Colors: Pink, green, crystal; some Delphite, amberina red, and ice blue.

Distinctive crystal Windsor items continue to be discovered that are not found in pink or green. The one-handled candle stick and 10½" pointed edge tray are a couple that come to mind. There are many collectors for colored Windsor, but less collect crystal. Color was discontinued about 1940, but crystal pieces were made as late as 1946. Redesigned moulds for the Windsor butter, creamer, and sugar were later conveyed to the Holiday pattern when that was introduced in 1947. There are two styles of sugars and lids. One is shaped like Holiday and has no lip for the lid to rest upon; the pink sugar on page 241 represents the second style with lip. The pink sugar and lid shaped like Holiday are hard to find.

Square relish trays can be found with or without tab (closed) handles. Pictured top of 241 are relish trays with tab handles; the large one holds two sizes of relishes without the tabs. Trays without handles commonly appear in crystal, but pink trays without handles are seldom found. Two styles of sandwich plates were made. The normally found one is 10¼" and has open handles. The later discovered tray is 10" and has closed handles.

Green Windsor tumblers are elusive. The water tumbler, commonly found in pink, is scarce. Mould roughness is found on seams of tumblers; and Windsor tumblers have an inclination to chip on the protruding sides. The diamond pattern juts outward, making the sides an easy target for chips and flakes. Check these seams cautiously before you buy. There are color variations in green; be cognizant of that.

The pink 13⅝" plate is often found as an underliner tray for a beverage set with a pitcher and six water tumblers. This set may have been a premium item since so many pitchers and water tumblers are available today. Green sets do not experience this abundance.

The 8" pointed rim bowl is rarely seen in pink, but is pictured on the bottom far right of page 241. The large bowl in crystal, along with the comport, make up a punch bowl and stand. The upended comport fits inside the base of the bowl to keep it from sliding. In recent years, there have been newly made comports in crystal with sprayed colors that have a beaded edge. This recently made version will not work as a punch stand because the beaded edge will not fit inside the base of the bowl.

A different style pink ashtray and a tab-handled berry bowl can be seen in the *Very Rare Glassware of the Depression Years, Second Series*. While looking there, check out the blue Windsor butter dish. In the Fifth Series of that book, there is an oval, handled, four-footed bowl pictured. Was this mould rejected, a worker's plaything, or shipped elsewhere?

Windsor always brings a feeling of satisfaction when it comes up on my computer screen since it signals the end of current updating information about patterns, now for the fifteenth time. The publisher moved up deadlines a month and "encouraged" two more books than usual; I really have been exceedingly pushed to get this done under deadline once again. I do most sincerely hope you enjoy the effort put forth!

	Crystal	Pink	Green
* Ashtray, 5¾"	13.50	38.00	55.00
Bowl, 4¾", berry	4.00	12.00	12.00
Bowl, 5", pointed edge	9.00	33.00	
Bowl, 5", cream soup	7.00	24.00	29.00
Bowls, 5⅛, 5⅜", cereal	8.50	22.00	30.00
Bowl, 7⅛", three legs	9.00	30.00	
Bowl, 8", pointed edge	18.00	60.00	
Bowl, 8½", large berry	10.00	25.00	25.00
Bowl, 9", 2-handle	10.00	22.00	25.00
Bowl, 9½", oval vegetable	8.00	22.00	30.00
Bowl, 10½", salad	15.00		
Bowl, 10½", pointed edge	32.00	150.00	
Bowl, 12½", fruit console	30.00	135.00	
Bowl, 7" x 11¾", boat shape	20.00	40.00	40.00
Butter dish (two styles)	28.00	60.00	95.00
Cake plate, 10¾", footed	8.50	25.00	28.00
Candleholder, one handle	15.00		
Candlesticks, 3", pair	25.00	100.00	
Candy jar and cover	20.00		
Coaster, 3¼"	6.00	15.00	20.00
Comport	10.00		
** Creamer	5.00	14.00	18.00
Creamer (shaped as "Holiday")	7.50		
** Cup	5.00	10.00	12.50
Pitcher, 4½", 16 ounce	27.50	125.00	
*** Pitcher, 6¾", 52 ounce	25.00	35.00	60.00
Plate, 6", sherbet	2.50	5.00	8.00
Plate, 7", salad	4.50	20.00	25.00

	Crystal	Pink	Green
** Plate, 9", dinner	10.00	27.00	25.00
Plate, 10", sandwich, closed handle		25.00	
Plate, 10½", pointed edge	10.00		
Plate, 10¼", sandwich, open handle	6.00	18.00	25.00
Plate, 13⅝", chop	15.00	35.00	42.00
Platter, 11½", oval	15.00	25.00	25.00
**** Powder jar	15.00	60.00	
Relish platter, 11½", divided	15.00	225.00	
Salt and pepper, pair	20.00	45.00	55.00
Saucer, ice blue $15.00	2.50	5.00	6.00
Sherbet, footed	3.50	14.00	15.00
Sugar & cover	12.00	30.00	33.00
Sugar & cover (like "Holiday")	15.00	125.00	
Tray, 4", square, w/handle	5.00	10.00	12.00
Tray, 4", square, w/o handle	10.00	50.00	
Tray, 4⅛" x 9", w/handle	4.00	10.00	16.00
Tray, 4⅛" x 9", w/o handle	12.00	60.00	
Tray, 8½" x 9¾", w/handle	6.50	24.00	35.00
Tray, 8½" x 9¾", w/o handle	15.00	95.00	
** Tumbler, 3¼", 5 ounce	12.00	25.00	35.00
** Tumbler, 4", 9 ounce, red 55.00	7.00	20.00	30.00
Tumbler, 5", 12 ounce	10.00	35.00	52.00
Tumbler, 4⅝", 11 ounce	9.00		
Tumbler, 4", footed	8.00		
Tumbler, 5", footed, 11 ounce	11.00		
Tumbler, 7¼", footed	18.00		

* Delphite $45.00   ** Blue $65.00   *** Red $450.00   **** Yellow $175.00; Blue $185.00

REPRODUCTIONS

NEW "ADAM" PRIVATELY PRODUCED OUT OF KOREA THROUGH ST. LOUIS IMPORTING COMPANY ONLY THE ADAM BUTTER DISH HAS BEEN REPRODUCED.

The reproduction Adam butter dish is finally off the market as far as I can determine. Identification of the reproduction is easy. Do not use any of the following information for any piece of Adam save the butter dish.

Top: Notice the veins in the leaves.

New: Large leaf veins do not join or touch in center of leaf.

Old: Large leaf veins all touch or join the center vein.

A further note about the original Adam butter dish: the veins of all the leaves at the center of the design are very clear cut and precisely moulded; in the new, these center leaf veins are very indistinct - and almost invisible in one leaf of the center design.

Bottom: Place butter dish bottom upside down for observation. Square it to your body.

New: Four arrowhead-like points line up in northwest, northeast, southeast, and southwest directions of compass. These points still head in the wrong directions. There are very bad mould lines and a very glossy light pink color on the butter dishes I examined.

Old: Four arrowhead-like points line up in north, east, south, and west directions of compass.

NEW "AVOCADO" INDIANA GLASS COMPANY Tiara Exclusives Line, 1974 – 1980s

Colors: Pink, green, and fifteen additional colors never made originally.

In 1979 a green Avocado pitcher was produced. It was darker than the original green and was a limited hostess gift item. Yellow pieces are all recently made. Yellow was never made originally.

The old pink color Indiana made was a delicate, attractive pink. The new tends to be more orange than the original color. The other colors shown pose little threat since none of those colors were made originally.

I understand that Tiara sales counselors told potential customers that their newly made glass was collectible because it was made from old moulds. I don't share this view. I feel it's like saying that since you were married in your grandmother's wedding dress, you will have the same happy marriage for the 57 years she did. All you can truly say is that you were married in her dress. I think all you can say about the new Avocado is that it was made from the old moulds. Time, scarcity, and people's whims determine collectibility in so far as I'm able to determine it. It's taken nearly 50 years or more for people to turn to collecting Depression glass — and that's done, in part, because everyone remembers it; they had some in their home at one time or another; it has universal appeal. Who is to say what will be collectible in the next 50 years? If we knew, we could all get rich! Now, that Tiara bit the dust, perhaps some of their wares will become collectible. Unhappily, there are many collectors who were taken in by some of this glass represented as old, and most of them have long enough memories to avoid it during their generation.

If you like Tiara products, then of course buy them; but don't do so depending upon their being collectible. You have an equal chance, I feel, of going to Las Vegas and depending upon getting rich at the blackjack table.

NEW "CAMEO"

Colors: Green, pink, cobalt blue (shakers); yellow, green, and pink (children's dishes).

I hope you can still see how very weak the pattern is on this reproduction shaker. It was originally made by Mosser Glass Company in Ohio, but is now being made overseas. Also, you can see how much glass remains in the bottom of the shaker; and, of course, the new tops all make this easy to spot at the market. These were to be bought wholesale at around $6.00 but did not sell well. An importer made shakers in pink, cobalt blue, and a terrible green color. These, too, are weakly patterned. They were never originally made in the blue, but beware of pink.

Children's dishes in Cameo (called "Jennifer" by the manufacturer) pose no problem to collectors since they were never made originally. These, also made by Mosser, are scale models of the larger size. This type of production I have no quarrel with since they are not made to dupe anyone.

There are over 50 of these smaller pieces; thus, if you have a piece of glass that looks like a miniature (child's) version of a larger piece of Cameo, then you probably have a newly manufactured item.

243

REPRODUCTIONS

NEW "CHERRY BLOSSOM"

Colors: Pink, green, blue, Delphite, cobalt, red, and iridized colors.

Use information provided only for the piece described. Do not apply the information on the tumbler for the pitcher, etc. Realize that with various importers now reproducing glass, there are more modifications than I can possibly scrutinize for you. Know your dealer and *hope* he knows what he is doing.

Due to all the altered reproductions of the same pieces over and over, please understand this is only a guide as to what you should look for when buying. We've now seen some reproductions of those reproductions. All the items pictured on the next page are easy to spot as reproductions once you know what to look for with the possible exception of the 13" divided platter pictured in the center. It's too heavy, weighing 2¾ pounds, and has a thick ⅜" of glass in the bottom; but the design isn't too bad. The edges of the leaves aren't smooth; but neither are they serrated like old leaves.

There are many differences between old and new scalloped bottom, AOP Cherry pitchers. The easiest way to tell the difference is to turn the pitcher over. The branch crossing the bottom of my old Cherry pitchers looks like a branch. It's knobby and gnarled and has several leaves and cherry stems directly attached to it. One variation of the new pitcher just has a bald strip of glass cutting the bottom of the pitcher in half. Further, the old Cherry pitchers have a plain glass background for the cherries and leaves in the bottom of the pitcher. In the new pitchers, there's a rough, filled in, straw-like background. You see no plain glass.

As for the new tumblers, look at the ring dividing the patterned portion of the glass from the plain glass lip. The old tumblers have three indented rings dividing the pattern from the plain glass rim. The new has only one. Again, the pattern at the bottom of the new tumblers is brief and practically nonexistent in the center curve of the glass bottom. The pattern, what there is, mostly hugs the center of the foot.

2 handled tray — old: 1⅞ lb.; ³⁄₁₆" glass in bottom; leaves and cherries east/west from north/south handles (some older trays were rotated so this is not always true); leaves have real spine and serrated edges; cherry stems end in triangle of glass. *new:* 2⅛ lb.; ¼" glass in bottom; leaves and cherries north/south with the handles; canal type leaves (but uneven edges; cherry stem ends before canal shaped line).

cake plate — new: color too light pink, leaves have too many parallel veins that give them a feathery look; arches at plate edge don't line up with lines on inside of the rim to which the feet are attached.

8½" bowl — new: crude leaves with smooth edges; veins in parallel lines.

cereal bowl — new: wrong shape, looks like 8½" bowl, small 2" center. **old:** large center, 2½" inside ring, nearly 3½" if you count the outer rim before the sides turn up.

dinner plate — new: smooth edged leaves, fish spine type center leaf portion; weighs one pound plus; feels thicker at edge with mould offset lines clearly visible. **old:** center leaves look like real leaves with spines, veins, and serrated edges; weighs ¾ pound; clean edges; no mould offset (a slight step effect at the edge).

cup — new: area in bottom left free of design; canal centered leaves; smooth, thick top to cup handle (old has triangle grasp point).

saucer — new: offset mould line edge; canal leaf center.

The Cherry child's cup (with a slightly lopsided handle) having the cherries hanging upside down when the cup was held in the right hand appeared in 1973. After I reported this error, it was quickly corrected by re-inverting the inverted mould. These later cups were thus improved in design but slightly off color. The saucers tended to have slightly off center designs, too. Next came the child's butter dish that was never made by Jeannette. It was essentially the child's cup without a handle turned upside down over the saucer and having a little glob of glass added as a knob for lifting purposes.

Pictured are some of the colors of butter dishes made so far. Shaker reproductions were introduced in 1977 and some were dated '77 on the bottom. Shortly afterward, the non-dated variety appeared. How can you tell new shakers from old — should you get the one in a million chance to do so?

First, look at the tops. New tops could indicate new shakers. Next, notice the protruding edges beneath the tops. In the new they are squared off juts rather than the nicely rounded scallops on the old. The design on the newer shakers is often weak in spots. Finally, notice how far up inside the shakers the solid glass (next to the foot) remains. The newer shakers have almost twice as much glass in that area. They appear to be ¼ full of glass before you ever add the salt.

In 1989, a new distributor began making reproduction glass in the Far East. He made shakers in cobalt blue, pink, and a hideous green, that is no problem to spot. These shakers are similar in quality to those made before. However, the present pink color is good; yet the quality and design of each batch could vary greatly. Realize that only two original pairs of pink Cherry shakers have ever been found and those were discovered before any reproductions were made in 1977.

Butter dishes are naturally more deceptive in pink and green since those were the only original colors. The major flaw in the new butter is that there is one band encircling the bottom edge of the butter top; there are two bands very close together along the skirt of the old top.

REPRODUCTIONS

NEW "FLORAL" IMPORTING COMPANY OUT OF GEORGIA

The important news in Floral is that reproduction shakers are now being found in pink, red, cobalt blue, and a dark green color. Cobalt blue, red, and the dark green Floral shakers are of little concern since they were never made in these colors originally. The green is darker than the original green, but not as deep as forest green. The pink shakers are not only a very good pink, but they are also a very good copy. There are a lot of minor variations in design and leaf detail to someone who knows glassware well; but I have always tried to pick out a point that anyone can use to ascertain legitimacy. There is one easy way to tell the Floral reproductions. Take off the top and look at the threads where the lid screws onto the shaker. On the old there are a pair of parallel threads on each side or a least a pair on one side which end right before the mold seams down each side. The new Floral has one continuous line thread that starts at one side and continues around the shaker until it ends above the beginning line on the other side. There is approximately one inch of overlapped thread making two lines for that inch; but the whole thread is one continuous line and not two separate ones as on the old. No other Floral reproductions have been made as of May 2001.

NEW "FLORENTINE" NO. 1 IMPORTING COMPANY OUT OF GEORGIA

Although a picture of a reproduction shaker is not shown, I would like for you to know of its existence.

Florentine No. 1 shakers have been reproduced in pink, red, and cobalt blue. There may be other colors to follow. I only have examined one reproduction shaker, and it is difficult to know if all shakers will be as badly molded as this is. I can say by looking at this one shaker that there is little or no design on the bottom. No red or cobalt blue Florentine No. 1 shakers have ever been found; so those are no problem. The pink is more difficult. I compared this one to several old pairs. The old shakers have a major open flower on each side. There is a top circle on this blossom with three smaller circles down each side. The seven circles form the outside of the blossom. The new blossom looks more like a strawberry with no circles forming the outside of the blossom. This repro blossom looks like a poor drawing. Do not use the Floral thread test for the Florentine No. 1 shakers, however. It won't work for Florentine although the same importing company out of Georgia makes these.

NEW "FLORENTINE" NO. 2 IMPORTING COMPANY OUT OF GEORGIA

A reproduced footed Florentine No. 2 pitcher and footed juice tumbler appeared in 1996. First to surface was a cobalt blue set that alerted knowledgeable collectors that something was strange. Next, sets of red, dark green, and two shades of pink began to be seen at the local flea markets. All these colors were dead giveaways since the footed Florentine No. 2 pitcher was never made in any of those shades.

The new pitchers are approximately ¼" shorter than the original and have a flatter foot as opposed to the domed foot of the old. The mold line on the lip of the newer pitcher extends ½" below the lip while only ⅜" below on the original. All of the measurements could vary over time with the reproductions and may even vary on the older ones. The easiest way to tell the old from the new, besides color, is by the handles. The new handles are ⅞" wide, but the older ones were only ¾" wide. That ⅛" seems even bigger than that when you set them side by side as shown below.

The juice tumbler differences are not as apparent; but there are two. The old juice stands 4" tall and the diameter of the base is 2⅛". The reproduction is only 3¹⁵⁄₁₆" tall and 2" in diameter.

REPRODUCTIONS

NEW "IRIS" IMPORTING COMPANY

New tumblers have two distinct differences. First, turn these upside down and feel the rays on the foot. New rays are very sharp and will almost hurt your finger if you press on them hard. Old tumbler rays are rounded and feel smooth in comparison. The paneled design on the new tumbler gets very weak in several places as you rotate it in you hand. Old tumbler paneled designs stay bold around the entire tumbler.

New dinner plates have two characteristics readily discerned from the old. The extreme edge of the pattern on the new dinners is pointed outward (upside down V). Old dinner plate designs usually end looking like a stack of the letter V, though optical illusions sometimes distort that a bit. Also, the inside rim of the new dinners slopes inward toward the center of the plate, whereas original inside rims are almost perpendicular and steeper.

In the fall of 2000, several large lots of Iris coasters appeared on an Internet auction site. All of these coasters had origins in Ohio and were like the tumblers and dinner plates in one major respect. The crystal color was too good. If you take any old piece of Iris and place it on a white background, it will have a gray or yellow tint to it. If you place the new dinner plates or iced tea tumblers on white, they have no tinted hue of any sort. The coasters are the same — no tint. The other sure-fire way to tell these newer coasters is to look from the side across the coaster. New ones look half full of glass or slightly over. The older ones are only a quarter-full of glass. You can keep up with current reproductions through a website where I have posted pictures. For additional photos, go to www.glassshow.com and go to the Reading Room. Click on Reproductions and keep up with the latest information available.

Iris 6½" footed ice tea tumblers (new on left).

Iris coasters (new on left).

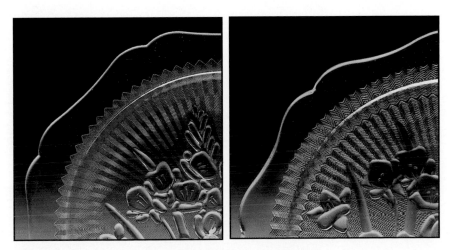

Iris dinner plate (new on left).

REPRODUCTIONS

NEW "MADRID" CALLED "RECOLLECTION" Currently being made.

I hope you have already read about Recollection Madrid on page 123. Indiana Glass made Madrid in teal after making it in blue, pink, and crystal. This light teal color was never made originally; so there is no problem of it being confused with old. The teal was sold through all kinds of outlets ranging from better department stores to discount catalogs. In the past couple of years we have received several ads stating that this is genuine Depression glass made from old moulds. None of this is made from old glass moulds unless you consider 1976 old. Most of the pieces are from moulds that were never made originally.

The light blue was a big seller for Indiana according to reports I am receiving around the country. It is a brighter, more fluorescent looking blue than the soft, original color. More and more of it is turning up in antique malls. Buy it if you like it, just don't pay antique prices for it.

Look at the picture below. Only the cup, saucer, and oval vegetable were ever made in old Madrid. The new grill plate has one division splitting the plate in half, but the old had three sections. A goblet or vase was never made. The vase is sold with a candle making it a hurricane lamp. The heavy tumbler was placed on top of a candlestick to make this a vase/hurricane lamp. That candlestick gets a workout. It was attached to a plate to make a pedestal cake stand and to a butter dish to make a preserve stand. That's a clever idea, actually. You would not believe the mail spawned by these two pieces.

The shakers are short and heavy and you can see an original style pictured on page 124. The latest item I have seen is a heavy 11 ounce flat tumbler being sold in a set of four or six called "On the Rocks." The biggest giveaway to this newer pink glass is the pale, washed out color.

The only concerns in the new pink pieces are the cups, saucers, and oval vegetable bowl. These three pieces were made in pink in the 1930s. None of the others shown were ever made in the 1930s in pink; so realize that when you see the butter dish, dinner plate, soup bowl, or sugar and creamer. These are new items. Once you have learned what this washed-out pink looks like by seeing these items for sale, the color will be a clue when you see other pieces.

The least difficult piece for new collectors to tell new from old is the candlestick. The new ones all have three raised ridges inside to hold the candle more firmly. All old ones do not have any inside ridges. You may even find new candlesticks in black.

REPRODUCTIONS

NEW "MAYFAIR" IMPORTING COMPANY

Colors: Pink, green, blue, cobalt (shot glasses), 1977; pink, green, amethyst, cobalt blue, red (cookie jars), 1982; cobalt blue, pink, amethyst, red, and green (odd shade), shakers 1988; green, cobalt, pink, juice pitchers, 1993.

Only the pink shot glass need cause any concern to collectors because that glass wasn't made in any other color originally. At first glance, the color of the newer shots is often too light pink or too orange. Dead giveaway is the stems of the flower design, however. In the old that stem branched to form an "A" shape at the bottom; in the new, you have a single stem. Further, in the new design, the leaf is hollow with the veins moulded in. In the old, the leaf is moulded in and the veining is left hollow. In the center of the flower on the old, dots (anther) cluster entirely to one side and are rather distinct. Nothing like that occurs in the new design.

As for the cookie jars, at cursory glance the base of the cookie has a very indistinct design. It will feel smooth to the touch; it's so faint. In the old cookie jars, there's a distinct pattern that feels like raised embossing to the touch. Next, turn the bottom upside down. The new bottom is perfectly smooth. The old bottom contains a 1¾" mould circle rim that is raised enough to catch your fingernail in it. There are other distinctions as well; but that is the quickest and easiest way to tell old from new.

In the Mayfair cookie lid, the new design (parallel to the straight side of the lid) at the edge curves gracefully toward the center "V" shape (rather like bird wings in flight); in the old, that edge is a flat straight line going into the "V" (like airplane wings sticking straight out from the side of the plane as you face it head on).

The green color of the cookie, as you can see from the picture, is not the pretty, yellow/green color of true green Mayfair. It also doesn't glow under black light as the old green does; so, that is a simple test for green.

NEW "MAYFAIR"

The corner ridges on the old Mayfair shaker rise half way to the top and then smooth out. The new shaker corner ridges rise to the top and are quite pronounced. The measurement differences are listed below, but the diameter of the opening is the critical and easiest way to tell old from new.

	OLD	NEW
Diameter of opening	¾"	⅝"
Diameter of lid	⅞"	¾"
Height	4¹⁄₁₆"	4"

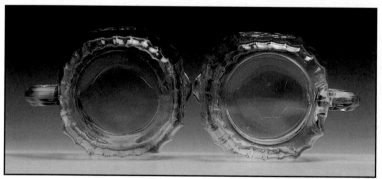

OLD   **NEW**

Mayfair juice pitchers were reproduced in 1993. The old pitchers have a distinct mould circle on the bottom that is missing on the newly made ones. This and the oddly applied handles on the repros make these easily spotted. The blue pitcher is the old one in the photos.

250   **OLD**   **NEW**

REPRODUCTIONS

NEW "MISS AMERICA"

Colors: Crystal, green, pink, ice blue, red amberina, cobalt blue.

Miss America reproduction cobalt creamers and sugars are smaller than the originals; Miss America was not made in cobalt. Other colors have followed. These creamer and sugars are poorly made. There are many bubbles in the glass of the ones I have seen.

The reproduction butter dish in the Miss America design is probably the best of the newer products; yet there are three differences to be found between the original butter top and the newly made ones. The obvious thing is how the top knob sticks up away from the butter caused by a longer than usual stem at the knob.

Pick up the top of the new dish and feel up inside it. If the butter top knob is filled with glass so that it is convex (curved outward), the dish is new; the old inside knob area is concave (curved inward).

Finally, from the underside, look through the top toward the knob. In the original butter dish you would see a perfectly formed multi-sided star; in the newer version, you see distorted rays with no visible points.

Miss America shakers have been made in green, pink, cobalt blue, and crystal. The latest copies of shakers are becoming more difficult to distinguish from the old. The measurements given below for shakers do not hold true for all the latest reproductions. It is impossible to know which generation of shaker reproductions that you will encounter, so you have to be careful on these.

New shakers most likely will have new tops; but since some old shakers have been given new tops, that isn't conclusive at all. Unscrew the lid. Old shakers have a very neatly formed ridge of glass on which to screw the lid. It overlaps a little and has rounded off ends. Old shakers stand 3⅜" tall without the lid. Most new ones stand 3¼" tall. Old shakers have almost a forefinger's depth inside (female finger) or a fraction short of 2½". Most new shakers have an inside depth of 2", about the second digit bend of a female's finger. (I'm doing finger depths since most of you will carry those with you to the flea market, rather than a tape measure.) In men, the old shaker's depth covers my knuckle; the new shaker leaves my knuckle exposed. Most new shakers simply have more glass on the inside of the shaker — something you can spot from 12 feet away. The hobs are more rounded on the newer shaker, particularly near the stem and seams; in the old shaker these areas remained pointedly sharp.

New Miss America tumblers have ½" of glass in the bottom, have a smooth edge on the bottom of the glass with no mould rim, and show only two distinct mould marks on the sides of the glass. Old tumblers have only ¼" of glass in the bottom, have a distinct mould line rimming the bottom of the tumbler, and have four distinct mould marks up the sides of the tumbler.

New Miss America pitchers (without ice lip only) are all perfectly smoothed rimmed at the top edge above the handle. All old pitchers that I have seen have a hump in the top rim of the glass above the handle area, rather like a camel's hump. The very bottom diamonds next to the foot in the new pitchers squash into elongated diamonds. In the old pitchers, these get noticeably smaller, but they retain their diamond shape.

NEW "ROYAL LACE" IMPORTING COMPANY

Colors: Cobalt blue.

The first thing you notice about the reproduced pieces is the extra dark, vivid cobalt blue color or the orange cast to the pink. It is not the soft cobalt blue originally made by Hazel Atlas. So far, only the cookie jar, juice, and water tumblers have been made as of May 2001.

The original cookie jar lid has a mould seam that bisects the center of the pattern on one side, and runs across the knob and bisects the pattern on the opposite side. There is no mould line at all on the reproduction.

There are a multitude of bubbles and imperfections on the bottom of the new cookie jar that I am examining. The bottom is poorly moulded and the pattern is extremely weak. Original bottoms are plentiful anyway; learn to distinguish the top and it will save you money.

As for tumblers, the first reproduction tumblers had plain bottoms without the four-pointed design. The new juice tumbler has a bottom design, but it is as large as the one on the water tumbler and covers the entire bottom of the glass. Originally, this design was very small and did not encompass the whole bottom, as does this reproduction. Additionally, there are design flaws on both size tumblers that stand out. The four ribs between each of the four designs on the side of the repro tumblers protrude far enough to catch your fingernail. The original tumblers

have a very smooth, flowing design that you can only feel. The other distinct flaw is a semi-circular design on the rim of the glass above those four ribs. Originally these were very tiny on both tumblers with five oval leaves in each. There are three complete diamond-shaped designs in the new tumblers with two being doubled diamonds (diamond shapes within diamonds); and the semi-circular design almost touches the top rim. There's at least an ⅛" of glass above the older fan.

Also, on the bottom of the tumblers, the four flower petal center designs in the old is open-ended leaving ⅛" of open glass at the tip of each petal. In the new version, these ends are closed, causing the petals to be pointed on the end.

NEW "SHARON" Privately Produced 1976...(continued page 253)

Colors: Blue, dark green, light green, pink, cobalt blue, opalescent blue, red, burnt umber.

A blue Sharon butter turned up in 1976 and turned my phone line to liquid fire. The color was Mayfair blue — a fluke and dead giveaway as far as real Sharon is concerned. The original mastermind of reproductions did not know his patterns very well and mixed up Mayfair and Sharon. (He admitted that when I talked to him.)

When Sharon butters are found in colors similar to the old pink and green, you can immediately tell that the new version has more glass in the top where it changes from pattern to clear glass. It is a thick, defined ring of glass as opposed to a thin, barely defined ring of glass in the old. The knob of the new dish tends to stick up more. In the old butter dish there's barely room to fit your finger to grasp the knob. The new butter dish has a sharply defined ridge of glass in the bottom around which the top sits. The old butter has such a slight rim that the top easily scoots off the bottom.

In 1977 a cheese dish appeared having the same top as the butter and having all the flaws inherent in that top which were discussed in detail above. However, the bottom of this dish was wrong. It was about half way between a flat plate and a butter dish bottom — bowl shaped; and it was very thick, giving it an awkward appearance. The real cheese bottom was a salad plate with a rim of glass for holding the top inside that rim. These round bottomed cheese dishes are but a parody of the old and are easily spotted.

REPRODUCTIONS

NEW "SHARON" (Continued)

Some of the latest reproductions in Sharon are a too light pink creamer and sugar with lid. They are pictured with the "Made in Taiwan" label. These retail for around $15.00 for the pair and are also easy to spot as reproductions. I'll just mention the most obvious differences. Turn the creamer so you are looking directly at the spout. In the old creamer the mould line runs dead center of that spout; in the new, the mould line runs decidedly to the left of center spout.

On the sugar, the leaves and roses are "off" but not enough to describe it to new collectors. Therefore, look at the center design, both sides, at the stars located at the very bottom of the motif. A thin leaf stem should run directly from that center star upward on both sides. In this new sugar, the stem only runs from one; it stops way short of the star on one side; or look inside the sugar bowl at where the handle attaches to the bottom of the bowl; in the new bowl, this attachment looks like a perfect circle; in the old, its an upside down "v"-shaped teardrop.

As for the sugar lid, the knob of the new lid is perfectly smooth as you grasp its edges. The old knob has a mould seam running mid circumference (equator). You could tell these two lids apart blindfolded.

While there is a slight difference between the height, mouth-opening diameter, and inside depth of the old Sharon shakers and those newly produced, I won't attempt to upset you with those sixteenths and thirty-seconds of an inch of difference. It is safe to say that in physical appearance, they are very close. However, when documenting design on the shaker, they're miles apart.

The old shakers have true appearing roses. The flowers really look like roses. On the new shakers, the roses appear as poorly drawn circles with wobbly concentric rings. The leaves are not as clearly defined on the new shakers as the old. However, forgetting all that, in the old shakers, the first design you see below the lid is a rose bud. It's angled like a rocket shooting off into outer space with three leaves at the base of the bud (where the rocket fuel would burn out). In the new shakers, this bud has become four paddles of a windmill. It's the difference between this ✿ and ✿ this.

Candy dishes have been made in pink, green, cobalt blue, red, and opaque blue that goes to opalescent. These candy jars are among the easiest items to discern old from new. Pick up the lid and look from the bottom side. On the old there is a 2" circle ring knob below the knob; on the new, that ring of glass below the knob is only ½". This shows from the top also but it is difficult to measure with the knob in the center. There are other major differences, but this one will not be mould corrected easily. The bottoms are also simple to distinguish. The base diameter of the old is 3¼" and the new only 3". On the example I have, quality of the new is rough, poorly shaped and moulded; but I do not know if that will hold true for all reproductions of the candy. I hope so.

Florence's Glassware
PATTERN IDENTIFICATION Guide
Gene Florence

Gene Florence's *Glassware Pattern Identification Guides* are great companions for his other glassware books. Volume I includes every pattern featured in his *Collector's Encyclopedia of Depression Glass, Collectible Glassware from the 40s, 50s, and 60s*, and *Collector's Encyclopedia of Elegant Glassware,* as well as many more — nearly 400 patterns in all. Volume II holds nearly 500 patterns, with no repeats from Volume I. Carefully planned close-up photographs of representative pieces for every pattern show great detail to make identification easy. With every pattern, Florence provides the names, the companies which made the glass, dates of production, and even colors available. These guides are ideal references for novice and seasoned glass collectors and dealers, and great resources for years to come. No values.

Vol I: ISBN: 1-57432-045-9 • #5042 • 8½ x 11 • 176 Pgs. • PB • $18.95
Vol. II: ISBN: 1-57432-177-3 • #5615 • 8½ x 11 • 208 Pgs. • PB • $19.95

Anchor Hocking's
FIRE-KING & More, 2nd Edition
Gene Florence

From the 1930s to the 1960s Anchor Hocking Glass Corp. of Lancaster, Ohio, produced an extensive line of glassware called Fire-King. Their lines included not only dinnerware but also a plethora of glass kitchen items — reamers, measuring cups, mixing bowls, mugs, and more. Instead of Depression and Elegant glassware, many collectors are now turning to the glassware from the 1940s to the 1970s. Due to this growing popularity and the success of his other books which feature several Fire-King patterns, Gene Florence has compiled a second edition of his bestselling book on Fire-King. This is the essential collectors' reference to this massive line of glassware. Loaded with hundreds of new full-color photos, vintage catalog pages, company materials, facts, information, and values, this book has everything collectors expect from Gene Florence. 2000 values.

ISBN: 1-57432-164-1 • #5602 • 8½ x 11 • 224 Pgs. • HB • $24.95

KITCHEN GLASSWARE of the Depression Years, 6th Edition
Gene Florence

This exciting new edition of our bestselling *Kitchen Glassware of the Depression Years* is undeniably the definitive reference on the subject. Many new photographs and new discoveries and information make this book indispensable to all glass collectors and dealers. More than 5,000 items are showcased in beautiful professional color photographs with descriptions and values. Many new finds and exceptionally rare pieces have been added. The highly collectible glass from the Depression era through the 1960s fills its pages, in addition to the ever-popular Fire-King and Pyrex glassware. This comprehensive encyclopedia provides an easy-to-use format, showing items by color, shapes, or patterns. The collector will enjoy the pages of glass, from colorful juice reamers, shakers, rare and unusual glass knives, to the mixing bowls and baking dishes we still find in our kitchen cupboards.

ISBN: 1-57432-220-6 • #5827 • 8½ x 11 • 272 Pgs. • HB • $24.95

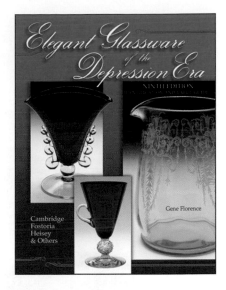

ELEGANT GLASSWARE of the Depression Era, 9th Ed.
Gene Florence

Gene Florence is America's foremost authority on collectible glassware made from the 1920s through the 1970s. His nineth edition of *Elegant Glassware of the Depression Era* holds hundreds of new photographs, listings, and updated values, and features the handmade and acid-etched glassware that was sold in department and jewelry stores from the Depression era through the 1950s, as opposed to the dimestore and give-away glass known as Depression glass. As always, Florence has added many new discoveries, several new patterns, and re-photographed many items from the previous book. Large, full-color group settings are included for each of the more than 100 patterns, as well as close-ups to show pattern details. The famous glassmakers presented include Fostoria, Cambridge, Heisey, Tiffin, Imperial, Duncan & Miller, U.S. Glass, and Paden City. In addition to his interesting discussions of each pattern, Florence provides a list of all known pieces, with colors and measurements, along with values for the year 2001.

ISBN: 1-57432-195-1 • #5682 • 8½ x 11 • 240 Pgs. • HB • $19.95

Collectible
GLASSWARE of the 40s, 50s, & 60s, Sixth Edition
Gene Florence

Covering collectible glassware made after the Depression era, this is the only book available that deals exclusively with the mass-produced and handmade glassware from this period. It is completely updated, featuring many original company catalog pages and 14 new patterns — making a total of 102 patterns from Anniversary to Yorktown, with many of the most popular Fire King patterns in between. Each pattern is alphabetically listed, all known pieces in each pattern are described and priced, and gorgeous color photographs showcase both common and very rare pieces.

ISBN: 1-57432-236-2 • #5897 • 8½ x 11 • 240 Pgs. • HB • $19.95

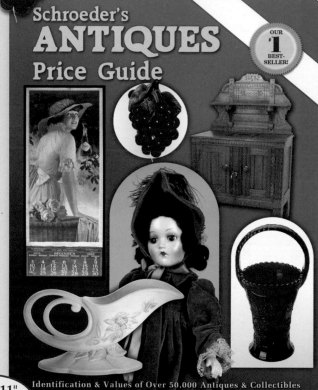